TRIUMPH OF THE NOMADS

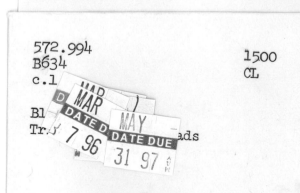

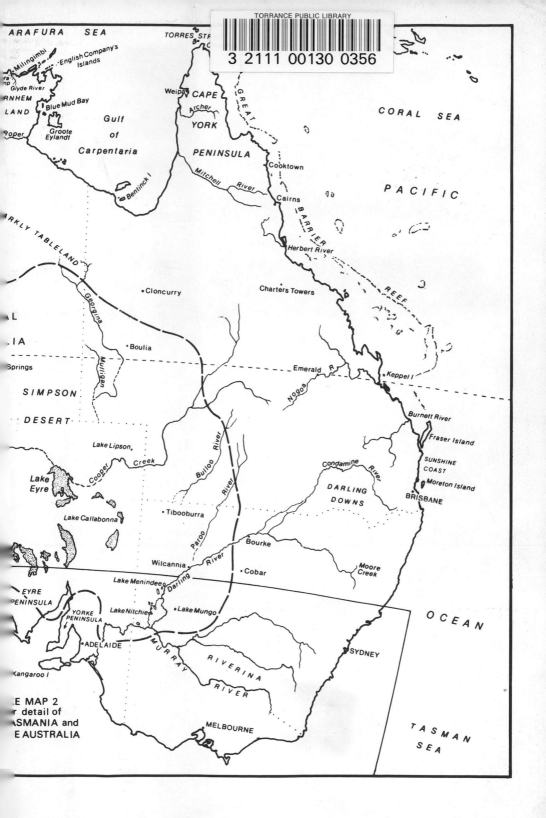

ARAFURA SEA

Milingimbi

English Company's
Islands

Glyde River

ARNHEM
LAND

Blue Mud Bay

Roper

Groote
Eylandt

Gulf
of
Carpentaria

Bentinck I

TORRES STR

Weipa

CAPE

YORK

Archer

PENINSULA

Mitchell River

CORAL SEA

PACIFIC

Cooktown

Cairns

Herbert River

BARRIER

REEF

RKLY TABLELAND

Georgina

Cloncurry

Charters Towers

AL

IA

Springs

Boulia

Milligan

Emerald R

Nogoa

Keppel I

SIMPSON

DESERT

Lake Lipson

Cooper

Creek

Bulloo River

Burnett River

Fraser Island

SUNSHINE
COAST

Condamine River

Moreton Island

BRISBANE

Lake
Eyre

Lake Callabonna

River

Tibooburra

DARLING

DOWNS

Paroo

Wilcannia

River

Bourke

Moore
Creek

Cobar

EYRE
PENINSULA

Lake Menindee

Darling

YORKE
PENINSULA

Lake Nitchie

Lake Mungo

OCEAN

ADELAIDE

MURRAY

RIVERINA

RIVER

SYDNEY

Kangaroo I

E MAP 2
r detail of
ASMANIA and
E AUSTRALIA

MELBOURNE

TASMAN
SEA

TRIUMPH OF THE NOMADS
A History of Aboriginal Australia

GEOFFREY BLAINEY

The Overlook Press
Woodstock, New York

First published in 1976 by
The Overlook Press
Lewis Hollow Road
Woodstock, New York 12498
Copyright © text and maps by Geoffrey Blainey
Library of Congress Catalog Card Number: 75-37122
ISBN: 0-87951-043-9

Printed by The Studley Press, Inc.

Preface

Long before the rise of Babylon and Athens, the early
Australians had impressive achievements. They were the
only people in the world's history to sail across the seas and
discover an inhabitable continent.* They bred a brave
procession of coastal and inland explorers; they were brown
Columbuses, Major Mitchells and even Dr Livingstones,
I presume. The aboriginals who occupied Australia also
found, over a long stretch of time, many edible plants,
valuable mines which they worked, new medicines and drugs,
manufacturing techniques, and a miscellany of resources
ranging from the raw materials of their cosmetics to the
hidden pools of water in deserts. They succeeded in adapting
their ways of life to harsh as well as kind environments; and
several large regions of Australia supported more people in
ancient times than they have supported in recent times.

In one sense the aboriginals resembled today's nations of
Europe rather than Asia, for the growth of their population
was slow and their material standard of living was relatively
high. Indeed, if an aboriginal in the seventeenth century had
been captured as a curiosity and taken in a Dutch ship to
Europe, and if he had travelled all the way from Scotland

* The Americas were entered first by 'Indians' who almost certainly
walked on dry land from Siberia to Alaska at a time when America
was part of Asia. Columbus re-discovered the Americas. Likewise
Dutchmen and Portuguese—and probably Indonesians and perhaps
Chinese before them—re-discovered Australia perhaps 40,000 years
after the real discoverers had settled in the land.

to the Caucasus and had seen how the average European struggled to make a living, he might have said to himself that he had now seen the third world and all its poverty and hardship.

Aboriginals also had vital knowledge which Europeans, when they arrived, rarely tried to acquire. Parties of white men crossing dry plains died of thirst within a mile of hidden water which, with the aid of aboriginals' knowledge, they could have tapped. Lost, they wandered aimlessly through countryside which displayed the invisible weathercocks and compasses of the aboriginals. Some died from exposure because they were unable to light a fire without the aid of tinder box or matches. Some died from starvation because they did not know that many kinds of plants they trod on were edible and because—without their firearms—they were unable to catch game. Some were ill, not knowing that they could be healed by the herbal skills of the aboriginals. They often concluded that the land was mean and hungry, not realizing that some regions in the course of four seasons provided a wider variety of foodstuffs than a gourmet in Paris would eat in an extravagant year.

For a long time the economic life of the aboriginals was mainly ignored or dismissed. Their land, after all, provided the world with only a few useful new plants, though if it had been colonized by Europeans four centuries earlier it could have offered the first tobacco as well as other novel plants. Aboriginals, being nomads, owned no treasures that could appeal to the first European visitors. Australia had no men of property, no brown Forsytes. Their wandering existence seemed escapist and haphazard, but an examination of their regular movements across country reveals pattern and purpose. They were not drifters; they reigned over the continent, and displayed a surprising mastery of its resources.

The terrain covered in this book is primarily the present Australia and Tasmania, though New Guinea appears intermittently because it was joined to the Australian land-

vi

mass for most of its human history. Ancient Australia had such diversity in social customs and languages that the unity of the continent was mainly artificial. One thousand, or ten thousand, years ago the contrast between the economic life of the desert people and people on the wider rivers was sharper than the present contrast between the economies of Australia and China. Moreover, Australia was split into hundreds of mini-republics, each conscious that its own traditions and people were unique. To see ancient Australia as an entity is to see it more through our eyes than the eyes of aboriginals who fought one another so frequently. When, after the British arrived, aboriginal tribes from scattered corners sometimes came together, they usually treated one another as foreigners. Thus Victorian aboriginals on the River Loddon met for the first time aboriginals who had travelled less than 100 miles from Lake Buloke, and they viewed the visitors as if they were migrants from outer space: 'they are foreign in speech, they are foreign in countenance, they are foreign altogether—they are no good.'

The book relies heavily on the recent research by archaeologists, anthropologists, prehistorians, anatomists, marine scientists, geologists, botanists, zoologists, linguists and others who have studied aboriginal history. My debt is set out in many of the following chapters and in the notes at the end of the book. In places the book offers conclusions which run counter to the main currents of learned opinion. These conclusions affect such themes as warfare and plagues, trade, population history, the standard of living and the possible effects of the great rising of the seas.

I am grateful for help given by many people. Isabel McBryde, an archaeologist at the Australian National University, and Jim Watson, a veterinarian at the University of Melbourne, read many chapters and pointed out weaknesses which I hope I have repaired or deleted. Dick Roughsey, Rhys Jones, Stephen Murray-Smith, Patrick Singleton, Judith Wiseman, Mary Turner Shaw, Carrick

Preface

Chambers, Harold Hort, Alan Beever, Daryl Forde, Kelvin
Rowley and Anna Blainey gave me useful information or
showed me where to find it. Bernard Joyce discussed his
research on the dating of volcanoes in western Victoria.
Joyce Wood designed and drew the maps, Lee White made
valuable editorial comments, Mrs J. Edgar typed the
manuscript, and Miss Marjorie Harrison compiled the index.

Displays of aboriginal items in museums in Australia
taught me much: so too did students in my classes. In fact
the seeds of the book were lectures given to undergraduates.
I used to begin a course on Australian economic history
in the accepted manner with the European explorations of
the eighteenth century until one day the archaeologist, John
Mulvaney, in conversation enquired what I said about the
earlier 99 per cent of time embraced by the human history
of Australia. He pointed out that the ancient and recent
history of Australia had continuous as well as broken threads,
and he pointed to some of the threads, and so the book owes
much to his original comment and his later encouragement.

Geoffrey Blainey.

University of Melbourne.
May 1975.

Contents

Contents

Maps

PART ONE

The Invaders

CHAPTER ONE

Fire on the Lake

The lake lies on the hot plain in south-eastern Australia.
The wide bed is edged by blunt cliffs, and from the centre of
the lake you see the sun rise over a high dune of sand. The
sand dunes form the eastern rim of the lake and follow the
shore for perhaps fifteen miles. Seen in the sharpened
shadows when the sun is low, or traced as an outline on the
edge of the blue sky, the rim of sand and clay resembles a
long defensive wall. It has for some time been known as The
Walls of China.

From the wide rampart of the wall the view is desolate in
most seasons of each year. Though sixty miles to the south-
west is the junction of two of Australia's longest rivers, the
Murray and the Darling, no expanse of water is visible from
the ramparts of The Walls of China. When the westerlies
blow, the only spray from the lake below is grit and dust;
except in times of flood the lake's only ripples are made of
sand.

Lake Mungo is like a deserted arena which carries traces
and echoes of events of long ago. In July 1968, on the sandy
shore near the dunes, human bones were uncovered. The
fragments of skeleton and skull were carbonate-encrusted; in
fact the body had been cremated and then the bones had
been crushed and buried in a shallow hole scooped from the
sand. The nomads who long ago burned the corpse thereby
provided vital evidence of the antiquity of the aboriginals'
existence in Australia.

II

The death and burial of the nomad at Lake Mungo took place so long ago that the climate of the plains was different. The summer days then were cooler and the winter nights were frostier; the annual rain too was probably more plentiful or the rivers were wider. Whatever the exact blend of climatic conditions, the result was often a full lake. Today Lake Mungo is one of a chain of dry lakes, each with its sandy Wall of China on the eastern shore, and each lake linked to the next only during those rare months when the Willandra Billabong Creek actually flows. But in the last glacial age that creek—in effect a great billabong of the Lachlan River—often flowed slowly across the plains towards the Murrumbidgee and Murray. For long periods the lakes were full forming a chain covering hundreds of square miles. Whenever a lake was brimful with brown water the overflow streamed south to replenish the next lake. The overflow was essential to the marine life and the shore life, for it flushed out the salt and so aided the freshwater fish and the trees and shrubs along the shores.

About 17,000 years ago the vital flushing became less frequent. The annual flow of water came from the Great Dividing Range but perhaps less snow fell on the mountains with the waning of the last ice age. The freshwater mussels died in the lake; the seeds of the great eucalypts on the water's edge probably ceased to germinate; the beds of rushes on the banks wilted; waterbirds flew away to other swamps and rivers; and the sappy smell of lush grass was replaced by the sniff of dust.

Long before the lakes dried, the aboriginals often visited the shores, the glow of their small fires beaming across the water at night. That they camped and ate there is undeniable. Scraps and debris of their meals still survive thousands of years later. From the blackened remains of the food archaeologists have been able to piece together some of

4

the hunting and eating customs of these nomadic people. In mud near the shallows the aboriginals collected freshwater shellfish, the shells of which have survived in fragments. In the late winter they raided nests of the giant emu and took the blue-green eggs. They captured the bettong, a small bounding animal about the size of a hare, and they hunted kangaroos, brown hare wallabies, western native cats, hairy-nosed wombats and small birds. They were also fishermen, and the fossil relics from their ancient meals reveal that they caught golden perch weighing more than thirty pounds. The same fish, birds, and animals formed a large part of the diet of aboriginals along the rivers of the same region when the first white men arrived hundreds of generations later. But one animal, sometimes seen long ago when Lake Mungo was brimming, will not be seen again—the Tasmanian tiger or thylacine. One jawbone found recently on the dry lake was unmistakably that of a Tasmanian tiger, a species extinct on the Australian mainland long before the coming of the first Europeans.

On the surface of the ground, parallel to the dry beach, stone tools were also found late in the 1960s. More tools were discovered in the circular charcoal-specked patches that had once been hearths; tools that could cut, scrape and pummel flesh and skin. They were samples of a tool-making tradition which survived in Tasmania until the nineteenth century. The quantity of stone tools and food bones unearthed, and the character of the geographical surroundings, suggested that long ago one or two dozen aboriginals had sometimes camped by the lake in the course of their seasonal wanderings.

The young woman who had been burned and buried less than a stone's throw from some of the hearths at the lakeside would seem to have belonged to this nomadic group. It would be fitting to describe how, thousands of years ago, her life's journey had ended on the shores of the still lake but her journey had not ended. In 1969 her burnt and broken bones were uncovered, put in a suitcase, and carried away to a laboratory.

She was given the name of Mungo 1. As one-quarter of her bones and three of her teeth had survived she deserved a name; but the impersonal label of a laboratory exhibit was perhaps inappropriate for one who had lived her life in a tightly-knit society. After an examination of her remains the anatomist A. G. Thorne was able to cull conclusions which were astonishing in their detail. She had been 'fully-fleshed' when cremated. The fire, however, held sufficient heat to singe only the bones of her back and neck. Before the half-cremated body was buried the skull and face were deliberately hammered and crushed: from her cranium alone, 175 fragments were gathered in 1969. 'In some instances', wrote Thorne, 'the direction of the blow can be deduced'. When, in the laboratory, the crushed bones were cleaned in a bath of weak acid, they emerged, in the anatomist's words, as the remains of a young adult, 'of gracile build and small stature'. *Gracile* means slender: in tone it hints at the gracefully slender, suggesting that she should have been christened Miss Lake Mungo.

The most surprising discovery was simply how long ago she had lived near the freshwater lake. According to radiocarbon dating, her remains were older than 25,000 years. Some carbon-encrusted shells, which seemed to be the result of a man-made fire at the same site, were at least 31,500 years old; and the nearby debris from others meals of shellfish were perhaps 38,000 years old. If that assessment was accurate, the aboriginals had lived in Australia far longer than had previously been known. They had lived in Australia far longer than man had lived in South America, longer in fact, than man had lived in any part of the Americas.*

* In the autumn of 1975 Jim Bowler, the geologist who found the first human remains at Lake Mungo, revealed that an even older burial had been uncovered in the sands of the lake. The skeleton—of a man about six feet in height—was some 30,000 years old.

III

In that epoch when Lake Mungo was full and the golden perch were cooked in hot ashes on the shore, the climate of every continent was probably colder than today. The world, 25,000 or 30,000 years ago, was in the concluding phase of the long glacial or Pleistocene epoch. Those fires burned at Lake Mungo in the last of the many ice ages. For perhaps two-million years there had been a succession of ice ages, each punctuated by a warmer era; and one effect of those momentous changes had been to favour the multiplying of some animal species and the decline or extinction of those species less capable of coping with the new condition. Mankind and his brain was probably the most dramatic beneficiary of these changes. And one sign of man's ability to cope with the new conditions was his migration—during the last of the ice ages—to the continents of America and Australia.

During the last glacial phase the ice of the Arctic and Antarctic was thicker than today. Arctic icebergs drifted far into the temperate zones, often floating as far south as the Azores. The area of the earth covered by ice was much larger than today. At the height of the latest ice age one quarter of the land surface of the globe was covered with ice, but the ice in our time covers only one-tenth of the land. In the last year of the life of Miss Lake Mungo at least one glacier was probably still active in Tasmania, less than 400 miles directly to the south. On the high tablelands and mountains of southern Australia, the cold was often intense. About 30,000 years ago, during a phase of increasing cold, the temperatures in the valleys at Canberra were probably about the same as those recorded in our time on the highest mountain in Australia, Mount Kosciusko. The intense cold may have deterred the first Australians from living on the tablelands of the south-east but not from travelling there in search of food during the mildness of summer.

7

Triumph of the Nomads

The climate was colder in the world's temperate zones 30,000 or 20,000 years ago. But to estimate the temperature and rainfall in specific Australian regions, or at scattered points during those thousands of years, is often to make half-informed guesses in the present state of knowledge. More is known about temperatures in Europe and North America 30,000 years ago, but to transfer them to an Australian region is hazardous. These oscillations of temperature, it is said, were probably more drastic in lands bordering the Atlantic than on the Pacific lands, and might have had scant effect on equatorial lands. Moreover local geographical influences, then as now, softened or accentuated the effect of these climatic changes.

When the human race first entered Australia the sea was almost certainly colder and the level of the sea was certainly lower. The colder water and lower seas were causally connected. The seas shrank as the ice sheets became thicker in the far north and south of the globe. During the latest ice age the level of the sea was probably 400 or 600 feet lower than today. Because of the rise or fall of continental shelves or the effects of sedimentation, earthquakes or local tides, it is dangerous to offer a global generalization about the average level of the seas, but the evidence is overwhelming that in nearly every part of the world the sea was shallower. The Australian beaches where waves broke about 30,000 years ago are now far beneath the sea.

The levels of the sea then were so low that most of the narrow sea lanes which have dominated naval strategy and funnelled commerce since the time of Christ were dry. The narrow straits between the islands of Java and Sumatra and between Sumatra and the Asian mainland were probably forest—they certainly were not sea. Indeed, Java and Sumatra and Borneo were part of the Asian mainland. So too was America; there was no Bering Sea, and men and animals could walk from Siberia to Alaska and continue into the Americas through an ice-free inland corridor. So the first

8

intercontinental missile was probably a spear or stone, which happened to be thrown in those months when the Americas and Asia were narrowly parted at high tide.

Men could walk with dry feet from Trinidad to South America. They could, without the aid of miracles, walk across what is now the North Sea, though they would have had to paddle across both the Thames and the Rhine because those rivers then flowed far north. It was possible to walk from Yorkshire to Esthonia, providing the rivers could be crossed and the marshes skirted. Today fishing vessels occasionally trawl from the bed of the North Sea the flint tools made by early men or the stumps of trees which grew there. Our custom of indicating altitude by stating that Canberra and London are so many feet above sea level spuriously implies too much stability in the sea heights.

Australia was very different in surface shape from the present continent. An Australian map in that epoch would not at first be recognizable to our eyes. The continent was much larger. The hunters of Lake Mungo by walking south, could have travelled all the way to Tasmania. If they set out to walk north they could have walked overland to New Guinea. Torres Strait and the Great Barrier Reef were dry land at that period. What are now the mouths or estuaries of the main rivers were then far from the ocean. If the hunters of Lake Mungo had heard of the ocean and if they decided to visit it they would have followed their billabong until eventually they reached the Murray River and followed that river far past its present mouth. At that time the continental shelf around Australia was probably above water in most places; great coastal indentations of our map were less prominent; Carpentaria did not exist and the Great Australian Bight was less arc-like. The most conspicuous bulges or gashes on the coastline were probably the long Tasmanian peninsula falling like an udder to the south-east and a great gulf in the north-east. That gulf, forming part of the present Coral Sea, consisted of an enfolding coast stretching from

9

the south-eastern tip of Papua around to central Queensland coast. As large perhaps as the Gulf of Mexico is today, that Coral Gulf was the outlet for the Fly River which of course must have been a longer river with a mouth much further to the east.

It is impossible to specify exactly the position of the coast-line of much of Australia during the last ice age. It is safe, however, to suggest that the main harbours of today were far from the sea. The sites of Melbourne, Adelaide, and Darwin then were probably as far from the sea as Canberra is today. If an opera house had been built on the jutting point of land in Sydney it would have looked down on a dry gorge; and anyone who walked along that gorge might have taken several days to reach the sea. Twenty thousand years ago the land mass of Australia and New Guinea occupied perhaps an additional one-seventh of territory which the rising sea was later to drown. But any estimate of how much land was drowned floats on a raft of supposition and guess.

IV

When the shores of Lake Mungo were inhabited, volcanoes were possibly active less than 300 miles to the south. On the wide basalt plains near the southern border of South Australia and Victoria the eruptions of at least five different volcanoes were almost certainly witnessed by aboriginals. And if the aboriginals were in possession of those plains for a period of 30,000 years then, according to the geologist Bernard Joyce, they might have seen perhaps a dozen volcanic eruptions.

At least two volcanoes of relatively recent times emitted lava. Mount Napier and Mount Eccles both stand on the plains to the south of Hamilton, and when they erupted their molten lava glided like a long molten snake across the plains. One flow of lava from Mount Eccles was only about 100 yards wide in places but extended for about thirty miles.

10

Aboriginals were probably living within sight of these volcanoes when the lava flowed; for the westerns plains were fertile, the game was plentiful, and a variety of edible roots and greens and grains could be harvested. As scores of generations must have passed between each of the five eruptions, and as the volcanoes were scattered spots on a wide plain, there was no reason for abandoning the region. Each volcano, moreover, was not like a cauldron which, over the ages, cooled intermittently before returning to the simmer. This type of volcano, from initiation to final extinction, had a short life ranging from perhaps a month to ten or twelve years. It devastated and died.

As the same kind of volcano exploded within a day's drive of Mexico City, and was observed minutely, we have some idea of what might have happened in south-eastern Australia. At Paricutin, in Mexico, the tremors began in a cornfield on 5 February 1943. They became so frequent that a fortnight later about 300 were recorded in 24 hours. On the following day a small fissure was observed in the corn field—a slit which made a hissing noise and began to emit smoke, sparks and dust. Within a few hours of the splitting of the ground a thin column of smoke was rising and red hot stones were thrown up. By the following morning a volcanic cone stood about thirty feet high; by noon its height had trebled. The lava started to flow from the volcano, and the noise of the eruptions could be heard 200 miles away. The cone of volcanic clay and cinders continued to rise, and by the end of the year it was a molten hill rising about 1,000 feet above the buried cornfield. The Mexican eruption finally ceased in 1952, after nine years.

On the pleasant plains of western Victoria the explosion of Mount Eccles and Mount Napier must have been frightening for those aboriginals who fled to safety or saw the eruption from afar. By day the molten hill might not have been a spectacular sight unless white clouds happened to be above, their whiteness reflecting the red below. But at night the red rim of the cone and the flank down which the lava flowed could have been a fierce red.

While these two volcanoes released ash as well as lava, three other volcanoes were essentially great explosions of ash, leaving one or more craters which in time were filled with water. Mount Schank (S.A.), erupting after several hundred generations of aboriginals had lived nearby, emitted its great clouds of hot ash, and a trickle of lava, perhaps 18,000 years ago. Only a few hours' walk to the north, Mount Gambier violently erupted less than 5,000 years ago—it could even have been only 1,400 years ago. Whatever the correct date, it appears to be the most recent volcano in the continent. Further to the east, the crater of Tower Hill was the result of an explosion estimated to have occurred between 5,000 and 6,000 years ago. The rims of these craters can be seen, in the course of two hours of driving, along the coastal highway between Adelaide and Melbourne.

These volcanic explosions were usually preceded by warning. Aboriginals had time to leave. If they panicked, however, they might leave behind an old man or woman too feeble to move rapidly. Kangaroos, wallabies and most birds would have taken to flight though slower creatures such as snakes and wombats would have been trapped. This kind of eruption resembled a black thunder-cloud, and the sight of the explosion of hot ash was perhaps more frightening than the noise; the sound itself was probably not unlike the firing of artillery or the clap of thunder. Meanwhile a rising rim of ash, like the edge of a saucer, was formed around the scene of the explosion, and from the crater came the acrid smell of gas and perhaps the taste of sulphur. As more and more ash was hurled upwards the wind carried it away from the crater and dispersed it on the trees and grasslands. Then, as now, the prevailing winds along that line of coast were westerly, and to the leeward of the craters fell a shower of lukewarm ash, burying the grass, stripping leaves from trees, and creating a wasteland of ash and dead trees. Nine feet below the ash of Tower Hill a grooved axe of stone was found in modern times—strong evidence that aboriginals inhabited the area before the eruption. It is even possible that the stone axe was discarded in the flight from the smouldering volcano.

How volcanic eruptions affected the few aboriginals in the vicinity can be easily supposed. A flow of lava could block creeks and waterholes, ruin patches where edible roots and vegetables grew, drive game from an area. A cloud of ash settling on land could make it barren though in the long term the ash could turn into rich soil that nourished grasses and attracted game. On plains which were more vulnerable to bushfires than almost any other terrain in the world, some of the volcanic eruptions in summer could have started massive bushfires that spread far. But the effect of these volcanoes on the aboriginals' views of the universe, nature, man, causation and all that we loosely call religion could have been long-lasting. As aboriginals tended to cloak every mountain, creek, crag and marsh with legend, the new mountain cones or the rims of craters appearing in their own lifetime could not have been meaningless, for they towered above their own tribal territory and happened in the centre of their world.

We have long believed* that during the time of the aboriginal possession of Australia their way of life did not change and nor did their landscape. They were said to be static people living in a static environment. But their environment could change, and at times it changed violently and dramatically. For the small wandering bands on the basalt plains of that part of south-eastern Australia, which was later named Australia Felix, their world was violently affected by volcanoes. For all the peoples living within one

*This is still the belief of the average educated Australian, long after the excavations of H. Hale and N. B. Tindale (1930), F. D. McCarthy (1948) and many others had given evidence of how stone and bone implements, for example, had slowly altered in 'static' Australia.

13

mile of the ocean—and for some who had never seen the sea
—a more shattering change was to affect their landscape and
way of life: that change was the rising of the sea and the
drowning of their hunting grounds. Nothing in the short
history of white men in Australia can match those physical
changes. The recent clearing of extensive forests, the building of a million miles of fences, the making of railways and
roads and artificial lakes—none of these changes which
dominate the modern history of Australia can be compared
with the ancient rising of the seas, the shaping of thousands
of new harbours, the swamping of scores of tribal territories
and the wiping out of the evidence of the aboriginal life
once lived on those drowned lands.

CHAPTER TWO

The Discoverers

The first Australians came across the stepping stones from south-east Asia during an epoch when the level of the ocean was lower. The sea-straits were narrow but the voyages were courageous. The slow eastward movement of these peoples was one of the great events in the history of man.

II

The south-eastern shores of Asia were then much closer to Australia. At the time of the migration Java was part of the landmass of Asia and even Bali was not yet an island. From Bali, however, the sea bed fell away steeply, and to the east the Lombok Strait was several miles deep. The strait between Asian Bali and the island of Lombok marked a zoological boundary which was first described by Robert Wallace, the English naturalist. Wallace's Line loosely divided the flora and fauna of Asia and Australasia. Thus on the mountains of Bali, to the west, tigers are still found. On Bali are the nests of woodpeckers and fruit thrushes, and on Lombok are the nests of cockatoos and honeysuckers; and many birds of the one island are rarely seen on the other. To the east, for millions of years, the sea has protected marsupials from the predators which flourished in Asia. While Wallace pencilled that north-south boundary more sharply than the evidence merited, he nonetheless pointed to a long-lasting barrier against the migration of large animals. That

15

barrier, with Bali and Borneo on the Asiatic side and the Celebes and the Philippines on the outer side, was the first strip of sea which had to be crossed by those Asians whose descendants ultimately pioneered Australia.

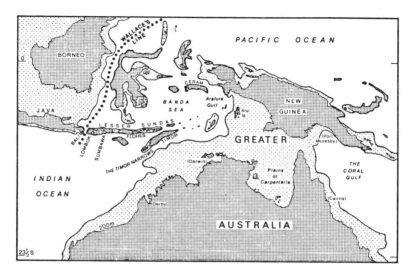

The Shallow Seas

One possible way to Australia was to cross the deep water to Lombok, follow the chain of islands to the east, and then perhaps cross from the mountainous island of Flora to Timor. The sea crossings on that line of advance to Timor were well within the capacity of fragile rafts or canoes. On each voyage the land on both sides would have clearly been in sight unless heavy rain, mist or darkness fell. Even at today's sea-levels no voyage along that course exceeds twenty miles from Timor. However, the voyage to Australia would have been hazardous. In that era Australia was much closer to Timor, but the gap of deep sea could still have been 70 or 100 miles wide. As the Australian coastline opposite Timor had no high mountains, the first voyagers to cross the inter-

16

vening sea cannot have been inspired by the certainty that land lay ahead.

Another possible line of island-hopping was on the other side of the equator. Professor John Mulvaney, in his excellent book *The Prehistory of Australia*, thought the ocean between Timor and Australia was too wide an obstacle. Instead he suggested the possibility of the first migrants reaching the continent somewhere near the western shore of New Guinea or near the mountains which are now the Aru Islands. He briefly charted a possible route—predominantly overland—from South China and Taiwan through the Philippines and Borneo and the Celebes. At that time part of the west coast of the Celebes was probably in sight of Asia while to the east stretched stepping stones which were just within the sea-range of a lucky vessel. J. N. Jennings, a specialist on sea levels, has suggested that each stepping stone would have provided a glimpse across the sea to the next. 'If', he added, 'the sightings of smudges of land on the horizon was a necessary prompter for primitive men to venture forth on logs or rafts, then the necessary stimulus of a chain of intervisibility would have existed through the Celebes and Moluccas to New Guinea.'

Between the coast of south-east Asia and the Australian continent lay so many islands, big and small, that a map-gazer could pencil scores of different routes for this slow migration. With the help of hindsight it is easy to imagine the stone-age migrants moving along the shortest possible route to Australia, but there is no reason why they should have taken the shortest route. Australia was merely the chance terminus of a series of voyages and migrations spread in all probability over many generations. The eastward movement might have been more like a zigzag than a straight line. Through the whims of winds and currents some islands might have been bypassed and then settled hundreds of years later. The seafarers might even have reached Australia centuries before they reached Timor.

Many of the vital voyages were probably not intended. Men swimming behind a push-along raft or roped logs were perhaps crossing a river when the tide pulled them out to sea. A lone fisherman, paddling his bark canoe near a reef, might have been caught by an offshore wind and swept far out to sea: next morning the nearest land was a strange jungle towards which he nervously pushed his canoe. Hunters who every spring visited the rocky coastline of a nearby island to raid the nests of sea-birds might have been marooned for days by choppy seas, might have gone inland in search of edible plants and fruits, and decided henceforth to spend several months of each year on the island.

There is no record of the voyages by which people discovered the succession of islands. At least no record is needed to sense the frequent terror of the voyage: the fear that rising seas would capsize the raft or flimsy canoe, the fear of falling asleep through exhaustion and slipping into the ocean, the anxious baling of water from a canoe, the increasing thirst and hunger, the sense of bewilderment as familiar land sank from sight. Even the delights of smelling the green growth from some near land before the dawn, of slowly recognizing the faint silhouette of mountains in the first light of morning, must have been quickly checked by fear that the unknown land held wild animals or unfamiliar tribes.

Even the narrow straits, where land was seen throughout the crossing, could be hazardous. Some were scoured by swift tides which could easily overturn or swamp a small vessel. In northern Australia, in living memory, even after the aboriginals acquired those dug-out canoes which were more seaworthy than any craft of the Pleistocene epoch, the hazards of crossing the narrow seas were high. We have a vivid account, from Arnhem Land, of a party of aboriginals setting out in their dug-out canoe to reach an island where turtles were abundant. The strait was about four miles wide and sometimes ripped by a wild tide. On this still day the canoe was packed with perhaps twenty men, women and children, 'their heads just peeping out over the rim as they huddled down in the bottom.' The mat sails were raised and the canoe moved along with her rim barely above the water. Then one of those south-easterlies known as a 'morning glory' began to blow. White clouds raced across the sky. The navigator hoped to reach the island before the seas began to rise, so he took in no sail. The wind increased, the mast snapped. The adults jumped into the sea to lighten the canoe and to hold her bow towards the waves. The waves became higher and at last the canoe was swamped. And we learn from the white observer, Bill Harney, that the only man who reached the shore was the navigator, a child held in his arms.

The coastal Tasmanians experienced the kind of dangers which early seafarers must have encountered in their short voyages to the west of Wallace's Line. As the vessels of Tasmanians were often despised by Europeans as the flimsiest of the flimsy they might have been no safer than those used in the era of the migrations; they might have been comparable. The raft-canoes in the south of Tasmania were made of elongated rolls of bark, bound together with grass cord. Four rolls of bark, tightly corded together at each end to form a pointed stern and bow, could not easily be upset in a light sea. On the rocky south coast of Tasmania some of these craft were as capacious as a whaleboat and could carry seven or eight adults, the men sitting in front and the women behind. In these vessels the southern Tasmanians went out to Maatsuyker Islands, killed seals on the rocks and beaches, and carried the meat back to the mainland. Occasionally they crossed to Eddystone Rock to kill the wallowing seals. That rock is so far from the most southerly point of Tasmania, the South East Cape, that it is not marked on most maps of Australian territory. The distance is about fifteen miles and there the ocean touches one of the most exposed stretches of the entire coastline. The journey can only be called heroic. On the sealing expeditions to offshore rocks and islands the casualties must have been many. One Tasmanian aboriginal recalled in the 1830s that many hundreds of his people had been drowned on these crossings. The aggregate statistic was probably exaggerated, but the risks of such a voyage were not. For any accidental voyage, as distinct from a planned voyage, the risks of drowning must have been higher.

To suggest that many voyages of discovery were unintentional is to go only a small way towards explaining the eastward migration towards Australia and New Guinea. The unintentional voyagers who escaped death at sea and landed safely on new ground were not likely to populate the island quickly. As fishing or canoeing was more usually a male occupation, the men who were accidentally marooned on new islands must have rarely been accompanied by women. Some of the discoverers might have lived out the remainder of their life, celibate, on the new island. Many presumably tried to return to their own land, and some must have lost their life in the attempt. Those who did return safely to their home islands of the Indonesian archipelago provided information which was useful if overpopulation or another thrusting force tempted some inhabitants to emigrate. Even if the discoverer of an island did not dare the seas again in order to return home he often conveyed unintentionally the news that his island had sufficient food to sustain life. The smoke from his fires, especially if he tried to burn part of the forest, must have sometimes been visible from his old land if the two places were not far apart.

In the slow emigration across the islands from south-east Asia, random sea voyages were possibly important in bridging land as well as sea. Even if the rain-forest and undergrowth on islands nearer the equator were not quite as thick during the lower temperatures of the last glacial epoch, they were still obstacles. In mountainous islands or in large masses of land such as the Western Celebes and Ceram, the sea provided easier pathways whenever wide bights or gulfs cut inland.

III

Circumstantial evidence suggests that the migrations to Australia were aided both by accidental and by planned voyages, and that the one promoted the other. The accidental voyages provided, at a heavy cost in drownings, useful information about the fertility of the islands that stood to the east. And when pressures arose in the settled islands—pressures such as famine or warfare—some people probably attempted to sail to the islands in the east, especially to islands about which favourable information was known or inferred.

A comparable situation probably existed thousands of years later in Polynesia where island after island was settled by voyagers who often had sailed hundreds of miles from the nearest island. Recent research suggests that accidental voyages often found islands which later became the goal for deliberate Polynesian voyages. The history of mineral discovery is also analogous to the discovery of islands, for every new mineral field is an island of promising ground in a sea of barren rock. Often in the mining history of Australia a new field was discovered accidentally and tentatively by a traveller not primarily interested in minerals; and his discovery was at first ignored and became the goal for mineral-seekers from other places only when economic pressures—drought or trade depression—spurred emigration.

The deliberate—not the accidental—voyage to new islands was the more conducive to the spread of the human race. Such a voyage was likely to include one or two women, and thus could lead to a natural increase of population on the new shore. The intentional voyage was more productive because it was also more likely to succeed. The rafts or canoes had probably been made with more care for a riskier and longer voyage. They probably also carried food and water.

Nothing aided the safety of the planned voyage so often as

the timing. The people who came east must have been mostly shore-dwellers: fishermen and hunters whose daily catches depended on their skill in observing wild life and weather. In planning a voyage they would choose the time when wind, current and the smoothness of the sea were most likely to favour them. Of their ability to predict weather we have no certain knowledge; but many bushmen and hunters labelled by city-dwellers as 'primitive' and 'ignorant' had a sophisticated knowledge of weather and seasons. G. A. Robinson, who in the 1830s camped nightly with Tasmanian hunters, respected their knack of reading the clouds and moon and stars and thereby forecasting the weather of one of the most changeable climates in Australia. 'I have seldom found them to err', he wrote.

Deliberate migrations—where the risk of death is high—require strong motives. Were such motives present in the Indonesian islands? To know why people emigrated we have to know much about their society—their standard of living, birth rate and death rate, medical knowledge and sexual practices, natural catastrophes, their attitude to climate and clan and homeland. Unfortunately we know little about these driving forces in the Indonesian islands more than 30,000 years ago.

Defeat in warfare, the threat of banishment, or fear of punishment might have forced some men to emigrate. Obviously the men had to abduct a woman—or be exiled with a woman—if the new settlement was to flourish. If it so happened that the eastward drift of men towards Australia was in part caused by acts of banishment it would not be the last time that Australia was peopled by exiles.

Over-population in several islands of the Indonesian archipelago might have caused some emigration to the east. Changes of climate and sea-level near the end of the last ice age might have reduced the supply of food and therefore provided incentive to migrate to those lands that were visible on the horizon. We cannot be sure, however, that famines arose. Moreover if a scarcity of food arose from changes in sea level or in temperature, the scarcity would have come slowly rather than dramatically, spreading its effects over many generations. As we will see later, hunting societies had various ways of preventing the number of mouths from exceeding the available mouthfuls of food. Their methods of restricting population might have largely avoided that abnormal famine for which one solution was emigration.

In the Banda Sea, perhaps 200 miles west of what was once the coastline of the united continent of Australia and New Guinea, a pinkish-white volcanic cone rises straight from the ocean. Passed today by ships sailing between Sydney and Hong Kong, this uninhabited island of Manuk is one of the vivid clues to another force which may have promoted the movement of man between south-east Asia and Australia. The Indonesian archipelago has experienced more volcanic eruptions in historic times than any other zone of the earth: seventy-eight volcanoes have erupted. Possibly the largest eruption in the last few thousand years was on the island of Sumbawa, where in 1815 a towering volcanic cone was violently blown away. As many volcanoes were astride the line of islands that form stepping stones between Bali and Sumbawa and Timor, it is conceivable that active volcanoes might at times have inspired, at times deflected, or even for a time reversed, the eastward advance of man towards Australia.

The journey to what was then the single continent of Australia-New Guinea was one of the momentous events of world history. That series of crossings must have surpassed any previous achievement in seacraft; indeed it could even have embraced the first long sea voyages in the history of man. It also marked the expansion of man beyond that single mass of land to which he had previously been confined: a continent embracing Africa, Asia, Europe, much of Indonesia and of course the Americas. A more significant event than any of the discoveries of Australia by Spanish,

23

Dutch or British navigators in recent centuries, it was brilliantly set in perspective by an Australian archaeologist, Rhys Jones, in 1969. He argued, in the year when man first walked on the moon, that man's first voyage across Wallace's Line had been the passing of a barrier no less formidable.

The real discoverer of the new continent probably waded ashore somewhere on the north-west coast. He might have landed near the present New Guinea rather than the present Australia or he might have landed on the western coast that then linked the two lands. One of a host of people taking part in a long, long relay race that perhaps extended over thousands of years, he simply happened to be carrying the torch when the new continent was reached. Perhaps he came ashore as the result of an accidental voyage, his raft blown by wind or drifting with the current. Perhaps he lived for many years in the new continent, all alone, unwilling or unable to attempt the voyage back to his own island. Where he landed and where he lit his first fire will never be known, for the shore was long ago drowned by the rising seas.

IV

The oldest known camp-site in northern Australia was occupied at least 22,000 years ago. It is near the Oenpelli Mission on the East Alligator River and—as the geese fly— lies 150 miles east of Darwin. When the cooking fires first burned in that camp the seacoast was much further away than it is today: the sea, now only a few days walk away was then far away. Only when the sea slowly advanced into Arnhem Land thousands of years later, did the addition of shellfish to the diet provide preservative which accidentally embalmed the food debris in the old camp-sites at Oenpelli. Thanks to the work of archaeologists and the preservative effect of sea shells, we have evidence that at least 7,000 years ago the aboriginals at Oenpelli ate tortoises, bandicoots, possums, boned fish, shellfish, nuts and the root-like stem of the lotus lily. We now also know some of the stone implements which were used to prepare and gather food about 22,000 years ago. Stone pounders and grinders were used, presumably to pulverize seeds and other vegetable foods into wholemeal or a moist paste. The stone flakes probably cut or scraped meat, skin and plant foods, and the stone axes were used to chop wood or shape wooden tools. The axes were impressive, and their cutting edge had been shaped and sharpened by a grinding process which, by the standards of that time, was sophisticated. Similar ground-edge axes, perhaps five or seven thousand years younger than those at Oenpelli, have been discovered in the Niah Cave in Borneo. Carmel White, the finder of these tools at Oenpelli, suggests that edge-ground axes were more likely to be found in the tropics than in temperate zones. Perhaps they were essential where the forests were damp, fast-growing, and dominated by trees which were less inflammable than the eucalypts further to the south. When aboriginals migrated from the tropics to the cooler parts of Australia the edge-ground axe appears to have been abandoned, giving way to the firestick.

Eventually camp-sites older than Oenpelli will be found and excavated in northern Australia. They will reveal much about the way of living of the first immigrants, but already some evidence has been pieced together. An ingenious survey by Jack Golson suggests that the early aboriginals probably had no difficulty in finding familiar foods in the new country. Even if they had not previously seen kangaroos and many of the other marsupials, and at first had refused to eat them, they must have known many shellfish and swimming fish. Moreover they probably would have found many fruits and vegetables which they had eaten in their home island.

Golson devised a simple way of estimating how many Australian foods must have already been familiar to them. He first made a list of the food plants eaten by aboriginals in Australia in recent times and then found how many of them were also growing in Indonesia, Malaysia and the Philip-

pines. Of the food-plants eaten in recorded times by aboriginals in Arnhem Land, at least twenty-nine are well known in
the zone of tropical lands from which the first Australians or
their ancestors had come. Another eight of the aboriginals'
food-plants also grow in New Guinea, and that territory was
possibly traversed by some of the first migrants coming
towards Arnhem Land. It is reasonable to assume that many
of those food-plants which today are common to northern
Australia and the adjacent islands were growing there 30,000
or 40,000 years ago, thus providing familiar foods for the first
migrants to reach Australia. Several of the plants, however,
might have reached Australia later, having been carried here
by people, birds or tides. Thus Golson argued that the noble
tamarind trees, whose fruits were eaten by aboriginals, probably reached northern Australia only about two centuries ago
when Indonesians began to come on regular fishing
expeditions.

Golson's survey of plant-foods suggests that the aboriginals
of Arnhem Land followed the food preferences and cooking
methods of the islands from which they had originated long
ago. These customs moreover continued to the end of
nomadic life in Arnhem Land, where aboriginals tended to
eat those plant-foods which also happened to grow in Indonesia, New Guinea and Malaysia rather than the numerous
edible plant-foods which were unique to Australia. Moreover
in removing the toxin from edible yams, mangrove seeds and
palm nuts, they followed the methods of heating and leaching which even in recent times were practised in islands of
Indonesia. This evidence is suggestive rather than conclusive,
but it hints at the power of tradition in those parts of
tropical Australia where aboriginals could choose between
Australian foods or old island foods.

When aboriginals moved south, either following the coast
or pushing into the interior, they could no longer find so
many of the plants which they had eaten in the tropics. They
were forced to experiment, and began to eat yams and seeds

and greens which in the tropics they had shunned or neglected. In the dry interior they eventually fed more on seeds; and various seeds of grasses and acacia became vital, though the seeds remained unpopular as food in the tropics. How long was spent in the process of experimenting with strange foods is impossible to say. Some seeds might not have been eaten regularly until thousands of years after the arrival of aboriginals. All we know is that on the dry sweeping plains they came to rely on many plantfoods which did not grow in the earlier homeland of their ancestors.

We know nothing of the thrust or impetus behind the occupation of the whole continent. Archaeology in the last few years suggests that aboriginals lived in the remote south-west and south-east of the continent more than 30,000 years ago, but how many years—or thousands of years—were spent in that slow southwards trek across the continent is a mystery. It would be surprising, however, if the exploring of greater Australia was completed in less than 400 or 500 years.

The few immigrants who had landed on the north-west coast would at first have hugged the coast. As they had come from the shores of islands, their skills and tastes had equipped them for winning food near the sea rather than inland. If, after living for generations on the coast of Australia-New Guinea, the pressure of feuds or famine compelled many small groups to move inland, they were unlikely to move far. Even when forced to live in the interior they probably tried to spend at least one season of each year near that sea which traditionally had provided them with much of their food. For breakaway groups the tendency was possibly to move along the coast rather than into the interior, so long as empty coast was there to be occupied.

Any group which decided to occupy new territory in Australia needed, by present standards, a large area for every ten people. As aboriginals kept no livestock and gardens, and rarely hoarded food, they roamed over a wide terrain in search of food. Their roaming was based on wide knowledge of plants and animals and seasonal gluts. They could acquire that knowledge and live that orderly form of nomadic life only after they had explored a region and found many of its foodplants, found axe-quarries and ochre mines, and closely observed the fish, animals and birds. Droughts or over-population were probably the main stimulus to their exploration and their occupation of new areas.

V

Small bands of nomads, coming together only during a seasonal abundance of food, were the typical economic organization when aboriginal life was recorded first by Europeans. The bands must have been typical for a long time. Being small and flexible, they were ideal for exploring new territory. The members were skilled in living off the land, they travelled lightly, and were observant of new land-marks and sources of food. The smallest of these bands probably consisted of one family: a husband, a wife and sometimes second and third wives, and children. Except when food or water was scarce a family did not probably live and travel on its own. For much of the year in many parts of Australia, three or four families moved over the countryside together. That group held perhaps twenty to fifty people. It is estimated that 5,000 or 10,000 such groups or economic communities inhabited the continent in the year 1800. Un-fortunately the groups have no accepted name. A. R. Radcliffe-Brown called them 'hordes' and the name often appears in learned books; but a 'horde' sounds like a multi-tude and so is not suitable for such small bands of wanderers.*

*Radcliffe-Brown used the word 'tribe' to denote the larger group which spoke a common language and the word 'clan' to describe the group which owned the territory. In general discussion 'tribe' is still a useful word, if it means nothing more than a band of aboriginals linked by social and economic ties.

The bonds which tied together a small mobile community probably varied greatly from area to area. The links might be of blood and marriage, or simply personal preference. M. J. Meggitt, observing desert peoples during the tail-end of their traditional life, noticed that brothers-in-law and their wives and children often lived and worked together; the women foraging together, the men hunting as a group. Sometimes an unmarried woman went with her sister, or a married man and his wife joined his father's party. Sometimes blood brothers and their retinue formed a common encampment; the brothers, Meggitt noted, often seemed willing to swap wives, and were thus able to 'enjoy male companionship and sexual variety simultaneously.' In abundant seasons many of the groups would come together and form a larger camp of several hundred people, but the available food could rarely support such a large gathering for more than a week. In these temporary camps most people probably were related to each other. If they were not directly related by blood or marriage they were sometimes united by the belief that they had a common totem ancestor who had pioneered that territory long ago and whose influence on the living was powerful.

A cluster of these nomadic groups usually held the communal right to gather food and to hunt in a specific belt of land. The right to the food also imposed an obligation to carry out those religious ceremonies which were intended to keep the land fertile and the animals abundant. These territories, however, did not have the tight physical boundaries and the family unity of a city state or nation state. While many aboriginals spent every month of their life in their traditional territory, others might spend most of their life in alien territory. In most regions the marriages were between people of different territorial groups or clans, and accordingly the children might have hunting rights in two distinct territories. Furthermore during times of scarcity or abundance the nomadic groups might move, either by invitation

29

or by force, outside their own territory. Even the boundaries of many territories were vague. By our standards the social groupings of aboriginals were complicated; and a chart of their social organization would seem, especially in relation to the small number of people involved, more complicated than the organization chart of General Motors or the Polish Communist Party. But during the first occupying of the land, the social groupings were probably less intricate and less rigid.

VI

It is unlikely that the slow aboriginal invasion of the interior of the continent was systematic or orderly. Some groups were probably driven out of the territory which they had discovered, explored and named. Other groups probably retreated voluntarily from regions which they had once occupied. Sometimes, in the slow southwards movement, a crust of ranges or a bare plain was leap-frogged and not occupied permanently until much later. The first aboriginal settlers probably skirted the deserts, perhaps wandering into them in the rare year of heavy rain but not attempting to live there permanently until thousands of years had passed.

So, in time, forgotten men and women discovered the Pacific Ocean and probably thought nothing of their find. They tasted for the first time the fruit of the towering Bunya Bunya pines, drank the warm water of the lazy rivers of the inland, found tracks across the spine of the eastern dividing range, ran forefingers on the salt which lay on the white rims of shallow lakes and waded into the cold waters of the Southern Ocean. They saw the footprints of strange animals and they peered into forests of jarrah or eucalypt which were taller than any trees which they or their line of ancestors had ever climbed. They felt the winds blowing in winter from the Antarctic, and for the first time they saw a white cape on the mountains and wondered what could be so dazzling and white, for snow was unknown to them.

To visualize that slow flow of people across the Indonesian islands, across New Guinea and Australia, is to see one of the great treks in the history of the human race. Eventually, however, the flow was halted. Small, flexible bands of people became attached to their own loose area of territory.

By the time the vanguard of aboriginals had reached the sites of Perth, Adelaide and Sydney, so many generations might have elapsed that the people in each of those three localities were speaking their own distinct dialect. Irrespective of whether one language or many languages had entered the continent, each language in the course of thousands of years nursed offspring, and the offspring were married or divorced, and eventually the continent was fragmented by the sheer variety of its languages. In most areas an aboriginal could understand the dialect of neighbouring people but he could travel no more than perhaps 100 miles before meeting people whose speech was unintelligible. Nonetheless a skill in speaking foreign languages was more common amongst the average tribal aboriginal than amongst the average Australian today.

According to cautious counts the continent eventually had more than 300 languages, and the number would be much larger if sharp differences of dialect were included. Tasmania alone had five distinct languages. Even the two facing shores of Sydney Harbour were, in languages, far apart. In 1969 a linguist discovered, partly from clues in the hand-written notes of a dead missionary, that the language spoken on the site of the present opera house was not spoken on the facing shore. An aboriginal paddling his canoe across to the north shore had to speak not merely a different dialect but a different language. The high sandstone cliffs rising on each side of the Sydney heads formed a linguistic chasm as deep as the Straits of Dover. Throughout the continent were similar barriers of language, geography, mythology or blood which divided the land into hundreds of fluid republics.

31

CHAPTER THREE

The Tasmanians: Outline of a Puzzle

One question was persistently asked by inquisitive Europeans who made early visits to Australia, Where, they asked, did the dark Tasmanians come from? The question, perplexing today, was even more perplexing then. The Tasmanians seemed so different in appearance from the aboriginals on the Australian mainland that different sources had to be supposed for the two peoples.

Tasmanians were first seen by Europeans in March 1772. The Frenchman, Marion du Fresne, called at the east coast of Tasmania while on a voyage from Mauritius to Tahiti, and he attempted to land on a long beach to the north of Eaglehawk Neck. There his crew was attacked with spears and stones. They replied with their muskets, killing one Tasmanian man. The naked corpse, eagerly examined by the Frenchmen, was smallish in stature and about 5 feet and 2 or 3 inches high. The skin appeared to be black, though according to the log of the voyage 'we could see that their natural colour was reddish and that it was only their habit of keeping close to a smoky fire that blackened them thus.' The chest had ceremonial scars, being 'slashed like a Mozambique Kaffir's.' The head was well shaped with a flattish nose, thick lips and magnificent teeth, but the eyes, we are told, were ill-tempered and reddish. The roots of his hair were smeared with red pigment and the hair itself was short and woolly.

The woolliness of the hair of the dark Tasmanians was

often described. Their hair, in the opinion of European visitors, had no superficial or innate resemblance to that of the overwhelming majority of aboriginals on the Australian continent whose locks were straight or curly, soft or coarse, black or dark brown, but rarely if ever woolly.* The hair of the Tasmanians grew in ringlets, tightly coiled; the shaft of the hair was oval rather than rounded, and it resembled more the hair of the negritos of New Guinea or the Bushmen of southern Africa. The hair of the Tasmanians, more than any other characteristic, suggested to early theorists that this race had not originated in the same land as the Australian aboriginals.

II

The riddle of where the Tasmanians originated and how they reached their new land tantalized learned men of the nineteenth century. In courageously seeking an answer to these questions, scholars were blindfolded by at least three closely-woven strips of cloth—blindfolds which have since become transparent.

The first blindfold was an ignorance that the sea-level had risen at the end of the last ice age. Scholars of the nineteenth century, not knowing that fact, had no alternative but to suggest that the first Tasmanians arrived only after braving long sea voyages. As Bass Strait can be one of the roughest stretches of sea in the globe, the first arrivals, it was inferred, must have been able seamen who sailed perhaps from a remote land. This supposition at the time seemed reasonable. It was not until 1895—long after the start of the debate about the origins of the Tasmanians—that the scientist Nathaniel Shaler pointed out that the melting of some great

*Fair hair, even flaxen hair, has often been recorded in aboriginals of central Australia. Professor A. A. Abbie, an Adelaide anatomist, reports that in certain tribes four of every five children under ten years of age had fair hair. By the age of twenty, however, blondeness was unusual.

ice sheets at the end of the ice age would raise the height of the oceans throughout the world. That discovery meant that Bass Strait was a relatively recent strait. We now know that the strait was formed long after man had settled in Australia and that therefore the Tasmanians probably came overland before the separating strait was formed.

Another blindfold was ignorance of the length of the span of human history. The events told in the Book of Genesis influenced the belief that the history of the world was short. As the Great Deluge and the launching of Noah's Ark had reputedly taken place only 4,200 years ago, and as the subsequent scattering of the human race to the corners of the world was probably slow, most scholars reasoned that Tasmania must have been settled hundreds rather than thousands of years ago. This hypothesis was widely held even towards the close of the nineteenth century. As the history of mankind was erroneously seen as short, it was impossible to envisage that the Tasmanians had lived long on their isolated island and that their language and culture and perhaps even their physique might have changed during their enforced isolation. In fact, the Tasmanians had 'probably one of the longest periods of isolation ever recorded in human history'.

There was a third blindfold on the eyes of those who were intrigued by the origins of the Tasmanians. That blindfold arose from a belief that the surviving primitive peoples and their way of life were eternally static. The Tasmanians of 1800 A.D. were assumed to have virtually the same physique, language, and hunting skills as their ancestors—wherever those ancestors might have lived. Tasmania was thus viewed with fascination as a museum case in which early human society had been preserved. Tasmania was seen as the home of living mummies. Sir John Lubbock—the English scholar who in 1865 coined those words, 'palaeolithic' and 'neolithic', which became the hourhands of archaeologists—believed the Tasmanians were vital evidence of what people in Europe had once been like. Their language, skills, ways of hunting and cooking, rituals and beliefs were usually seen as facets imported wholly from foreign lands and preserved in a new environment.

Naturally, these assumptions steered the enquiry about the origin of the Tasmanians. As it was believed that they had not lived long in Tasmania and that their way of life was static, identification of their ancestors was not expected to be difficult. The race to which the Tasmanians were related would presumably speak a similar language and have similar beliefs, customs, skills. As the Tasmanians used neither boomerangs nor spear-throwers, the related race was expected to have a very small armoury of weapons. Moreover their physique would also be similar to that of the Tasmanians since the two races had not long been separated. As the Tasmanians did not physically resemble any known aboriginal group on the mainland, most scholars assumed that they must have migrated from a faraway land.

III

Africa was seen as one possible homeland of the Tasmanians. Perhaps the Tasmanians were simply African negroes who had been driven west by storms. The prevailing westerly winds in the Southern Ocean made that theory plausible; and Robert Fitzroy, an English naval captain who knew the winds, was one of the first to argue that Tasmanians were negro castaways. An African homeland was also advocated in 1886 by Edward Micklethwaite Curr in his four-volumed work, *The Australian Race*. Curr argued that in language, customs and skills the aboriginals of Australia and the negroes of east Africa had much in common. They had similar practices of circumcision, of scarring the body ornamentally, piercing the septum of the nose, knocking out the front teeth of children, and shared many customs in marriage and burial. The boomerang, he decided, was the Australian variation of a weapon copied from Ethiopia. In his vigorous search for evidence Curr reflected the belief that human history was short and that primitive people and their languages and skills were mummified.

Curr found many of his illustrations of African behaviour in travellers' books on Africa, especially the writings of David Livingstone who in the popular imagination was the cosmonaut of that era. Curr was quick to detect resemblances, real or imagined. In Australia he had seen thirsty aboriginals wade into a waterhole, lower their right hand, and scoop water into the mouth, so he was delighted to read the following passage in Livingstone's story of his travels on the Zambesi:

> One of the Makolo ran down in the dusk to the river, and, as he was busy tossing the water to his mouth with his hand, in the manner peculiar to the natives, a crocodile rose suddenly from the bottom and caught him by the hand.

Curr repeated the sentence in his book as evidence of the likenesses between Africans and Australians but forgot to mention what happened to the hand that was gripped by the crocodile's jaw. Curr was obsessed by his studies. He was obsessed too by the idea that the first Australians came either directly from Africa or from some land that was the cradle of the negro race. He thought all the tribes of mainland Australia were descendants of negroes crossed by another unknown race of lighter-skinned, straight-haired people. They were, he believed, the descendants of those whose ship or canoe had landed on the north-west coast of Australia. Likewise the Tasmanians, added Curr, were of 'mixed negro' descent; they had crossed with another race and independently reached their island home.

Other investigators decided that the Tasmanians came not from Africa but from southern Asia. Racial links have long been detected between Tasmanians and the smallish people who inhabited the Andaman Islands—a chain of high hills and coral beds specking the Bay of Bengal. It would be intriguing to know why the Andaman Islands should have been so persistently linked with Tasmania, for those islands are as close to Istanbul as to Tasmania. One clue may lie in the quaint notes written about the Andaman Islanders in the ninth century: 'They are black, with woolly hair, and in their eyes and countenances there is something quite frightful.' The woolly hair and the facial features, probably stimulated the hypothesis that they and the Tasmanians had once formed part of a race which, in south-east Asia, had split by emigrating in different directions. Perhaps the idea was encouraged by the simple technology as much as the woolly hair of both peoples. At the close of the last century two Australian anthropologists—H. Ling Roth and William Howitt—were inclined to think that the original Tasmanians had been more closely related to the pygmies of the Andamans than to the people of any other race. A version of the idea is still viewed with respect. Visitors to a famous museum in London in the early 1970s could see, prominently displayed, the suggestion that the Andaman Islanders may be a dwarfed residue of the Melanesian stock which was said to have inhabited Tasmania.

Languages as well as the texture of hair were eagerly analyzed as a possible clue to the origin of the Tasmanians. If the vocabulary and grammar of the brown Tasmanians could be studied, similarities might be found with the language spoken by races in other parts of the world, thus suggesting a race with whom the Tasmanians had been in contact at an earlier period. Captain Cook, who in 1777 spent several days on the east coast of Tasmania, tried to test his belief that there was originally a common mother language for all of the islands stretching across the Pacific from Australia to Easter Island. To his disappointment, however, those first Tasmanians whom he met on the beach at Bruny Island seemed to comprehend no words of the two or three South Sea languages spoken to them. Eleven years later

William Bligh, calling on the same east coast during the voyage that was to end in mutiny, saw twenty brown-skinned Tasmanians emerge naked from the forest. From the ship's boat, only a spear's throw from the surf beach, he threw them gifts wrapped in paper and watched them take the beads, nails and trinkets from the packages and place them on their heads as if they were hats. Their voices, he wrote vividly, sounded 'like the cackling of geese'. It is the sound of the voices which lingers, outlasting the tumble of the surf:

> When they first came in sight, they made a prodigious clattering in their speech, and held their arms over their heads. They spoke so quick, that I could not catch one single word they uttered.

When over the years the words they uttered were caught and recorded, five groups of languages were recorded in Tasmania alone—languages so distinctive that many aboriginals from one part of Tasmania could not readily understand the speech of those from another part of the island.

The recorded vocabularies of the dying Tasmanians were examined to see whether they resembled the languages spoken in parts of mainland Australia or other parts of the world. Any affinity would be a valuable clue to the origin of the Tasmanians. In the 1840s Robert Gordon Latham, the young professor of English language and literature at University College, London, examined specimens of Tasmanian languages and decided that they had similarities with the language spoken in New Caledonia. He decided that the original Tasmanians had probably crossed the Pacific from New Caledonia, sailing about 1,500 miles in fragile rafts or boats from the tropics to the cold temperate zone. As the Tasmanians had woolly hair the evidence of contact with New Caledonia was even stronger in Latham's eyes.

Latham's theory had a long and tempestuous voyage, but remained buoyant even after the linguistic raft had sunk. As recently as 1934 the idea of New Caledonia as the homeland of the first Tasmanians was revived in a more sophisticated form by the persuasive Australian anatomist, Professor F. Wood Jones. In his theory the body had replaced the tongue as the crucial evidence.

While some theories argued that the Tasmanians came directly from a remote homeland, other theories saw them as the original Australians who had been expelled from the mainland by later invaders. This idea is feasible. Perhaps the Tasmanians were driven south, though it is slightly more plausible to suggest that they were pushed south not by the invasion of a new race but by the invasion of the sea onto plains which they had long inhabited.

If the Tasmanians were to be seen as the first invaders of the continent, a superior people had to be selected as their conquerors. Southern India was increasingly seen as the source of the new conquerors of Australia. In 1869 Thomas H. Huxley, the celebrated biologist, suggested that the Australian aboriginals were difficult to distinguish physically from the tribes in the Deccan, the region of south India. From Robert Caldwell, Bishop of Madras, came the supporting suggestion that the languages of tribes of southern and western Australia used almost the same words for *I*, *Thou*, *He*, *We*, and *You* as the fishermen on the Madras coast. The idea of a link between Australian languages and the Dravidian languages of southern India won more and more converts. The Dravidian family of languages, of which Tamil is spoken the most, had defied attempts to prove that it had affinity with Asian languages as far apart as Burma and the Urals. Such a mysterious language was thus a ready-made ally for Australian tongues.

The Dravidian theory, in its most respectable form, appeared in the famous Cambridge edition of the *Encyclopaedia Britannica* in 1910. There the Australian boomerang and canoe were added to language and physiology as further evidence of the affinity between Dravidian and Australian peoples. The rare boomerang, readers were informed, was thrown by 'the wild tribes of the Deccan'. The canoes used by aboriginals on Australian sheltered waters resembled those used on the Dravidian coast. The powerful argument set out in the encyclopaedia by Channing Arnold of University College, Oxford, ended in the firm conclusion: 'it seems reasonable enough to assume that the Australian natives are Dravidians, exiled in remote times from Hindustan, though when their migration took place and how they traversed the Indian Ocean must remain questions to which, by their very nature, there can be no satisfactory answer'. He was inclined, however, to the view that they sailed and drifted by way of Ceylon in their bark boats, eventually landing on the west or north-west coast of Australia. He suggested that the Dravidian people might have arrived in several ways and then slowly mastered the Papuan-type of man who had previously entered Australia from Flores, Timor, New Guinea and islands of the near north. Like the Celts retreating into Cornwall, the woolly-haired people fled to Tasmania and settled there.

While there was no accepted version of how man reached Australia, the Dravidian theory came closest to orthodoxy. In our generation few scholars still believe in that ancestral home in the Southern Indian hills. But the idea still lives, is taught in many Australian schools, is repeated in the hall of one of the great museums of Europe, and recently was affirmed by a gifted historian of Pacific exploration.

The long era of speculation about the origins of Tasmanians and Australians provoked many contradictory theories, but most theories assumed that different races had occupied Tasmania and Australia. Indeed the American anthropologist, Joseph Birdsell, suggested that three waves of migration came from south-east Asia across the chain of islands to Australia and New Guinea. And he suggested that within each of the three main regions of Australia the aboriginals had more physical resemblance to peoples of distant lands than to those of the neighbouring Australian region. To Birdsell the physical differences between say the aboriginals on the Murray River and the aboriginals of Arnhem Land was so marked that one could only conclude that they had immigrated at different times.

Birdsell had first visited Australia just before the Second World War. He had arrived with the belief—common at that time—that the mainland aboriginals were homogeneous but fourteen months in the field changed his belief. He believed that he detected sharp physical variations from region to region; and a series of measurements ranging from the breadth of nose to the sitting height confirmed his faith in his ideas. He completed a Harvard thesis on the topic in 1941, and a quarter of a century later he reaffirmed his hypothesis that three distinct waves of aboriginals had peopled Tasmania and Australia.

The first major wave of migration, according to Birdsell, consisted of Oceanic Negritos. They were shorter, lighter in colour, than later migrants; and many had woolly hair. In Australia within living memory they survived only in a belt of rain forest near Cairns (Q.) but they had 'marked resemblances' to some tribes of the highlands of New Guinea and the Gazelle Peninsula of New Britain. The Tasmanians, he hinted, had belonged to this first wave of migration. The second wave of migrants occupied the south-east corner of the continent; as they flourished along the River Murray and its tributaries they were named Murrayians by Birdsell. They had larger heads and broader shoulders than those aboriginals which migrated in the other two waves. They were also very hairy, and were 'clearly related'—in Birdsell's opinion—to the Hairy Ainu of northern Japan. The third wave of brown migrants could be seen in modern times in Arnhem Land and northern Queensland. These 'Carpentarians' were tall and skinny, according to Birdsell's tape measure. Birdsell believed that they had some physical resemblance to the aboriginal tribes of southern India and Ceylon. Photographs which Birdsell published in 1967

South-East Australia showing present coastline and coastline of 20,000 years ago.

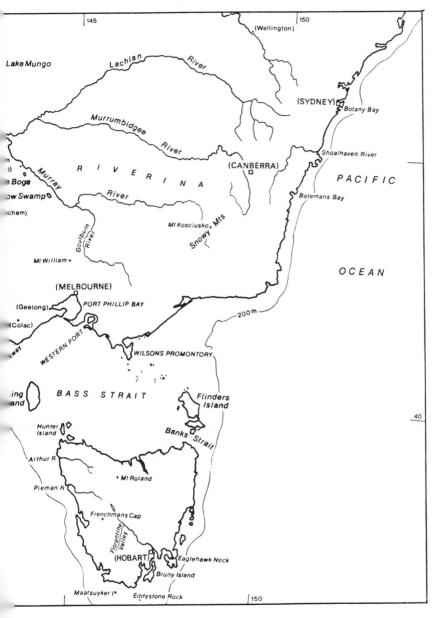

showed striking similarities, in face and body, between selected people from southern India and northern Australia.

Birdsell did not invoke a study of languages to support his argument. He was a physical anthropologist and kept to his speciality. His opinions about the origins of the Australians and Tasmanians belonged to an old tradition, and he had documented his argument more carefully and carried that tradition further than any of his predecessors. The strongest part of his case perhaps lay less in the origins of the migrants than in their racial diversity.

IV

No dramatic conclusion has emerged from two centuries of theorizing. The removal of the old ideological and geological blindfolds has allowed most of the old theories to wilt, though shreds of them survive in recent writings. All attempts to suggest that Tasmanians or Australians were closely related to peoples now living outside the region of Australia and New Guinea have either failed or remained fragile hypotheses. Circumstantial evidence suggests strongly that long ago the first Tasmanians and Australians came slowly along the stepping stones of the Indonesian archipelago but whether they belonged to the same race is still uncertain.

Even the once-trusted anatomical evidence is no longer the solution. In the second half of the nineteenth century, when the search for a missing link between ape and early man was strenuous, the skulls of dead Tasmanians had been measured to the nearest hair's breadth. Such was curiosity in medical schools and museums of Europe that the demand for Tasmanian skulls became stronger than the supply, which was limited by the traditional practice of cremating the dead, and by the rapid extinction of pure-blood Tasmanians. To meet the scarcity, Australian skulls were sometimes labelled 'Tasmanian' and sold at high prices. After 1876, when the last pure-blood Tasmanian died, Tasmanian skulls became as rare as the 'penny black' postage stamp. Moreover, anatomical collectors had been more interested in collecting skulls than whole skeletons; and only five 'whole skeletons' of Tasmanian aboriginals were preserved, so far as is known. Three of them were destroyed by air raids in Europe during the Second World War. Though the opportunity of carefully comparing the skulls and skeletons of the Tasmanians had diminished, the evidence at present suggests that they did not differ markedly from most Australian aboriginals on the opposite coast.

While most of the old theories about the ancestry of Tasmanians and Australians have been wrecked, a few spars can be salvaged. Furthermore, research and changing assumptions have given rise to two ideas which would have been perilous only half a century ago. The first idea suggests that the unusual physical characteristics of the Tasmanian could have evolved while they were inhabiting that isolated island. The second suggests, surprisingly, that physical differences between mainlanders and Tasmanians were not so sharp as between people of neighbouring regions of south-eastern Australia.

It is now possible to suggest, but not to prove, that the Tasmanians were mainland aboriginals who, isolated by the slow rising of the seas, developed different physical traits during their long era of isolation. Their crinkly hair, the colour of their skin, their slightly shorter physique and those other factors which apparently distinguished them from aboriginals on the mainland might have been the result of slow changes occurring over some nine thousand years in a relatively small group of people. Perhaps the Tasmanians were 'the descendants of Australian aborigines modified in isolation by random processes and possibly mutations.'

The Keppel Islands offer some support for the idea that in a relatively short span of time a small segregated race could be changed physically. These small tropical islands, which are now holiday resorts off the coast of central Queensland, once supported small groups of aboriginals. The twelve surviving skulls of aboriginals on the islands were reported on by Larnach and Macintosh at the University of Sydney in 1972. The skulls were unusually smooth and round, the forehead was high, and altogether they differed greatly from the skulls of the mainlanders and possibly the aboriginal skulls from any other region in Australia. According to the two anatomists the skulls were perhaps the result of micro-evolution amongst an isolated group of people who rarely, if ever, used swimming logs and rafts to cross the ten miles to the mainland, who rarely inter-bred with mainland aboriginals, and who therefore evolved in isolation. Undoubtedly the Keppel Islanders were not as totally isolated as the Tasmanians but fear of warfare with mainlanders who far outnumbered them might have kept the islanders at arm's length. As the Keppel Islanders were said to have spoken the same language as the people on the coast, they were perhaps not as isolated for as long as the theory of micro-evolution would require. Nonetheless the explanation of Larnach and Macintosh, to a layman, is fascinating for its confident assumption that isolation can conceivably lead to physical divergence in the space of a few thousand years.

That Tasmania was completely isolated for at least twelve thousand years is almost beyond dispute. The present Pygmies of Africa, it is now argued, were the product of dwarfing tendencies which had run strongly for only about the same length of time. The Tasmanians might also have been the product of evolutionary changes which were less pronounced. Thus a Tasmanian beauty queen could have legitimately parried the question—'where did you get that Afro hair-style?' with the answer that it was only a question of time.

While a relatively small span of time could sharpen the physical differences between peoples, the same span could also eradicate differences. An astonishing discovery, made in the last few years, discloses that as recently as 10,000 years ago two distinct types of men were living in neighbouring districts of south-eastern Australia. At a time when aboriginals with 'modern' skulls were living in that area, settlements of people possessing relatively archaic features were living nearby. Near the River Murray, at Kow Swamp (V.), A. G. Thorne has found that 10,000 years ago the inhabitants there had the kind of skull which was believed to belong to an earlier period in the development of mankind. The skulls had sloping forehead, a small ridge of bone above the eyes, and large jaws and teeth. The most likely explanation of the existence, almost side by side, of two distinct physical types is that at least two races of people immigrated to Australia. Whether they kept to their own regions, whether they intermarried or whether they frequently fought each other must remain tantalizing and open questions. It is possible that the race bearing the more prehistoric features was slowly extinguished by direct and indirect competition from the existing aboriginal race. Conceivably the people buried on the shores of a lake—the present Kow Swamp—sometime between 9,820 years ago and 10,320 years ago were the descendants of the real aboriginals who discovered and first occupied the continent and held it for most of Australia's history. In probing the origins of the early Australians, Tasmania was perhaps ceasing to be the largest gap in the jigsaw.

V

Meanwhile, sparse evidence allows theories to proliferate. In filling the gaps our imagination is tinted or coloured strongly by prevailing religious, biological, racial, and historical views and vogues, many of which are fragile. In the nineteenth century every thoughtful explanation of the origins and route of migrations of the Tasmanians was influenced, understandably, by a reverence for the Book of Genesis, by a simplistic application of Darwin's theory of evolution, by an inflated pride in the achievements of European technology and a disdain for primitive cultures, or by theories in geology and linguistics and anthropology which have since been abandoned or refined. We are still presumably the prisoners of a variety of untested assumptions. Thus a popular myth today depicts aboriginals discovering the continent, holding it without challenge throughout the millennia, forming one proud race that spanned the continent, and living peacefully with one another—and with nature—until the British invasion began in 1788.

In puzzles where the evidence is sparse, the finding of one clue can shake all the reigning hypotheses. In the archaeology of Australia and New Guinea several vital clues may well be found in the following quarter century, and those new clues may make assumptions in this chapter seem archaic.

PART TWO

The Sway of Fire and Sea

CHAPTER FOUR

Death of the Giants

In the 1830s the bones of a puzzling creature were discovered in a cave near Wellington, west of the Blue Mountains. Part of the jaw was carried to Sydney and shipped to London where the anatomist Sir Richard Owen concluded with some excitement that it belonged to an animal hitherto unknown to science: he named it the diprotodon.* A few years later, in 1847, a complete skeleton of a diprotodon was collected from the banks of a tributary of the Condamine in southern Queensland and sold for about $100. In Sydney the enormous head, the tusk-like teeth, and the massive skeleton were marvelled at by those who crowded around as if they were seeing an exhibit in a side-show. Some of the bones, wrote the geologist Reverend W. B. Clarke, were so large 'as to show that some individuals of this genus might have attained a size much greater than that of the largest elephant.'

Amongst those who studied the head of the diprotodon in Sydney was the Prussian scientist, Ludwig Leichhardt. He had long been fascinated by the thought that Noah's Ark might not have succeeded as fully as the Old Testament claimed: all God's creatures might not have survived the deluge. In 1837 Leichhardt had seen near Bristol the bones of bears and elks which thousands of years ago must have inhabited the English countryside. Seven years later, near the Condamine River in southern Queensland, he saw the half-

---

* The name is usually pronounced dye-proh-tod-on; it comes from the Greek words for 'two teeth'.

51

buried bones of gigantic marsupial creatures which must have once flourished in the region. And yet the extinction of these gigantic creatures, he thought, might not have been long ago. He noticed that several of their bones were attached to mussel shells by a kind of cement, and the same mussels were still living in the freshwater holes of the creeks. Giant marsupials, he deduced, must have been alive in conditions not unlike those of today. Perhaps the drying of swamps and lakes in the region had exterminated them. As such big creatures must have been heavy consumers of water and herbage, they could have been slowly wiped out by the coming of a drier climate to southern Queensland. But if this hypothesis was correct there was no reason why the giant creatures might not still survive in Australian regions where the climate was moister. He decided in 1844 that the great diprotodons and giant kangaroos might still be discovered grazing on the lush grasses of an unmapped river. 'I should not be surprised', he wrote to Sir Richard Owen, 'if I found them in the tropical interior.' But in his long journey from the Pacific Coast to Port Essington on the Arafura Sea he failed to find them. Before he himself disappeared in the interior in 1848 he apparently had given up hope that he would find the giant marsupials alive.

Leichhardt was sound in his belief that the extinction of several species of giant creatures was a relatively recent event. The weight of evidence now suggests that several of these species were alive when the first aboriginals reached Australia. What caused their later extinction is not clear. One feasible answer is that some species were partly the victims of the aboriginal invasion.

II

Giant marsupials had evolved during the millions of years when Australia and New Guinea were isolated from Asia by impassable sea. Some of these marsupials dwarfed the surviving Australian species. There were giant emus and wombats. A species of rat kangaroo was as large as the present grey kangaroo. The largest kangaroos were about ten feet high; short faced, cumbersome creatures, they would have towered over the first aboriginals. The diprotodon was even heavier; nothing so large inhabited the islands from which the first aboriginals had sailed.

Even today the skeleton of a diprotodon is impressive. A cemetery of these animals was excavated in the 1890s at Lake Callabonna, where they had apparently been trapped tens of thousands of years ago in a marsh of sticky clay, and one skeleton was carried bone by bone past the Flinders Ranges to Adelaide, and reassembled on its four legs in the museum. Seen from a distance the living animal must have appeared squat and low, but when you approach the reconstructed animal in the museum you realize with surprise that the middle of its back is about six feet from the ground. Its colour and skin are unknown but it is likely that they rather resembled the wombat, to which it was related. The short tusks and stubby teeth look formidable but it was not a flesh-eater and might not have seriously menaced a human hunter. In weight and shape it was probably close to a giant rhinoceros. While it would have thumped the ground if it happened to charge an enemy, its speed judging by the legs and feet was not fast. Nevertheless, in the opinion of the naturalist, J. H. Calaby, it might have been faster than a man.

Whereas the diprotodon and most of the large mammals of Australia ate grasses and bushes, the marsupial lion possibly ate flesh. It is not clear whether the marsupial lion (*thylacoleo*) killed its own meat or fed on carrion; indeed one cannot be certain whether the marsupial lion was carnivorous. A fine skull can be seen today in the Western Australian Museum, side by side with the smaller, narrower, skull of a contemporary lion. The teeth, especially the two large protruding incisors of the marsupial lion, resemble the teeth of

53

a meat-eating animal but possibly they were used rather to slash soft foods such as melons. Moreover the marsupial lion's nearest surviving relatives are the possums, and they are herbivorous. The terrain inhabited by marsupial lions was large, and their bones have been excavated in places as far apart as the Nullarbor Plain and a valley within sound of Melbourne's airport.

Whether marsupial lions sometimes attacked aboriginal children or whether a diprotodon occasionally trampled on a hunter remains an open question. No human skull or crushed leg bone has yet been found beside the bones of a diprotodon. While it is easy to produce indirect evidence that aboriginals shared the continent with giant marsupials, the direct evidence is elusive. At Keilor near Melbourne, Dr A. Gallus excavated the bones of diprotodon and other extinct marsupials from strata which were about 31,000 years old; aboriginals had long ago camped on the same site but it is difficult to assess whether they were there at the time when the animals died. Edmund D. Gill investigated the bones of extinct species near lakes in western Victoria but again any association between the bones and aboriginal hunters is inconclusive. The excavating in 1974 of the bones of a small herd of diprotodon in a quarry near Bacchus Marsh (V.) raised the possibility that they were more recent than the first aboriginal invasion. They had died in a swamp—now a deposit of china clay—perhaps no less than 30,000 years ago, but a positive date is still awaited.

The most tantalizing evidence that man and giant marsupials shared the country comes from the west of New South Wales where remains of a giant kangaroo were found in the earthen oven of an old aboriginal camping site. According to radio-carbon dating the remains were 26,300 years old, plus or minus 1,500 years. The discovery justified a modest purr of triumph until a zoologist, Larry G. Marshall, produced evidence in 1973 suggesting that the question was still open. He revealed that the animal found in the aboriginal cooking place was conceivably a large member of a still-living species of kangaroo rather than one of the last members of an extinct species. For in the animal world in the late Pleistocene era the extinction of large species of marsupials was accompanied by the diminishing in size of several other species which survive to this day.

Perhaps the most comprehensive survey of the extinction of what are called 'megafauna' was made in 1967. In his presidential address to the Royal Society of Western Australia, D. Merrilees briefly assessed the antiquity of marsupial fossils found in eastern Australia and then turned to his own territory, especially to caves in desolate country near the Great Australian Bight. The most exciting evidence, he said, had been found near the Balladonia homestead and a lonely stretch of the east-west highway. There an excavation revealed the bones of animals long extinct in Australia—a Tasmanian devil, marsupial lion, a species of large wombat and possibly a diprotodon. The presence of stone implements in the same layer of rock which held the bones suggested that the giant marsupials had been alive at the time of the aboriginals' occupation of that region. Unfortunately the layer embedding the animals' bones and human implements contained no carbon from which the antiquity of the bones could be computed. The layer itself consisted of rounded pebbles and fragments of rock and grit, cemented together into a kind of conglomerate over a period of thousands of years. It is difficult to tell how many thousands of years were required for the forming of the cemented layer. It was therefore impossible to exclude the possibility that the bones had lain there for thousands of years, that aboriginals had chanced to discard their stone implements at that site, and that finally there had occurred the slow process by which clay and pebbles—and the bones and implements they enclosed— were hardened into a layer of conglomerate about two feet thick. Accordingly Balladonia, like every other discovery of the bones of extinct marsupials, did not yield the evidence enabling an archaeologist to state positively that the aboriginal implements were at least as old as the marsupials' bones.

Dr Merrilees argued that at least twelve species of the larger marsupials were 'present with man on the Australian mainland' but eventually became extinct. Merrilees not only believed that the aboriginals had inhabited Australia at the same time as these now-extinct marsupials; he suggested that the aboriginals had actually extinguished them. The title he gave to his presidential address was 'Man the Destroyer'. His emphatic headline was a slightly stronger conclusion than his evidence would justify.

Any detective investigating the death of the giant marsupials would have to include aboriginals on the list of likely suspects, especially now that an earlier suspect has been largely exonerated. For long suspicion had been directed towards a quieter, slower killer. A change in climate had once seemed the most reasonable explanation of the extinction of giant marsupials. It was suggested that over a long span the climate in Australia had become drier and that massive animals such as the giant kangaroo or diprotodon were decimated by the withering of pastures and by the evaporation of rivers and lakes. If the freshwater lakes became wastes of cracked mud in dry years, and if the grassy plains were shrivelled for much of the year, massive animals might not have survived the scarcity of food and water.

The suspicion that changing climate had killed the giant creatures was based on the assumption that their favoured habitat must have been lush and well-watered. Into that theory, however, the archaeologist Rhys Jones recently fired several bullets. He pointed out that the largest living marsupial is the red kangaroo and that it does not flourish in lush rainforest or river pastures. Instead it thrives on the dry plains of New South Wales. Moreover, the suggestion that the lumbering diprotodon could not tolerate dry conditions is also challenged by the discovery that their diet at

Lake Callabonna in their dying days consisted of vegetation akin to the saltbush and bluebush which feed sheep and kangaroos even today in arid areas. Of course the fossilized contents of the stomachs of the diprotodon might not indicate what they had normally eaten but what they were compelled to eat when vegetational changes perhaps challenged their existence. In the present state of knowledge there are few clear-cut answers to simple questions. That the change of climate killed some giant species is still feasible but not persuasive.

In many other lands the arrival of man certainly endangered species. The clumsy swan-like birds which were unique to the volcanic islands of Mauritius and Reunion were vulnerable when European sailors and settlers arrived; the pigs released in the forests often ate the conspicuous white egg which the birds laid; the birds themselves could not fly and many were shot; and by 1681 the last bird was dead and the name of dodo was about to become the pseudonym for extinction. The huge moa bird barely outlived the dodo; when the first Maoris reached New Zealand the moa became one of their meals and, being big and flightless, was easily hunted to extinction. In North America the camels and giant ground sloths and mammoths were flourishing as recently as 15,000 years ago but they were extinct long before the Vikings or Spaniards reached that continent. Their disappearance was, similarly, blamed on drought; but a search for evidence of drought has not been successful, tempting one American naturalist to quip that these animals were wiped from the plains 'not because they lost their food supply but because they became one'.

It is likely that some species, especially those confined to one or two islands, were eliminated by the arrival of man. The moa or dodo was more likely to be extinguished by the landing of a new predator if other factors, operating over thousands of years, had already reduced the number of birds to the brink of extinction. The final elimination of a species of bird or animal from the face of the earth is the dramatic, tragic event, but in the sequence of causation it may be less important than those quiet unrecorded forces which eroded the ability of the species to meet new dangers. As those unrecorded and slow forces of decline can only be guessed at, the temptation is strong to turn to the death-blow. Hence the popularity of the hypothesis that the extinction of the giant marsupials in Australia was mainly caused by change of climate. When that theory recently fell from favour, the aboriginal invaders were increasingly blamed. Both theories tend to single out one catastrophic cause, whereas in ecology a delicate mesh of many inter-woven causes is more usually found. But to trace that delicate mesh of causes is impossible when probing the extinction of creatures whose feeding and breeding habits were never recorded and whose chronology of decline and extinction is still a mystery.

III

In the wiping out of certain species of giant marsupials the arrival of aboriginals and their weapons and firesticks were possibly part of the web of death. Certainly there is no justification for the assumption—widespread in the 1970s— that the aboriginals lived in complete harmony with the natural environment. Their indirect effect on the living landscape mainland can also be glimpsed in the extinction of those two marsupials commonly called the Tasmanian tiger and the Tasmanian devil. Both creatures lived on mainland Australia long after the death of the giant marsupials, but were extinguished before the first European settlers arrived.

The Tasmanian tiger or thylacine resembled a wolf or big dog. It was variously named tiger or hyena because of the stripes on the top of the back and on the thicker part of the long tail. It is easily described because it existed in Tasmania as late as the 1930s. Several of the stuffed specimens in Australian museums still have glossy skins of fresh appearance with as many as sixteen stripes—dark brown stripes on a fawn or pale yellow background. The stripes of the Tasmanian tiger were neat and almost military-like. They were more numerous and regular than the stripes of the African tiger though not so vividly coloured. Being a marsupial, the Tasmanian tiger was not related directly to any animal outside Australia, and the formal Latin name announced its freakishness: 'pouched dog with a wolf head'. In the pouch the bitch carried the pups or cubs until they were old enough to be placed in a concealed cubby of grass and leaves; there they stayed when she went hunting. The main food devoured by the incredibly wide jaw of the full-grown animal were wallabies, ground-nesting birds, kangaroo-rats, a variety of smaller marsupials and, in the final century, European sheep and poultry. Thylacines like to hunt at dusk or in darkness. They appear to have picked up the scent of prey quickly. One would expect grown animals that were six feet from tip of nose to tip of tail to be fast runners but they were ungainly and not very fast.

During the long history of man in Australia, the marsupial tigers were present for at least five-sixths of the time span and perhaps for an even higher proportion. The decline of marsupial tigers was not rapid. About 10,000 years ago they lived in the highlands of New Guinea. Less than 4,000 years ago they lived on the Nullarbor Plain, and in several parts of Australia they were perhaps surviving as recently as 1000 years ago.

Recent inspections of art in remote corners of the mainland have even raised the possibility that marsupial tigers survived almost until the coming of the first Europeans. In the Pilbara region of Western Australia, just inside the tropic, several animals engraved on rock by aboriginal artists were more like the marsupial tiger than any other marsupial or mammal. The stripes are suggestive; even more so is the hang of the tail. Whereas the dingo's tail usually curls up or hangs down, the thylacine's tail often stuck out. The tail also had unusual rigidity: when a marsupial tiger was caught by the tail it reputedly was unable to turn around easily and snap at the captor. Likewise in western Arnhem Land are aboriginal rock paintings of a four-legged creature with hooped stripes and lowered tail. Aboriginals who were consulted about the faded red paintings said that they did not represent dogs or dingoes but an animal they had never seen. E. J. Brandl, writing in 1972 about these rock paintings he had discovered in Arnhem Land, offered no date for the paintings of the hooped animals but implied that they might have been painted in recent centuries. One of his sentences almost takes the breath away: 'nor can the possibility be entirely dismissed that thylacines still persist in remote parts of the western Arnhem Land plateau.'

Extinct on the mainland, the marsupial tigers survived only in Tasmania. There, a century ago, they were regarded as too plentiful. They were shot by the white farmers and sheep-owners, and hunted by professional trappers who received government bounties for the scalps of this proclaimed pest. In the undulating country near Hamilton in the 1860s the marsupial tigers were so numerous that shepherds had to lead flocks of sheep down from the higher ground where marsupial tigers hid in scrub beside the grasslands. Often the shepherds complained that the animals killed sheep not only for meat but for sport. War on marsupial tigers became more intense: after 1900 they were not often seen. In 1933 one was trapped in a snare in the Florentine Valley, wild country to the west of Hobart, and taken to that city to be exhibited. The last, perhaps, of a long line of hunters which at one time were to be found in many parts of Australia, its death aroused little interest in 1933. Since then scores of sightings of marsupial tigers have been reported: most of the stories reflect weak sight or strong imagination. But as late as 1961 two men fishing at night on the west coast near the mouth of the Arthur River, heard the noise of an animal trying to eat their fishing-bait which lay in a bucket outside their hut.

One of the men went outside and with a lump of wood clubbed the animal. Samples of hair and dry blood were sent to Hobart for analysis and were interpreted as evidence that the animal was a marsupial tiger. Since that year many rumours of sightings have been reported. In 1972 a French expedition briefly searched for the animal and returned without even a rumour.

The marsupial tiger, like so many Australian species, had lived in a continent to which no powerful intruder had come for perhaps tens of thousands of years. The species was perhaps vulnerable. But the fierce challenge to its survival probably began with the arrival of dingoes in Australia. The evidence is overwhelming that dingoes did not reach Australia until long after aboriginals had occupied the continent. Perhaps they were imported to Australia by a later wave of migrants. Perhaps they arrived on the log rafts which were accidentally blown by strong winds from the Moluccas or Timor to the Australian coast. Wolf-like animals, the dingoes probably reached Australia after the rising seas had separated Tasmania from the mainland. The time of their arrival is uncertain; the oldest dingo remains so far found in Australia were near Mount Gambier (S.A.) and were said to be about 8,300 years old but that date is sometimes dismissed as too old.

Dingoes did not reach Tasmania, and the marsupial tiger and marsupial devil continued to survive on the island. In contrast dingoes flourished in many regions of Australia and the two marsupials died out. These facts spurred the conclusions that dingoes were the destroyers. The case, however, is not conclusive and can't be conclusive until we know with more accuracy when the first dingoes reached Australia and when the marsupial tigers and devils within the continent became perilously low in numbers or finally vanished. It is still conceivable that these species were virtually extinct within Australia, indeed were doomed, before the howl of a dingo was heard in the land. It is even feasible that dingoes

61

multiplied quickly in Australia because a suitable niche was made available by the earlier decline of the marsupial tiger, especially in the warmer parts of Australia.

The weight of evidence suggests that the dingo became a dangerous competitor of the marsupial tiger. Adult dingoes had no powerful natural enemy within the continent. Dingo pups—and only one litter was born annually—seem to have had only one strong enemy, the wedge-tailed eagle, but cubs of the marsupial tiger might have been prey to the same huge bird. As both the dingoes and marsupial tigers were eaters of meat they were possibly competitors for the same foods, and during a drought the marsupial tigers might have suffered in the competition for scarce game. Contrary to the popular impression the two species of animals did not occupy different terrain. While the marsupial tigers are popularly imagined to have hidden themselves in the dense Tasmanian rain-forest they had no alternative, in fact, but to inhabit the more open country. As meat-eaters they would have starved if they had spent most of their time in the heavy under-growth of the rain forests. Since open, grassy country was their natural habitat during their long existence on the mainland, they would often have competed with dingoes for the same supply of meat.

If one of the reasons for the extinction of the marsupial tiger on the Australian mainland was the coming of the dingo, then part of the blame could rest with aboriginals. Possibly the dingoes' acclimatization within this continent, and their slow spread to the most southerly edges of land, owed much to the pettings and favours of aboriginals. In times of scarcity dingoes were eaten by aboriginals but they were normally protected because of the minor functions they performed around the camp. For they were watchdogs and pets; they cheerfully served as nightly blankets in winter; and they were useful on hunting expeditions; being quick to spot goannas, possums, wallabies and other game which aboriginals could then chase and kill. Generally the dingoes

around a camp were fed infrequently though women sometimes took up a motherless pup and suckled it with their own
milk. The wilder dingoes who lived beyond the aboriginals'
moving camps were often fatter than the camp dingoes, and
from those wild dogs the aboriginals stole young pups in
order to replenish the tame pack.

Dingoes never seemed to be far from man. At night in
many parts of the continent the most common noise was the
long howl of dingoes. Wild dingoes were attracted to the
camps and human tracks even when their only welcome was
death. Professor F. Wood Jones, an anatomist who wrote
eloquently about Australian mammals, described in the
1920s the way in which a dingo often followed the horse and
cart of European travellers in the outback:

> The Dingo, even in the most remote places, still has a curious
> hankering after man and his fleshpots. He still falls in behind
> the buggy, still follows the traveller at a discreet distance,
> still has a leaning towards hanging on to his camp—and this
> despite the fact that he is always killed at sight for the price
> set on his scalp.

Even today men hiking through the rugged parts of the
Cape York Peninsula are followed by dingoes for days on
end, the dingoes remaining just out of sight, their high howl
heard clearly in the darkness. Are the dingoes following the
men in the hope of scavenging scraps of food at the camping
sites? Percy J. Trezise, who knows that peninsula, thinks the
food scraps are less important than the dog's hankering for
companionship: 'one gets the feeling that the dogs are
yearning after the company of man.'

IV

The alliance of aboriginals and dingoes might have also
hastened the extinction of another carnivorous marsupial in
mainland Australia. The Tasmanian Devil (*Sarcophilus har-
risii*) is less than half as long as the marsupial tiger and only

63

about ten inches high, with a head resembling a pig, stiff black hairs fringing its snout, a big mouth and very large teeth. This black tough scavenger still inhabits the wilder parts of Tasmania and was living in south-eastern Australia not long before the arrival of Europeans. It was alive in Arnhem Land no more than 3,000 years ago, and was probably abundant in some regions about 7,000 years ago. At that time an aboriginal near Lake Nitchie (N.S.W.) was ceremonially buried, and on his neck hung one of the most impressive necklaces so far found in Australia—a string of 178 pierced teeth from Tasmanian Devils. Such a necklace suggests that about 7,000 years ago the animal was abundant; on the other hand the teeth might have been scarce by that time and therefore a rare treasure fit to be buried with a man of importance.

The reasons for the vanishing of the marsupial tigers and devils from the continent are likely to be complicated. Certainly the slowness of the process of decline and extinction forbids dramatic explanations. Both marsupials survived the coming of man for perhaps 30,000 years, and so man alone cannot be blamed. Both marsupials might also have survived the coming of dingoes to mainland Australia for a thousand years or more, and so the dingo alone cannot be safely blamed. Moreover the decline of a species cannot be attributed solely to new predators or to changes of climate. The peculiarities of a species may make it either vulnerable or immune to new competitors; and the fall of the marsupial tiger must have been hastened by some of its own feeding and breeding habits, and by its relative lack of prowess in running, fighting, hearing or sniffing. Little is known yet of several facets that appear to have endangered marsupial tigers but which now appear to have proliferated some of the docile species of kangaroos.

It is easy to overlook the fact that while aboriginals and their technology endangered some species they must have favoured others. Understandably those flourishing species excite only a fragment of the wonder which they would have excited if instead they were now on the verge of extinction. It is also easy to overlook the possibility that changes during the aboriginals' occupation affected the tiny species more than the huge. In the study of history we are mesmerized by what was large. We see great events and large creatures as intrinsically more interesting: moreover they leave behind ample evidence of their existence after they have ceased to exist. It is likely, however, that the way of life of the aboriginal pioneers had stronger effects, directly and indirectly, on tiny plants and small insects than on the spectacular diprotodons and marsupial tigers. After all there were many more of the smaller species.

Recent research, for example, suggests that the bush fly—the small insect which is a plague in many parts of the continent—was multiplied drastically by the coming of man. In eastern Australia the bush flies breed mainly in the cattle dung. Two hundred years ago Australia had no cattle but now nearly 30 million cattle feed on Australian grasslands and in the course of a day they drop some 300 million pats of dung in which the bush flies can breed. Douglas Waterhouse believes that before the coming of cattle and sheep to Australia the plague of bush flies must have been smaller and less frequent, for the main grazing animals were kangaroos, and their manure rarely bred flies outside those short periods of spring and autumn when pastures were lush. Before the arrival of Europeans and their grazing animals, the ideal breeding ground for bush flies was probably the dung of dingoes. The arrival of the first dingoes, their dispersal across the continent, their frequent presence in aboriginal camps, and the probable appearance of more and more bush flies on the faces and hands of aboriginals, were perhaps one of those sequences which defy the simple idea that aboriginals were living in harmony with a static environment.

An even more dramatic sequence of changes probably stemmed from man-made bushfires. The main weapon which came with aboriginals was not a spear but a fire, and their fires ravaged and possibly changed much of the countryside.

CHAPTER FIVE

A Burning Continent

The eagerness with which aboriginals set fire to the country was noticed by the first Europeans who visited the south-east of the continent. Even when their ships lay well out to sea they saw the smoke and recorded it in their journals. What the smoke signified they could not at first tell. Perhaps it was the inhabitants' way of signalling; perhaps they were cooking a large breakfast; perhaps the smoke came from fires started by lightning. Certainly storms started some fires, but if all the fires had been ignited by a flash of lightning then this must have been the most thunderous region in the whole Pacific.

II

Abel Janszoon Tasman, sailing from the Mauritius where the yellow-winged dodo was on the verge of extinction, discovered the island of Tasmania in 1642. He sent men ashore to scavenge timber, fresh water and greens; and they returned with the news that the trunks of many trees had been deeply burned and that patches of earth had been baked hard by fire. There was no sign of the Tasmanians but the smoke of their fires could be seen from the ship when she anchored in the bay or sailed along the east coast. More than a century later William Bligh, calling at the same coast for fresh water and wood during his breadfruit voyage to Tahiti, saw the pinpoints of fire on the shore at night and evidence of fire on the shore by day. Whereas Tasman had come in summer

Bligh was a winter visitor but even then he realized how destructive were the fires of the Tasmanians. And so, when he planted fruit trees and seeds which he carried from the Cape of Good Hope—plums, peaches, apricots, apples, grape vines, pumpkin seeds, and other vegetables—he wondered whether they would resist the fires and so provide food for passing ships. He observed that 'in the dry season, the fires made by the natives are apt to communicate to the dried grass and underwood, and to spread in such a manner as to endanger every thing that cannot bear a severe scorching.'

When Captain Cook in the *Endeavour* in 1770 became the first European to see the Pacific coast of Australia he and his crew saw the autumn fires burning in the bush on most days as they sailed northwards. On several days they saw large fires, on other days smaller fires—the smoke conspicuous against the blue hills even when the ship was far out to sea. When they went ashore at Botany Bay, and when nearly two decades later the founders of the first British settlement also went ashore, they saw aboriginals carrying lighted sticks. Aboriginals fishing at night in a tiny bark canoe would keep alight a small fire on a patch of wet clay in the bottom of the canoe. Or roaming the countryside with a smoking firestick in their hand aboriginals were often to be seen casually setting fire to tufts of grass or bark. Many of the early European settlers who ventured a short way inland were surprised to see wide tracts of blackened country —the tree-trunks charred, the grass burned, and the stones on the surface blackened. Their fires seemed to be lit more frequently on windy days; on some days of summer the valleys were infernos.

The carrying of firesticks was so common that some foreigners wondered whether the original Australians were incapable of making fire. Perhaps fire was a precious gift which, once received, had to be guarded nervously. To educated Europeans the classical myths of how fire first came to man suddenly acquired new meaning: perhaps to primi-

tive man, as to the Australian aboriginals, the source of fire
was a mystery? While the Australians actually had a variety
of methods of making fire, and those methods were soon
detected by white men curious enough to look or to ask,
the ability of Tasmanians to produce a fire was seriously
doubted by several skilled observers. George Robinson, making long journeys to gather up the last of the Tasmanians,
recorded how they hunted with a waddy in one hand and a
lighted torch in the other, and how they carried torches in
cold weather to warm themselves and also—he was informed
—to preserve the flame:

> As the chief always carried a lighted torch I asked them what
> they did when their fire went out. They said if their fire went
> out by reason of the rain they was compelled to eat the
> kangaroo raw and to walk about and look for another mob
> and get fire of them.

The skills and way of life of these people might already
have been crumbling under the shock of invasion when
Robinson made his observations. By then, apparently, the
Tasmanians he travelled with had so little command of fire
that they were chained to his own tinderbox. On the west
coast of Tasmania in mid-winter, by those beaches where
the surf pounded during the westerlies, he was careful to
pour water on his fires when he moved camp. He was thus
more likely to persuade Tasmanian aboriginals, who lacked
the comfort of their own fire, to join his party.

The common Australian method of making fire was by
rubbing wood against wood, and it is still employed sometimes by aboriginals in the desert near the border of Western
and South Australia. First they looked for a dead branch of
mulga, usually of medium length and preferably dry; that
timber could usually be split lengthways without much
trouble. Splitting open one of the branches, they arranged
it so that the split faced upwards. While one man anchored
the branch by setting a foot firmly on each end, the other

began to make friction by rubbing crossways on the split wood. The simplest friction device was the sharp edge of a wooden woomera or throwing stick. It was drawn rapidly backwards and forth across the piece of split mulga—so rapidly that a spectator, at a casual glance, might think that the aim was to saw through the mulga. The sawing soon heated the wood and the adjacent kindling in the fork of the split mulga. The kindling was usually a pinch of dry kangaroo dung or powdered wood-dust. Within twenty or thirty seconds of the start of the sawing motion, the dung—if everything went well—commenced smouldering. Once the dung was aglow, a few shreds of dry grasses were gently arranged on top. A few delicate puffs of breath, and a pinch of the skill that is sometimes called luck, and the grass was set alight.

In contrast the twirling of a fire drill, with a piece of paperbark as kindling, was the only method of making fire in many parts of Arnhem Land. The northerly location of the regions which preferred that technique suggests that the fire-drill was a later entry into Australia. In addition to friction, fire was sometimes made by percussion. The striking of iron pyrite with a flint gave off sparks which could ignite dry grass, feathers, teased bark and other light kindling. Percussion was probably the sole way of lighting a fire in Tasmania according to a German museum director who has recently studied the meagre evidence; no European is known to have observed a Tasmanian light a fire.

Knowing their ways of lighting a fire we still cannot be sure why the nomadic groups of aboriginals carried it wherever they went. Admittedly, to make fire was a tedious chore if the appropriate timber was scarce or sodden, but on most days of the year it was a tiny chore compared to hunting, vegetable-gathering, and fetching of timber and water. Significantly it seems to have been a male task; men made fire and women usually carried it from camp to camp. The laziness of men therefore might have inspired the custom that women should carry the fire when the group travelled. In addition, if the women reached the new camping site first because the men had made a detour to hunt possum or wallaby, the women could light their own fire. If the men returned with game the hot coals would be ready to singe the fur of the slaughtered animal.*

Fire was central to their way of life, affecting nearly every activity. Fire should still be ranked as the greatest of man's conquests, and in the way of life of the aboriginals fire had no rival. It was the core of their technology though, like the core of our advanced technologies, it was sometimes master as well as servant.

The variety of uses of fire possibly explains, more than any other reason, why aboriginals carried it everywhere as if it were their prized possession. Fire grilled or roasted their meat and fish; it cooked some of their vegetables. In many regions fire burned the dead and raised the ornamental scars on the living. Fire deterred the evil spirits from approaching a camp at night. A flaming stick, it was often believed, would curb the wind or halt the rain. Smoke was the most popular insect repellant, and in parts of Arnhem Land smoking fires were kept burning all night under a kind of stilt but known as a 'mosquito house' in order to protect sleepers from mosquitoes. Near Cape York the smoke of slow-burning fires served the same purpose in igloo-like huts. Flames were used to drive snakes from long grass where nomads hoped to camp that night; and in parts of the River Murray hot ashes were used as a poultice on human limbs bitten by snakes.

Fire not only helped to manufacture spears and hafted

*The practice of carrying fire perhaps calls for no more elaborate explanation than the substitution of cigarette-lighters for matchboxes in recent decades. One of the early men to pasture sheep near the River Murray noticed how aboriginals were captivated by the predecessor of the safety match: 'Tobacco, iron tomahawks, and the tinder-box, which relieved the women from the trouble of carrying fire-sticks on the march, were indeed the three boons which the Blacks received from the Whites in compensation for endless disadvantages.'

axes; it was also used instead of an axe. If the camp lacked firewood, women would light a small fire near the base of a tree; and by carefully tending the fire they burned through the trunk until the tree toppled.

Except when the moon was full, fire was the only illuminant at night, lighting up the grounds for ceremonies or illuminating the outskirts of the camp when women went out to fetch more wood. On the coast of Arnhem Land it was a striking sight to see a Pandanus palm burning in the darkness—a beacon for a flotilla of canoes at sea. On the other side of the continent, when men fished at night, their light and warmth came from a fire sitting on clay on the floor of the canoe.

Fire warmed them on winter nights, for mid-winter in the centre and south can be intensely cold. Each aboriginal slept between two small fires. As the fire soon died without stoking, the sleeper had to stir himself and place a few more twigs and sticks on the fire several times during the night. The practice of sleeping very close to fires, and the presence of many warm heaps of ashes around a camp, meant that accident burns were common. Children often trod on hot ashes or fell in small fires: a burn-scarred child or adult was often seen.

As no clothes or skins were worn in winter in most parts of Australia the winds could be bitingly cold for travellers. One solution was to carry a blazing firestick. Charles Mountford, whose *Brown Men and Red Sand* is one of the most charming and sympathetic books about Central Australia, recalled that he had viewed the firestick as an inefficient method of heating until, on a very cold day, he was persuaded to carry one. He was surprised how much heat it gave his body, face and hands. He also realized that the holding of the stick required skill and that the penalties for clumsiness were burned fingers or a slow-smouldering stick.

Fire was also their radio and sometimes a two-wave radio. Wherever the white explorers moved they felt they were followed or preceded by smoke signals. A distant wisp of smoke, to an inexperienced explorer, was a sign that his party was closely watched. If the aboriginals knew something unexpected about the exploring party the knowledge was attributed to their skill in transmitting and reading smoke signals. For long the aboriginals were looked upon as magicians or devils in their ability to send signs, but most of their effective messages appear to have been the result of sensible forethought or deduction. In desert country in Western Australia an anthropologist who on three occasions saw the full sequence of events involving the sending and receiving of a smoke signal, concluded that magic was not needed in order to understand the sequence. When a few women, for instance, were foraging for food in the Clutterbuck Hills one decided to visit a specific area alone in search of ground fruits; and when leaving her friends she promised, if she found the fruit growing, to send up a smoke signal so that they could come across and help pick the fruit. In that situation a smoke signal had a clear meaning; moreover it was a vital aid to gathering the day's food with the minimum exertion in hot desert.

Perhaps the most detailed message which could be transmitted by smoke—unless alternative messages had been previously arranged—was the direction in which people were travelling. By lighting a fire every 400 or 500 paces they could indicate their course of travel to anyone in the vicinity. It is relevant to recall that some of the messages which astonished white men late in the nineteenth century were successful predictions by aboriginals that coast-hugging steamships were on their way, were delayed, or were in trouble. Aboriginals being observant of smoke, they knew that the smoking funnel of a steamship spoke their own language, and they often passed information about the passing or the direction of ships to neighbouring tribes by means of their own smoke signals. But when all allowance has been made for the aboriginals' gift for observation and deduction,

73

there remain authenticated stories of signalling which defy simple explanation or which suggest that our definition of intelligence or perception might be too narrow.

A vast area of Australia was ideal for smoke signals. The blue sky was infinitely more favourable for the visibility of smoke than the mists or haze of other climates. Dead timber or clumps of spinifex were plentiful, and a few dabs of a firestick into that coarse grass soon sent up a column of smoke that was thick and black. The flat country aided the visibility—except in dust storms—and columns of smoke could be seen as far away as twenty miles. Despite these advantages the messages must have sometimes been interrupted or altered by static or crossed wires. A cinder falling from a firestick could start a fire that was not intended. Or the staccato line of small fires which were believed to show the movements of one hunter might have been lit by another.

It is probable that smoke signals were most valuable in co-ordinating the hunting and gathering of foods in those dry semi-desert areas where distances were long and population and foodstuffs were both sparse. On the more favoured strips of tropical coast, where the standard of living was higher and probably sustained with less sweat and effort, the smoke signals were not so necessary but more sophisticated. Tribes or groups which spent much of the year in the one place could signal to each other with more accuracy and send a wider variety of pre-arranged messages. Jack McLaren who spent eight years in trying to run an isolated plantation near Cape York, continued to be impressed and mystified by the ability of aboriginals to send messages. 'Any morning', he recalled, 'I might see them make on the beach, close to the edge of the water—that being the position from where a signal could best be seen—a bright, quick-flaring fire which presently they would so overlay with green boughs that a thick grey mass of smoke went up.' Then for the following half hour two men intermittently placed a large sheet of

74

bark over the smoking fire to interrupt the upflow of smoke, thus transmitting the dots and dashes of their primitive smoke code. McLaren said he first heard of the outbreak of the First World War from aboriginals who said they had received the message by smoke signal.

Even on the hunt the firestick was occasionally used. Smoke could flush animals from burrows or suffocate bats in caves. By the lighting of fires in well-chosen places a sizable band of hunters, beaters and shouters, could drive wallabies towards a precipice. Tasmanian hunters, quietly approaching a grassy patch where kangaroos were grazing, sometimes tried to surround the kangaroo with a horseshoe of fire, leaving a small gap through which the animals would attempt to escape: at the gap several kangaroos would be easy targets for the weapons of hunters.

Only when you see a technology in its many ramifications do you begin to see those effects which may be unintended. In 1900 nobody could really envisage the range of un-intended effects of the internal combustion engine—the smogs in large cities, the traffic jams, the accidental deaths on roads, the fouling of beaches and the killing of fish when an oil tanker sinks, the difficulty of quarantining diseases now flown across the world in 24 hours, and many other effects, obvious or still hidden. Fire dominated the life of the aboriginals to an even greater degree than the motor-engine dominates western nations today. Fire too had its unintended consequences. In Australia every day for millions of days countless fires had been lit or enlarged for countless pur-poses, and many of those fires had unintended effects. Of one large, hot region of Australia a reliable observer com-mented that in the course of two seasons he did not once see an aboriginal put out a fire. A fire lit in order to smoke a possum from a tree or a rodent from a burrow would be left alight; if the wind sprang up the fire spread for miles. In the Warburton Ranges of Western Australia five aboriginal boys were seen using firesticks to hound wild cats from the grass and scrub, and during the course of the afternoon they caught three large cats. In the opinion of Richard Gould, an anthropologist who watched, the cost of that catch was the burning of nine square miles of country.

Campfires were normally abandoned with no attempt to cover them with sand or put them out: fires lit for signalling, for manufacturing, for warmth, for weather-control and for many other purposes burned themselves out or sometimes raced away, setting fire to the countryside. Some 'smoke signals' must have covered the length of a Marathon race, at three times the speed. The practice of carrying firesticks on journeys increased the amount of unintended burning. When the firestick seemed likely to stop smouldering it was placed against inflammable grass or bark in order to create a flame from which the firestick could be lit again. The fire so started was left to burn itself out. Perhaps never in the history of mankind was there a people who could answer with such unanimity the question: 'have you got a light, mate?' There can have been few if any races who for so long were able to practise the delights of incendiarism. To set fire to a dead bush or a tussock of dry grass and watch the flames spread often confers a stronger sense of omnipotence than its modern counterpart—driving a powerful car or motor-bike. In early Australia this power of the torch belonged not just to the fit and the rich but to tiny children and old people.

There was rarely a reason why the nomads should have put out a fire. They had few possessions. What they owned was portable, and in an emergency could be carried away from an approaching fire. As they did not try to fight a large bushfire—for they had neither sheep nor fences to protect—they were not likely to be burned in the attempt. Occasionally they might have been taken by surprise when a fire beyond control rushed towards them, but presumably they were usually protected by safety zones black from their own previous fires: the zones served as unintended firebreaks

76

over which the fire had difficulty in advancing. Perhaps in every century several raging bushfires trapped and incinerated a few aboriginals but the fires were less likely to be deadly in the widely-inhabited grasslands than in the southern eucalypt forests where few aboriginals lived in summer. A people so experienced in handling fire and so observant of all kinds of bushcraft were rarely likely to be overtaken by a fast fire.

III

The burning of large areas of Australia at least once in every few years was not simply the result of breakaway fires. In many regions the hunters seem to have set fire to grasslands for the same reason that farmers plough and fertilize the soil. They were cultivators, using fire in the hope of producing lush grass for the game when the next showers fell.

Robert Logan Jack, a Scottish geologist, made a long reconnaissance of the Cape York Peninsula in 1879 in the company of two brown and two white men. From the vicinity of the gold-rush port of Cooktown he rode north into rough terrain where no white men lived. On 19 August, moving between tussocky marshes and coastal sandhills, he saw the smoke of fires where natives 'were busy burning the grass'. On the following day he came to a long valley and he could trace its length by the smoke from fires, and for the last three miles of that day's ride he crossed the smoking embers of the grass fires. He saw grass fires on so many days of his expedition that in the end it was more newsworthy to record in his journal the strips of bush or spinifex which were unburned. A month out from Cooktown he wrote that they 'had neglected to burn the country passed over to-day'. He could see no evidence that their fires were attempts to impede his journey or to deprive his horses of feed. The burning was systematic and deliberate, carried out in a season when the grass, being dry, was of little value to kangaroos and wallabies but was easy to burn. Robert Jack had no doubts that the main aim of the burning was to produce sweet green shoots of grass soon after the first hard rain-shower. He was disappointed that this was their only method of farming and

> the alpha and omega of their simple notion of "doing their duty by their land".

Admittedly, another aim of the burning might have been to rouse out lizards and wallabies in the season when food was becoming less accessible. Either aim—whether hunting or firestick farming—would often have been met with the same burning.

Many alert European explorers or sheep-owners were convinced that the aboriginals in many parts of Australia burned the grass in order to encourage fresh growth for the kangaroo and other game. Their conclusions must have come more from close observation of the place and time of the fires than from specific information received by asking questions of aboriginals. It is doubtful whether aboriginals ever expressed the logical sequence of destruction and growth which the fire intiated: if they did express it, it was more in terms of their convention of causation. They simply knew that the burning was effective and they continued to light grass fires year after year. Nevertheless, simply because their own explanations of their fires are, by our criteria, not necessarily coherent, it would be unfair to conclude that they did not know what they were doing. More compelling is the evidence of old settlers who spoke their language, quietly watched them on their own hunting grounds in the first years of racial contact and, all in all, neither romanticized them nor belittled them. As Edward Curr, a Victorian squatter, recalled:

> there was another instrument in the hands of these savages which must be credited with results which it would be difficult to over-estimate. I refer to the *fire-stick*; for the blackfellow

78

was constantly setting fire to the grass and trees, both accidently, and systematically for hunting purposes. Living principally on wild roots and animals, he tilled his land and cultivated his pastures with fire; and we shall not, perhaps, be far from the truth if we conclude that almost every part of New Holland was swept over by a fierce fire, on an average, once in every five years.

Thousands of years of burning could not fail to affect the landscape and all that lived on it. The sheep-owners who came from Britain did not have the faintest idea of how long the aboriginals had occupied the land but they had a sound idea of the botanical effects that came within a few years of the cessation of burning. If five or ten years that experienced few fires could alter the vegetation of Australian forests and grasslands, it would not be surprising if thousands of years of fires had also altered the previous vegetation.

To the tourist there is something timeless in the wilder landscapes of Tasmania. The rainforest and its tangled undergrowth on the west coast is sometimes called 'primeval', and the grassy valleys in the midlands are sometimes likened to an unchanged Garden of Eden, quiet and serene, unspoiled by man. Some of the forest has tall lichen-spotted myrtle, fallen logs, matted vines and dense undergrowth, but it can scarcely be called primeval if in aboriginal times it was relatively open country and sufficiently grassed to attract game. Other parts of the thick rainforest of the west coast were dissected in aboriginal times by tracks kept open by repeated burning; when the Tasmania aboriginals vanished the forest closed in, and ironically the tourist literature now describes it as impenetrable forest, parts of which have never been explored. There is strong evidence that some of the button grass plains and the sedgeland on the west coast, some of the grassy patches at the headwaters of the north-flowing rivers, and the parkland or grassland of the midlands were the result of the persistent burning by the Tasmanian aboriginals.

79

On the Darling Downs in Queensland in the 1840s the glorious stretches of grass—growing like wheat and oats and nearly as tall as a sitting kangaroo—delighted the explorer Ludwig Leichhardt:

> This grass ripens in October and November, when the ground under the trees looks like an even, sweeping field of oats. In November and December the weather gets dry and bushfires break out. They're often a mile wide, and they clear the ground of grass and dead wood as they sweep through the bush. The ashes left behind are like manure to the sweet, tender grass that shoots up as soon as it rains . . .'

For countless generations the bushfires there had been mainly the result, intended or unintended, of the aboriginals' occupation of the downs. The grass—and the game it nourished—was multiplied by burning. Without those fires the grassy woodlands that occupied much of the fertile crescent in south-eastern Australia would have been scrub-land or forest. A period of fifty years was probably sufficient to change the character of that savannah country if no fires burned. Likewise rain forest, in the absence of burning, encroaches on open forest. The same moulding of the grass-lands had almost certainly been carried out in North America. In the north-east of the United States the fires lit by Red Indians allowed grass rather than brushwood to cover the floor of the forest, thus supporting much larger herds of deer. There is much evidence to suggest that the grasslands of the Great Plains were a monument to the firestick.

In arid parts of Australia the effects of fire were mingled with the lottery of rainfall and of course variations in soil. In the Gibson Desert the destruction of mulga shrubs by fire probably gave varieties of spinifex (*triodia* or porcupine grass) the chance to take over. If heavy rain fell soon after the burning, seedlings of mulga received their only chance to compete with the voracious spinifex. In turn a series of fires could completely destroy the spinifex, and when rain fell the sprouting spinifex would have to jostle with 'a

luxuriant crop' of annuals, perennials and subshrubs, turn-
ing the plain into a series of clumps of foliage growing one
or two feet high. Heavy rains for a few seasons would keep
alive the competitors but in dry years the spinifex would
dominate the hot plains—so long as no fire swept through.
To unravel the botanical and zoological history of any strip
of country in Australia is to sense the pervasive influence of
fire even if agreement on fire's exact effects is not easily
reached.

Repeated burnings helped to determine whether some
plants—and the insects and animals and birds dependent on
them—flourished or diminished. As the ashes of fires held
potash, calcium, phosphorus and other elements, they
fostered those grasses or bushes which required those elements. At the same time fires destroyed leaves, mulch, and
natural compost and so affected the topsoil and those plants
which it was likely to sustain. Likewise the thinning of the
layer of mulch must have affected the runoff of water to
creeks and rivers, making their flow less regular in dry
months and thus affecting the populations of reeds, frogs,
fish, and insects in the rivers and water-holes.

In Australia many abundant species of flora and fauna are
drought-resistant, and to that quality is often attributed their
proliferation. It is equally relevant to add that many species
are relatively fire-resistant, and their proliferation must be
partly assigned to the fires which became more frequent
when aboriginals arrived. Frequent fires aided the dispersal
of many kinds of eucalypts, especially in northern Australia.
There eucalypts shed their seeds in the dry season, but the
seeds did not travel far even when winds were strong. At
most, in fluttering down, they reached the ground only
twice as far from the tree as the tree was high, and so the
dispersal of seeds was slow. In time some of the new seeds
would grow into trees which in turn would shed their seeds,
and by that tedious process a species might migrate only a
few hundred feet in every century. A strong bushfire, how-

81

ever, could in one hour carry a seed distances which it might normally take six centuries to cover. A bushfire's heat could burst open the seed capsule, and the turbulent air currents generated by the fire picked up seeds, lifted them high, and carried them along. Moreover, frequent bushfires prepared a surface soil which was ideal for germinating the scattered eucalyptus seeds.

IV

The firestick was not the aboriginals' only influence on the landscape. They themselves killed a variety of birds, animals, fish and reptiles for food and so altered the balance of species. They destroyed what must in aggregate have been vast areas of forest by removing large sheets of bark for canoes, roofing material and other manufactures; like the birds they must have carried many seeds, roots and nuts to new parts of Australia; and by their digging and foraging for vegetables they probably cultivated some species unintentionally. But their playing with fire had, probably, the most pervasive effect on the natural environment.

Some of the species of giant marsupials might have been partly the victims of fire—not fierce naked fire but a slow combustion of factors often fanned directly and indirectly by fire: the decline of bushy vegetation on which certain species fed, or the greater scarcity of food or water in an extreme drought. The extreme conditions of course, provide the real threat to the continuation of a species. The giant marsupials possibly suffered a further handicap because frequent bushfires fostered erosion, and erosion led to the silting of waterholes, and sometimes silted waterholes ceased to offer sanctuary to large animals escaping from the bushfires. Whatever the sequence of causes, the fire which man carried to Australia could have been ecological dynamite.

A second effect of the firestick was, in all probability, more profound than the endangering of species. In altering the vegetation the aboriginals' fires altered their own food supply. When they turned forest into more open country, and scrubby land into grassland, they must have increased the feed of edible animals and therefore the potential food supply of meat for man. Grassland has always supported more grass-eating animals than could be supported in dense forest. The grasslands too offered more edible seeds for humans. As nearly all the native animals of size in Australia were grass-eating rather than carnivorous, they were more likely to flourish if grasslands were enlarged and the area of forest reduced. The effect of the firestick in the long term was therefore to enable more people to hunt and to forage a living in most but not all Australian regions.

It is almost invariably assumed that the population of Australia was static for thousands of years until the European ships arrived. The idea of static population assumed a static environment and static natural resources. This assumption can no longer be held. It is incinerated by the firestick.

If the hundreds of small independent aboriginal societies which once occupied Australia had adopted a coat of arms, an appropriate emblem would have been a firestick. It was a symbol of their technology, often a sign of their achievement, and a refutation of any suggestion that they were prisoners of their land. Fire was also an emblem of the collapse of their society. By helping to create many of the grasslands of the south-east, fire indirectly attracted the Europeans and their sheep and cattle to the interior and so quickly led to the extinction of a way of life which was essentially pastoral.

On those pastures Australian sheep in the nineteenth century quickly became the largest supplier of wool in the world, and the wool annually clothed millions of Europeans. This was an age when clothing was seen as a sure sign of civilization and nakedness as a sign of savagery. And so most Europeans disapproved and tut-tutted whenever they read of the nakedness of the brown Australians, for they did not realize that their own winter clothing was partly the product of pastures which generations of aboriginals had created.

CHAPTER SIX

The Rising of the Seas

The aboriginals imported botanical and zoological knowledge—practical lore about plants and animals of which the average educated Australian is now ignorant. They made stone and wooden tools for the hunting, digging or preparing of food. They almost certainly possessed a variety of skills for catching fish and many techniques of tracking and hunting animals and birds. They knew how to make fire. They probably had considerable knowledge of plants with medical properties and they probably knew how to harness certain poisons for their own use and to rid some toxic plants of poison. They must also have had impressive knowledge of how to build simple craft that could cross wide rivers and narrow seas. It is probable that they possessed all these skills before they reached Australia, and that in their long history in this land they increased some skills and allowed others to vanish.

They practised some of the rituals and skills which are usually called 'civilized'. Those aboriginals who at least 25,000 years ago cremated the young woman on the shores of Lake Mungo bequeathed perhaps the world's oldest known evidence of cremation. On the walls of Koonalda Cave, a flint quarry hidden in darkness below the Nullarbor Plain, are marks which probably represent human art of some 20,000 years ago. If they are the marks of artists they are an art more ancient than any firmly dated so far in Europe.

The cremation and the art might in part have been

responses to a strange environment, or they might have come with the first migrants from the Indonesian islands. They might even have been introduced by later migrants, for contact between the continent and the ancestral islands was probably sustained for several thousands of years after the first migrants arrived. So long as the level of the sea remained low, and so long as Australia and New Guinea were one, many new ideas from the outside world perhaps found their way to southern Australia. Likewise it was possible for skills and arts developed in Australia to radiate back to the ancestral islands and even, in slow stages, to southeast Asia so long as the intervening sea-straits were narrow.

As Australia was a cul-de-sac, a dead end, its proximity to the Indonesian archipelago was virtually its link to the outside world. The weakening of that link as the seas began to rise was one of the crucial events in the human history of Australia.

II

The end of the last glacial phase was accompanied by the rising of the seas. As parts of the ice cap were melting at the earth's poles, the release of water slowly raised the level of the ocean. The date when the rising seas were perceptible is not easily estimated, but perhaps 20,000 years ago some coastal lands in Australia were being slowly drowned. In parts of the interior this change was visible in the climate. There is evidence that the belt of territory near the latitude of Sydney or Perth had a moister climate than today, but 17,000 years ago that climate was perhaps no longer so wet. On the plains of south-western New South Wales the fish, and birds and animals in the rivers and billabongs were perhaps less prolific because the supply of water was less assured. Lake Mungo and the line of adjacent lakes were becoming saltier—a hint that fewer floods were rushing down periodically to flush out the salt.

As the level of the sea rose in the north-west of the united continent of Australia and New Guinea, it widened the straits between the Indonesian islands. A voyage which in predictable weather was safe became sometimes dangerous. A journey which once could be made by wading or swimming now required a raft. The increasing invasion of ocean into the tropical plains of the north-west cut Australia adrift from the western part of New Guinea which was on the pontoon of islands extending to Asia.

The seas continued to rise around the coast of the continent. They shaped new headlands, islands, and straits. Thus the low-lying bridge of land which linked Tasmania and Victoria was slowly narrowed by the invasion of the sea. About 14,000 years ago the once-dry land between King Island and Cape Otway was cut, and in stormy weather at full-moon it must have been frightening for tribes to see the surf licking grasslands where they had lived for generations. About 13,000 years ago the water also broke through the ledge of land linking Wilson's Promontory to Flinders Island. Bass Strait was still unformed or narrow, neither King nor Flinders Islands were yet surrounded by water, and 500 miles to the west 'Kangaroo Island' was still joined to South Australia. This chronology is tentative and may well be altered many times by the neap-tides of research.

After the waters of the Pacific and Southern Indian Ocean had come together to form Bass Strait, the narrow and shallow strait at first did not prevent contact between the new island of Tasmania and the mainland. At some points small watercraft were probably paddled to and fro. If, as seems likely, several aboriginal bands possessed territory which was now split by Bass Strait, they would have often crossed the strait as part of their seasonal wanderings in search of food. Indeed they might have walked and waded to and from Tasmania for some generations until at last the scouring effects of the tides and the slow rising of the sea made walking hazardous.

The Rising of the Seas

The strait between Tasmania and Victoria became wider; and sometimes the fierce rip tides cut it deeper. For a period as long as several hundred years, however, small canoes and bark rafts might have crossed from one side to the other in still weather or during low tides. At last the crossings became too dangerous.

The plains which now lie under Bass Strait were at one time probably fertile, for the Yarra and Tamar and other strong rivers crossed the plain towards the sea in the west. The flooding of that plain had possibly been the signal for the first migration into what is now called Tasmania. At the same time as Bass Strait was being formed, the warmer temperatures made the lower ground in northern Tasmania more habitable. So a few aboriginals were perhaps driven by rising seas and wooed by rising temperatures to settle in Tasmania. As their earliest camp sites near the receding beaches at the warmer northern end of the island lie far beneath the sea today, they are beyond the reach of archaeologists. The earliest evidence of the human invasion of Tasmania comes from the north-west corner, where bone and stone artifacts and food remains on Hunter Island are estimated to be about 18,000 years ago. The island—now separated from Tasmania by four miles of dangerous sea—was at that time far from the rising sea.

In the early phases of settlement the winds blowing from the Tasmanian mountains in winter must have been bitterly cold. The higher peaks still had sheets of permanent ice. As recently as 9,000 years ago the mountains around the Frenchman's Cap were not fully deglaciated, though before long they were to be free from ice and snow for part of the summer. Understandably the early Tasmanians must have clung to the warmer coastal lands, especially in the north. But the time was coming when these nameless men would explore much of inland Tasmania, naming those peaks and gorges which thousands of years later were to be explored again and given European names.

While Tasmania was being isolated, Australia was also being isolated from the Indonesian islands by the advancing ocean. And yet long after the ocean had begun to advance, occasional contacts continued between the single landmass of Australia-New Guinea and the islands towards Asia. As far as we can tell the first dingoes reached the continent less than 8,000 years ago, at a time when Bass Strait was wide enough to prevent them reaching Tasmania but when the island straits to the north-west of Australia were not yet so wide as to restrict crossings. The entry of these half-domesticated dogs suggests that long after the oceans had begun to advance, people and implements and ideas and at least one breed of animal were imported to Australia. If imports were possible so were exports: to discard the idea of two-way traffic is to believe that because Australia was technically backward in recent times, it must also have been technically backward ten thousand years ago.

For long, New Guinea and Australia had been joined by land which was too wide to be called a bridge. Now, as the level of the sea rose, it carved slices from the north and north-west of Australia. There the slope of many of the coastal plains was gentle, enabling the sea to encroach at a pace which was clearly perceptible in one lifetime and sometimes visible in the space of a week. A man could be hunting on grasslands one day, and in exactly the same place one month later he could be paddling in the Gulf of Carpentaria. A study of sediments scooped from the bottom of the Timor Sea suggests that at the extreme period of advancing seas the shore line there could have moved inland at a rate of three nautical miles in a year. Not only did the gradients of the shoreline affect the speed of the invasion but the sea itself was erratic in its rising. In some centuries it rose more than others: at times it paused; and possibly in several periods it even retreated. The average rise of the sea level over a span of ten to fifteen thousand years was perhaps half an inch or an inch a year. That meant that in the span of a lifetime many sea-crossings became hazardous. At the age of 15 a girl could walk at low tide across a sand pit without the water rising above her knees, but at low tide fifty years later she would have been drowned if she had made the same attempt.

When the sea finally divided Australia and New Guinea is not precisely known. J. N. Jennings, after carefully studying the meagre evidence available, concluded that Torres Strait was formed later than Bass Strait. He estimated New Guinea became an island probably between 8,000 and 6,500 years ago. At that time the southern regions of New Guinea were inhabited by people who must have had a strong physical resemblance to aboriginals of northern Australia. Moreover their ways of hunting and gathering and their social life must have had many similarities to the life of northern Australia.

III

In one way or other the rising seas disturbed the life of every Australian for thousands of years. Salt water drowned perhaps one-seventh of the land. Higher seas slowly upset the seasonal cycle of wanderings in coastal regions. For instance a tribe which traditionally spent a month at lagoons where yams and freshwater mussels were plentiful would find the old routine had become impracticable, because the sea had penetrated the lagoon, making the waters brackish and killing the old foods. The rising seas could silt a river mouth, thus creating coastal marshes in places where kangaroos had once grazed. The marshes themselves might become a breeding ground for birds which previously had not been attracted to that region, and the aboriginals eventually might have devised new snaring and hunting skills to catch the birds. The advancing tides must have affected the diets of the people. The taboos on certain foods required reconsideration. And so an inland tribe for whom mussels were taboo might, ten centuries later, be a coastal tribe for whom mussels were too vital a source of food to be rejected dog-matically. Local changes in climate, changes caused by the effect of the rising seas on the intensity and timing of rain-fall, could have had profound effects on a traditional way of life and on the ability of areas to support their people.

A tribe living so far from the coast that it had never heard of the sea could not escape these events. If its stone axes had come, century after century, from a remote basalt headland which was now cut off by rising water, obviously that tribe was now gravely inconvenienced. Its ability to hunt possums, to make implements or to cut bark canoes, was impaired until such time as suitable stone could be found elsewhere. Such changes were not very dislocating, however, compared to changes of climate. The rising of the seas was accompanied by, and largely caused by, warmer temperatures. The climatic changes differed from region to region. We know virtually nothing about them except for clues provided by a few discoveries at places such as Lake Mungo. The climatic changes were perhaps slow, being spread over scores of generations, but the adaption required might have been considerable.

Languages, marriage patterns, genetics, religion, mytho-logy and warfare—all must have been effected by the rising of the seas around Australia. The archaeological record so far has not even whispered about these effects. Anthropolo-gists have not yet begun to speculate about them. During thousands of years the forming of a wide bay could have permanently separated people who spoke the same language, and so the languages slowly diverged until they seemed to be foreign languages. The same intrusion of the sea could have permanently brought together tribes who henceforth mar-ried into one another, and so fostered other breeding patterns. The drowning of landmarks of mythological impor-tance, the invoking of explanations for that drowning, and the enforced mingling of different peoples must have fer-tilized many new legends and beliefs. The throwing-together

of separate peoples, and the parting of peoples who had long
been linked, must have characterized the long epoch of The
Rising of the Sea.

Every tribal group on the coast 15,000 years ago must
have slowly lost its entire territory. Compelled to move
inland, in order to survive, a tribe entered territory to which
few or none of its members normally had right of access. In
the Gulf of Carpentaria and other new gulfs, bays, and
straits, a succession of retreats must have occurred. The slow
exodus of refugees, the sorting out of peoples and the
struggle for territories probably led to many wounds and
deaths as well as new alliances. The violent deaths—if widespread—must have cushioned the pressure on foodstuffs in
some of the places of retreat.

Seven thousand years ago the sea had virtually completed
that slow rise which had been occurring for at least 13,000
years. The level of the sea was now only about thirty feet
below its present level. The continent was thus cut off, by
wide arms of the sea, from those Indonesian islands with
which its contacts, presumably, had always been most influential. The shortest distance between Australia and the island
of Timor was perhaps trebled. The gap between Arnhem
Land and New Guinea was now sea instead of land, and frail
rafts and canoes could no more venture across the new
Arafura Sea than across the old Timor Sea. That strip of
Australian coast which had long faced the islands of the
Indonesian archipelago and the powerful sources of new
influences was now effectively isolated from those sources.
Instead Australia's nearest access to those sources was the
roundabout link through West Irian and Papua.

Ironically the continent was cut off at the very time when
Asia—through the domesticating of plants and animals—
was beginning to change at a faster pace than ever before.

CHAPTER SEVEN

Birth and Death

Australia is said to have supported as many as 300,000 aboriginals before the first white settlers arrived. The aboriginals were widely dispersed then—more dispersed than is the Australian population today. Nearly every plain, tableland and valley was inhabited for at least part of the year. Every desert yielded food. Every district, even in drought, yielded raw material for making equipment. Amongst the areas which were closely settled were the banks and billabongs of the Murray Valley and favoured bays and rivermouths along the tropical coast.

An anthropologist, A. R. Radcliffe-Brown, made the often-quoted estimate that Australia held an aboriginal population of 250,000 or 300,000 at the time of the white man's arrival. Any such estimate* calls for boldness as well as detailed knowledge, for the continent really consisted of hundreds of self-supporting republics, embracing a diversity of terrain ranging from cool plains to tropical forest. Even allowing a margin of error of forty per cent, we probably do not know

---

*The implications of this estimate of 300,000 aboriginals become astounding when the date of aboriginal occupancy is pushed back further and further into antiquity. If the continent in say the last 30,000 years had held an average population of 250,000, and if the average span of life (assuming a high rate of infant mortality) had been 25 years, then 10 million people must have lived during each millennium. A grand total of 300 million aboriginals would thus have lived and died in Australia since 28,000 B.C. And millions more would have lived and died in the misty earlier era.

the population of more than a few of those territories at the time of the first European contact. If we were able to make an accurate census of Australia in 1788 we would not be sure how to answer the more tantalizing questions about the population in earlier centuries. For instance, was the population rising, falling, or relatively stable in the previous thousand years? Learned opinion is inclined to imply that the population of Australia had long been static, and that a rough balance had been attained between the level of population and each different environment.

Many customs curbed the increase of aboriginal population; so too did floods, droughts, diseases, and other natural hazards. It seems dangerous, however, to concentrate solely on these curbs and checks. The very idea of a relatively stable population usually reflects an undue emphasis on the brakes and a neglect of the accelerator. In Australia the brakes and the accelerator each had periods of dominance. The evidence suggests that the history of Australia's population was a complicated story of many fluctuations rather than a simple story of quick growth and then long stagnation.

II

Scarcity of food has long been seen as the highest barrier to the expansion of primitive populations. The famous exponent of this view was the Reverend Thomas Malthus, who from 1805 was professor of history and political economy at the East India College near London. In later editions of his *Essay on the Principle of Population* he gave many examples of how primitive societies were confined to small numbers by near-famine. One only had to observe the inhabitants of Tierra del Fuego, he said, to know why their population was sparse. Their 'very appearance indicates them to be half starved'. One rung higher up the ladder of wretchedness came the Andaman Islanders. Their faces, he said, were 'a horrid mixture of famine and ferocity'. Next came the Tasmanians and, a little higher, the Australians; and even they were barely above the level of starvation in a land where 'the supply of animal and vegetable food is so extremely scanty'.

Malthus's main source of information on the Australian aboriginals was the large book completed in London in 1798 by David Collins, who had just returned from a term as Judge Advocate of the British colony at Sydney. A glance at Collins's book quickly reveals that Malthus had read it with care: indeed he had copied out some of his comments word for word though without bestowing the courtesy of quotation marks. Collins himself had lived in the garrison town of Sydney and had little opportunity to travel more than ten miles inland, but he had diligently learned much about local hunting and eating habits. At that time the diet of the aboriginals near Sydney was lean. Perhaps tribal life and traditional ways of food-collection had collapsed quickly; perhaps the herds and gardens of the new settlers had occupied much of the ground where aboriginals had previously gathered roots and greens; or perhaps Sydney was one of the few districts in Australia where vegetables and fruits had long been only a minor part of diet. The aboriginal remnant near Sydney Harbour was mistakenly assumed to be living the kind of life typical of aboriginals everywhere, and that hungry precarious life was described often between 1790 and 1830. In Malthus's *Essay*—a book of indelible influence on the thought of the nineteenth century—the vivid detail he had gathered from Collins's book illustrated how 'the lowest stage of human society' fought with famine in every part of the world.

It is now impossible to accept the popular Malthusian picture that aboriginals were normally living on the edge of starvation. Famine was probably abnormal. Scarcity of food was probably not a frequent check on the expansion of population except perhaps in the thinly-populated deserts of the interior. In most parts of the continent only freak climatic conditions were a grave danger. Admittedly, during a span of history exceeding 30,000 years, catastrophic droughts even on the fertile coastal lands must have come many times. Even if the catastrophes came only twice, on average, in each millennium, that was sufficient frequency to mark a graph of population with drunken dips and dives. When exceptionally long droughts set in, or the supply of edible plants and animals was gravely upset by predators or diseases, the resulting famines must have seriously reduced the population of Australia and Tasmania.

The very old and the very young would be the main casualties. Fewer children would be born, and the death rate of infants would soar. If a dangerous disease arose during the famine it could severely cull out the young men and women, for their resistance then would probably be low. Most of those natural catastrophes might not have affected the food supply everywhere. In a land as big as Australia the famines were regional rather than continental; nonetheless they must have seriously lowered the population.

The fear of a shortage of food was probably not often present. Generation after generation probably passed through life without fearing famine. The main reason why that fear remained mostly in the background was the existence of customs which checked the population from rising rapidly. Adherence to those customs meant the difference between plenty and relative poverty for most aboriginal groups.

III

Abortion was perhaps common practice. During a medical survey of aboriginals in three settlements in Arnhem Land in 1948 those women who were questioned knew of methods of inducing a miscarriage. At Oenpelli at least half of the miscarriages appear to have been induced deliberately. In some regions certain herbs were eaten to promote abortions; and a planter on the western side of Cape York Peninsula believed that illegitimate births were rare because of the aboriginals' intimate knowledge of herbs. In the lower part of the Paroo River in the north-west of New South Wales—and perhaps in most regions—the common way of trying to bring on an abortion was to press the hands heavily upon the stomach of the pregnant woman.

A recent survey of 350 societies, all of which were pre-industrial, concluded that abortion was 'an absolutely universal' practice. This did not necessarily mean that the only motive of those who carried out the abortions was to limit the size of a family to manageable numbers; and in a nomadic society only one child-in-arms was manageable. The motivation was often individualist. At Oenpelli several aboriginal women in 1948 privately gave simple reasons for wanting no baby. They said they wanted to play about with men, not babies.

Most aboriginal women gave birth to babies with comparative ease. A group might be moving to another camping site and in the course of the day's walk through the countryside a woman might feel the labour pains. If the time had come she walked quietly away from the straggle of aboriginals, and in the shelter of a bush or tree she crouched down and quickly produced the baby. She herself tied the umbilical cord; and if water lay nearby she washed the baby before wrapping it in a skin rug. If the party was settled in a camp when a woman was about to give birth she disappeared into the bushes, taking another woman for companionship. The circumstantial evidence is persuasive that few aboriginal women died in childbirth. The relative ease with which they bore children may partly account for the frequency with which they delayed the destruction of an unwanted baby until after it was born.

Infanticide was practised throughout Australia and indeed in probably every nomadic society. The practice of killing new-born infants is at present mentioned infrequently in writings about the aboriginals' traditional way of life. Some

96

anthropologists and pre-historians delicately avoid the topic.
And yet the conclusion seems inescapable: over a long span
of time millions of new-born aboriginals must have been
deliberately killed by their mother or father. Infanticide was
almost certainly the strongest check on the increase of the
population of aboriginals.

One of the sharpest observers of tribal life thought that
the women of the Bangerang, a group on the plains of
northern Victoria, gave birth to six or perhaps even eight
children during the course of their life. Nearly half of those
babies, he estimated, were killed at birth.* He realized that
nomadic peoples had no alternative but to kill superfluous
babies. As a woman carried the camp chattels, often a firestick, and sometimes a basket of food when her group moved
camp, she could carry in addition only one child. In contrast
the aboriginals living near the Murray River and its swamps
walked shorter distances to find their daily food, moved camp
less frequently, and so were not compelled to kill so many
new babies or abandon so many old people. Their camps,
being more permanent, seemed to support more picaninnies
and many old people including some who perhaps were
70 years old and perhaps a few who were 80.

A mother normally fed a child at the breast until about the
age of 3: even a few 6-year-olds were partly fed from the
breast. As a child grew older the mother could not always
supply enough milk for one, let alone two mouths, to suck.
To abandon breast-feeding at an early age was possible but
risky. No animal milk was available in the continent. Easily-
digestible foods were not to be found during some months of
the year. Undoubtedly a long period of breast-feeding curbed
the mortality of infants. Moreover the prolonged breast-

*The observer was the sheep-owner, E. M. Curr. His actual sentence
leaves some doubt whether his infanticide rate of nearly 50 per cent
included abortions as well as the killing of new-born babies. In two
areas of South Australia independent estimates of the proportion of
babies killed at birth were about 30 per cent and 50 per cent.

feeding slightly reduced the mother's chances of becoming pregnant and so helped to space her births. If her pregnancies happened to come too closely together, and one child followed another in the space of eighteen months, the new baby probably was killed. A white man who for thirty years lived with aboriginals in the Geelong district explained that a new-born child could be saved from death by the decision of the father. He might refuse to sanction the killing if the new baby was a girl. In many other districts, however, a baby boy was more likely to be saved.

It was the custom to kill a deformed child at birth: a deformed child imperilled a nomadic society. If twins were born one was killed at birth. If babies were believed to have been fathered illegitimately, they were usually killed at birth, according to tribal practices operating as far apart as the Gulf of Carpentaria and Bass Strait. That practice possibly reflected a fear of the danger of inbreeding; it was therefore essential to the welfare of a society which periodically moved about in search of food.

Unwanted babies could be killed in a variety of ways. A baby's brains were bashed out with a piece of wood or stone, or it was suffocated when its mouth was stuffed with sand, or it was quickly strangled: strangulation was possibly the most frequent method.

The essential role of human milk in a continent where no animals were domesticated can be seen in some of the infanticide customs. In the Bunbury district of Western Australia and in the vicinity of Sydney—regions almost two thousand miles apart—an infant was usually killed if its mother died. In Sydney in the 1790s those spectators who, out of curiosity, attended the burial of an aboriginal woman were astonished to see the husband place the small baby in the grave alongside the mother. The father then dropped a large stone onto the baby, and other aboriginals quickly filled the grave before the white spectators fully realized what had happened. They rebuked the aboriginal father, one

Cole-be, accusing him of barbaric behaviour. He simply replied that he knew of no woman who would feed and nurse and carry the baby now that the mother was dead. To allow the baby to live, he said, was to condemn it to a lingering, more painful death than the one which he himself had precipitated. A little later in England the Reverend Thomas Malthus read of the incident and described it as a mirror of the sheer 'difficulty of rearing children in savage life'.

Curious clues about aboriginal mortality have come from the uncovering of a burial ground near the banks of the Murray River, upstream from Blanche Town (S.A.). There, beneath high limestone cliffs, the elbow-shaped bends of the river enclosed wide flats with great red-gums and sweeping beds of rushes; but the coming of European sheep, rabbits, wood-cutters and builders of river-lochs so altered the vegetation and the river-levels that the fertile Roonka flat was denuded, scoured and eroded. Eventually the skeletons of aboriginals which had lain for thousands of years in a high sand-dune beside the river were exposed. Between 1968 and 1973 Graeme Pretty of the South Australian Museum excavated more than one hundred graves. His first tentative report revealed 'frequent and profound changes in patterns of burials', including the practice—unusual in Australia—of burying a corpse in an upright position. The burial ground was a guide not only to ways of burial but to causes of death. Circumstantial evidence in different graves hinted at death in childbirth, death by genetic abnormality, the judicial execution of a young couple and death through disease and death through spearing—the bone spear-point could still be seen in the man's rib cage.

One grave held the body of a child resting on the left arm of the skeleton of a strong man; in the judgment of Graeme Pretty it was 'the most striking and elaborate tomb yet unearthed in this country'. His tentative interpretation of the treasures in the grave suggests that the man's corpse had been adorned richly before burial. Probably the corpse had been cloaked in an animal skin which was fastened with many bone pins and decorated with the feathers of birds. On the head was probably placed a chaplet of notched wallaby teeth and a headband made from the vertebrae of selected reptiles. The child too had a touch of ornament; a bird's skull was probably worn as a pendant and her feet had been painted with ochre, dabs of which are still visible after thousands of years of burial. Another grave enclosed the skeletons of an adult and a child, some elaborate ornaments, and the remnants of food offerings, prompting Pretty to suggest that this must have been the burial place for people of prestige. It is likely that the children in the double grave were victims of ritual infanticide. They had been sacrificed not because their mothers had died but because the beliefs and rituals of the group maintained that the burial of certain adults should be accompanied by the sacrifice of a child. How widely the Australians practised ritual infanticide is unknown. The ritual is illuminating, for it hints that the curbs on aboriginal population arose from social customs as well as from nomadic necessity.*

Their attitude to infants might often seem callous but generally they displayed tenderness towards children. Most observers of tribal life noted their kindness towards children, indeed their indulgence. Children were rarely scolded or punished. They were frequently allowed to impose themselves on their parents: a common sight was a mother 'carrying a stout young urchin who was too lazy to walk'.

The seasonal wanderings penalized the very old as well as the day-old. The aboriginals probably treated old people as favourably as white Australians treat their old today—a mixture of concern and neglect. The time came, however, when nothing further could be done: a skinny old man or

* Of course social customs often reflect economic necessity; and what we define as economically necessary is often influenced by social attitudes.

100

woman became too feeble to travel; the ground-down stumps of their teeth and their delicate digestion could no longer cope with the food they found or were offered. The very old were then treated with a kind of indifference. Their life had been lived; to prolong it was pointless and perhaps cruel.

When the explorer W. C. Gosse was leading an expedition to the south of Alice Springs in 1873 he came across a camp of about thirty aboriginals at a waterhole on the Alberga. It was summer and the ground felt like burning metal; and the aboriginals walked on grass or low bushes to protect their bare soles. There, on the burning sand, was an old woman, pitifully old, her skin tight against her bones, her teeth probably incapable of chewing the wallaby meat and the ground seeds which formed the bulk of the diet. Gosse's brother was sorry for her and boiled some wheaten-flour. Flour of the texture of fine powder is a luxury to those aboriginals who grind their own flour from desert seeds; and this old woman was so eager to dip her bony fingers into the hot gruel that she would have burned her hand if she had not been restrained. The kindness towards the woman, however, did not impress some of the aboriginals who observed the preparing of the gruel. The gift, they said, was misplaced; the gruel was wasted: 'it was no use giving her food as she was soon going to die.'

A woman too old to walk was deliberately killed by aboriginals near the lower reaches of the Goulburn River (V.) in the 1840s. She was placed on a pile of dry wood, the wood was set alight, and her companions promptly left the blaze and moved to another camp. That hasty cremation could have been partly a reflection of a culture which was crumbling with the coming of white men and sheep. On the other hand the aboriginals excused their conduct with the kind of arguments which their countrymen had used elsewhere to justify infanticide. They had decided to move camp, nothing could save her from dying, her groans and complaints distressed them. If she had died alone, they added, she would have been eaten by dingoes. The episode suggests a streak of fatalism in the attitude of the young to the old, and of the fit to the feeble: a willingness to accept prematurely the way in which a nomadic existence imperilled the life of the old. A London scholar, James Woodburn, warned recently of the danger of explaining the abandonment of the old and the lame in hunting societies as solely the result of 'ecological pressures'. Heartless pressures were also at work. Thus in some favoured regions of Australia the old were usually given the poorer scraps as food and—for blankets—the tattered animal skins.

If abortion, infanticide and the difficulties of caring for the very old and the very young had been the only curbs on a rising population, they would have gone a long way towards explaining the success of aboriginals in continuing to live in a land of relative plenty. These, however, were not the only customs which helped to ensure that people were usually less plentiful than food. Epidemics and warfare also pinned down the population. At present most of those who study nomadic societies are inclined to view wars and plagues as less deadly amongst nomads than in societies of farmers and herdsmen. Indeed the freedom of nomadic societies from serious plagues and wars is seen as one of their triumphs or good fortune. In nomadic Australia, however, there was no such good fortune.

Anthropologists tend to agree that epidemics were not frequent in societies of hunters and gatherers. Their grounds for this opinion, however, are open to challenge. For instance they argue that in Australia or Patagonia or other wandering societies the social groups are small; but is a small tribe necessarily less vulnerable to a plague than a populous city? Ten deaths in a nomadic tribe can be, statistically, as significant as 10,000 deaths in a mediaeval city. Those numbers might each represent one-fifth of the population and so serve equally as a brake on the natural increase.

The bands of hunters and gatherers in Australia often formed groups which were not much smaller than a cluster of peasant families in isolated parts of Europe in, say, the eighteenth century, but epidemics amongst the peasants were not unknown. Anthropologists also argue that a nomadic economy, because it consisted of isolated communities, was less likely to be swept by an infection. But the hundreds of isolated groups in Australia were not as isolated from one another as we imagine. They married into other groups, they met to fight and to trade, and even their economic boundaries were untidy. A virus which began in the Gulf of Carpentaria might have taken a long time to reach the Great Australian Bight but clearly a transcontinental crossing was possible along the web of contacts.

The isolation of the many bands of aboriginals did not prevent infections from spreading swiftly across south-eastern Australia early in the nineteenth century. The diseases might have arrived with Europeans or with Indonesian fishermen, and they infected a few aboriginals who had no immunity, and then began to spread through vast areas of the interior. William Buckley observed that the aboriginals, during his three decades with them near Port Phillip Bay, were generally healthy but he recalled how one infection swept through the countryside, catching the strong and the healthy, causing 'a dreadful swelling of the feet' and ulcerous sores, and taking many lives. The nature of that infection is a mystery. So too is the infection which resembled smallpox and travelled down the river to South Australia, perhaps in the 1820s. As the banks of the Darling, Murrumbidgee and Murray were relatively thick with people the riverside societies must have been a smooth ribbon for the spread of the infection. Later a pioneer sheepowner of the river region noticed that the skin of very old aboriginals was pocked, and they told him that a disease had spread downstream at the time of the spring floods. So many aboriginals had died of the disease that their society ceased to operate, and for a

103

time the bodies lay unburied, the sick were unattended, and the survivors fled. On present knowledge it is therefore not safe to assume that hunters and gatherers were much less likely than the later farming societies to be decimated by epidemics.

The question of whether epidemics helped to restrain the population is complicated by the isolation of the continent. Perhaps it could be argued that Australia was so remote that it was not likely to import contagious diseases until the coming of the Indonesians and Europeans in the eighteenth century. The land, however, was not completely isolated for most of its long human history. It is even conceivable that in every millennium at least five or ten people arrived from an eastern island of the Indonesian archipelago. Those islands in turn had occasional contact with a string of tropical islands which extended to the mainland of south-east Asia. Admittedly the rising of the seas and the widening of the Timor Sea and Arafura Sea lessened the chance of an accidental voyager landing in north-western Australia, especially between say, 8,000 B.C. and 2,000 B.C.; but even during that epoch of tighter isolation Australia was still not completely cut off. The people on Cape York Peninsula were in touch with the Torres Strait islands and with Papua; and of course Papua was part of that string of islands extending all the way to south-east Asia. Whereas the Timor Sea was a wide barrier, Torres Strait was more like a bridge. Human carriers could easily cross the bridge, conveying new diseases to Australia.

Even if there had been no contact for thousands of years between the aboriginals and outside peoples, infectious diseases could still enter Australia. Migrating birds arrived annually and could carry dangerous diseases. The Murray Valley encephalitis, which had a fatal outbreak in 1974, is believed to be carried south by migrating birds and spread by mosquitoes during summers of widespread flooding in the interior of eastern Australia. Even if, for thousands and

104

thousands of years, no infected bird and no infected Indonesian or Papuan had reached these shores, epidemics could still flourish. We are accustomed to thinking, erroneously, that aboriginal Australia had static population, static resources, and static ideas, and was incapable of originating anything, but that does not preclude the possibility that dangerous viruses might have originated in Australia. It is unlikely that in the long pre-history of Australia there was a complete absence of those infectious diseases which, even if confined to one outbreak, were more devastating than twenty massacres or battles.

The effect of epidemics on aboriginal population is not easy to assess. The effect of some epidemics, moreover, was probably compounded by the reprisals which they incited. Aboriginals believed that a fatal disease was the result of a plot of an enemy, and that the enemy therefore must be punished. The plague that followed the river settlements about the 1820s, for instance, was seen not as the result of a virus but rather as a malicious spell cast by hostile tribes from the upper rivers. Belief in the power of sorcery meant that some men and women, even though lightly infected, gave up hope, ceased to eat, and quietly prepared to die. Sorcery was a self-fulfilling prophecy because the victim almost willed himself to die and indeed would die unless a local medicine man was persuasive enough to convince him that the spell could be dispersed. The devastation of a plague was increased not only by the widespread belief in sorcery but also by the avenging expeditions which were set in motion after the plague had passed; ultimately the groups which had suffered from the plague felt strong enough to retaliate against the originators of the plague.

IV

While epidemics came irregularly, armed fights were more an annual event in many parts of the continent and Tasmania. Violent death—by spearing or clubbing—was a restraint on the growth of population. Occasionally there were pitched battles or raids in which many men took part. The casualties might not, at first sight, seem large; but the death of two men in a battle involving forty meant that casualties were approaching the scale of the Battle of the Somme. An aboriginal fight could absorb a large proportion of the adults within a radius of fifty miles—indeed could involve a far higher proportion of able-bodied adults than any war of the twentieth century could possibly involve.

The European who had the longest opportunity to observe the effects of warfare on aboriginals in southern Australia was William Buckley. He came originally from Cheshire and as a teenager he fought in the French Revolutionary Wars. In 1802, back in England, he was convicted of receiving a roll of stolen cloth and was transported across the world to the short-lived convict settlement at Sorrento, near the entrance to Port Phillip Bay. Soon he escaped. Walking about 100 miles around the bay, crossing the river where Melbourne was later to arise, he eventually fell in with aboriginals. When the convict settlement was removed from the bay, Buckley remained at large. Decade after decade he wandered with aboriginals, eating yams and eels, swan's eggs and possums. At last in 1835 the sheep-owners arrived to settle along the Victorian coast and Buckley returned to the clothes-wearing society, received an official pardon, and in old age reminisced about his experiences with aboriginals.

Buckley was a giant, standing 6 ft. 6 ins. in his large bare feet. Physically strong, a veteran of military engagements, he should not have been frightened by the warfare which he saw as he moved from place to place with aboriginal bands. And yet one of the strongest impressions of his memoirs is the fighting and bloodshed. He had not long been adopted by one group when a fight began with a neighbouring group. In the fight a man was speared in the thigh and a woman was fatally speared under the arm. A little later the seduction or abduction of women led to another fight in which two boys were killed. In a three-hour battle between neighbouring bands three women were killed. Buckley witnessed all these killings. In another fierce battle, men and women were so streaked with blood and they fought one another so indiscriminately that the scene, to his mind, was 'much more frightful' than anything he had seen in battles fought with powder and shot in the Netherlands in 1799. As a result of the battle two women in Buckley's group were killed. That night his group took revenge: they ambushed the sleeping enemy, beating three to death, wounding several more and putting the remainder to flight. The wounded ones were not spared. They were beaten to death, said Buckley, and their legs and arms amputated with sharp shells, flints and stone tomahawks.

As the people with whom Buckley roamed were few, and as the bands of his enemies appeared also to have been small, the reported deaths represented a high ratio of casualties. Moreover the massacres and ambushes so far culled from his reminiscences might well have happened in his first year with the aboriginals, a time which remained vivid in his hazy memories. Even if those violent deaths—numbering at least thirteen—had been spread over thirty years instead of one year they would have underlined the effect of warfare on a small population.

This casualty list does not exhaust Buckley's experience of aboriginal fighting. Near Mount Moriac and close to the present highway between Geelong and Colac, Buckley's group was temporarily weakened by the absence of most of the men on a hunting trip. His group, being vulnerable, was suddenly attacked, and a boy and a girl were speared to death. A raid to take revenge was successful, killing two of the enemy. Not long after, camped on a freshwater lake, Buckley and his friends heard uproar across the water and next day found people massacred in their sleep or drowned after fleeing into the reedbeds. How many women died is not recorded but Buckley saw 'many women and children' on the ground, 'wounded and sadly mutilated'. Near the shores of Lake Modewarre three men were speared to death and a four-year-old child was brained in a further episode of revenge. In another fight, ostensibly over the possession of women, one woman was killed and two severely wounded by the riverside somewhere near the present Queen's Park at Geelong. Later Buckley's party was again attacked, and his oldest friend was killed, along with wife and son: in the next round three of the enemy tribe were killed. In recounting these and other fights between wandering bands Buckley tended to remember himself as an armed peacemaker, a conscientious objector, or war correspondent.

A slow count of the deaths inflicted in the battles and raids described by Buckley reveals a total of at least thirty-seven, of whom ten were women and twelve were children. Furthermore an unspecified number had been killed or drowned in the massacre which he reported on the shores of the freshwater lake. Uncounted members of another group of copper-skinned aboriginals from the Otway Ranges had apparently been suffocated to death when Buckley's friends, surrounding them, had deliberately set fire to the bushes in which they were hiding. Even if we add only another thirteen deaths for the massacre by the lake and the fire-trap in the bush, that brings the total reported by Buckley to fifty. The list still excludes the fights—of which Buckley was not a witness—between other groups in the same region, and it excludes casualties which must have occurred during that long time when Buckley, tired of the wanderings and the revenges, lived alone near the sand dunes of the ocean.

The region over which Buckley's group wandered probably covered, at the most, about 1700 square miles. The probable population of that region was one inhabitant to each four, five or six square miles; and that would suggest a total of perhaps 280 to 420 people. If we go on to accept a very cautious estimate of the number of fighting deaths, we

arrive at the conclusion that the annual death rate in warfare equalled 1 for every 270 in the population. That death
rate was probably not exceeded in any nation of Europe
during any of the last three centuries.

Two thousand miles to the north an American anthropologist, Lloyd Warner, studying in the twilight of tribal
life, collected many details of aboriginals dying in warfare
during a period of twenty years. Many of the deaths were
the result of raids carried out to avenge an earlier death.
Thus thirty-five deaths arose from avenging expeditions in
which armed men quietly surrounded the camp of the
enemy and then killed the man they were searching for.
These raids were known as 'maringo', the word for death-
adder, because the raiders traditionally approached the
enemy's camp in a snake-like formation. Another twenty-
seven men were killed, probably while asleep, during smaller
raids of revenge. Twice in the period of twenty years a chain
of isolated killings had culminated in a pitched battle in
which two lines of warriors stood less than twenty paces
apart and threw short spears; as they carried no shields the
casualties were high. A pitched battle involving many clans
was seen as a way of bringing peace after the long snatches of
violence. It was a war to end wars, 'a spear fight to end
spear fights'. Two such battles, however, resulted in the
death of thirty-five men.

Warner concluded that a total of about 200 men died from
organized warfare in north-east Arnhem Land between 1909
and 1929. Those statistics, standing alone, may appear either
bloody or trifling. Warner sensibly let them stand, with little
comment. At the time when he wrote his book *Black Civilization*, unjustified contempt for the aboriginals and ignorance of their civilizing achievement was widespread. To
dwell too much on their deadly warfare—he perhaps decided
—was to tamper unfairly with a dice which was already
loaded.

As north-east Arnhem Land held only 3,000 people at

that time, the casualties of warfare were colossal. The effect of their fighting is realized if it is compared with the casualty statistics of the nations which suffered severely in the Second World War. Such comparisons reveal that the annual death-rate through warfare in that corner of Arnhem Land was nearly six times as high as that of the United States during an average year of its participation in the Second World War. Even the direct drain on Japan's population through the loss of fighting men in China, the Pacific and all other theatres of war between 1937 and 1945 was not quite as high as warfare's drain on the population of Arnhem Land. In the Second World War only the armed forces of the Soviet Union and Germany suffered losses of greater relative magnitude. In an average year of those two decades the north-eastern part of Arnhem Land lost through warfare one person in every 300.* In contrast one person of every 150 in Germany was killed in action or presumed killed in the average year of the Second World War. The direct losses of the Soviet Union—7,500,000 members of her armed forces were missing in action or killed—ran at the annual average of one in about 130.

Even these comparisons minimize the way in which war-fare reduced the population of north-east Arnhem Land, for we are really comparing their normal life with only the war years of the industrialized nations. If it were possible to measure the military casualties in Arnhem Land with those of advanced nations over many decades we would probably find that the spears of Arnhem Land were more deadly than the heavy artillery and machine guns of Europe. It is doubt-ful if even the Soviet Union lost a higher proportion of her population through the combined effect of the Russo-Japanese war of 1904-5, the First World War, the War of

* My conservative calculation of the violent-death-rate in Buckley's terrain—an area stretching from Geelong and Port Phillip Heads to Lake Corangamite—was 1 in 270, but it could have been 1 in 150 or the same as Germany's casualties in the Second World War.

Intervention and the Second World War than would have
been lost by Arnhem Land in the course of a normal half-
century of avenging raids and pitched battles. In essence the
steady casualties of warfare in Arnhem Land, year by year,
decade by decade, probably accumulated totals that exceeded
those inflicted on a European nation in the combined total of
peaceful and fighting years.

Whether fighting in Arnhem Land killed more warriors
in the years 1909-29 than in earlier years is impossible to
answer. Whether that region was more inclined to deadly
fighting than other regions of Australia is also an unanswer-
able question. But certainly the tabulation in two regions
suggests that warfare was one of the powerful curbs on the
growth of population.

At least the warfare amongst aboriginals rarely destroyed
sources of food. It rarely interrupted the process of gathering
food. As men were not indispensable as breadwinners the
loss of men through war did not necessarily deprive women
and children of food. Even the birthrate of aboriginal groups
did not always suffer through the loss of young men. In the
north-east of Arnhem Land polygamy was practised; the
average middle-aged man had three or four wives, so the
death of many young men in warfare and armed raids did
not lower the birthrate in the dramatic way experienced in
societies where each man had only one wife. On the other
hand warfare was a terrible scythe in those regions where it
killed women and children as well as men, because it thereby
affected the birth rate as well as the death rate.

These episodes of fighting in aboriginal Australia run
counter to the beliefs of most anthropologists. A New York
professor, recently surveying the attitudes of living anthropologists, concluded that they did not see war as major cause
of death amongst hunters and food gatherers: 'Whatever
evidence we have of armed conflicts among the contemporary
hunters and gatherers tends to support this view'. In fact the

evidence from a large part of Arnhem Land and Western Victoria defies this view.

War was a curb on the growth of population: on the other hand cannibalism perhaps had only a trifling effect on the death rate. The theme of cannibalism in Australia is slippery with emotion and morality, and is not easily grasped. So many of the Europeans who were curious about the morality of aboriginals questioned them intensely about cannibalism. Every generation seems to writhe under a different nightmare, and in the nineteenth century—that heroic era of inland exploration—many Europeans in their nightmare imagined themselves falling into the hands of cannibals. In that century cannibalism was often regarded as the greatest depravity, the antithesis of civilization, and was so viewed even by many who regularly took Holy Communion and believed they were thereby eating the body and drinking the blood of Christ. In fact, many aboriginals ate human flesh in the same spirit, believing that they thus acquired some of the strength of those who had died. In many tribal areas from the De Grey River near the Indian Ocean to headlands on the Pacific Ocean, pieces of flesh were cut from a dead enemy and eaten. There are also many records—some of them false or exaggerated—of aboriginals eating flesh which they had cut from those who had died peacefully.

Cannibalism probably was more often the ritual aftermath of a death than a motive of murder. On occasions, however, aboriginals were deliberately killed so that their flesh could be eaten. Thus Baldwin Spencer and F. J. Gillen reported from central Australia that occasionally amongst the Loritja-speaking people a very young child was killed so that its flesh could be fed to an older but weaker child. The Herbert River in north Queensland, the western district in Victoria, and several other districts yield convincing evidence that certain aboriginals committed murders in order to eat flesh. Carl Lumholtz, a Norwegian zoologist whose book recounting four years of travelling in Australia was rather sensationally entitled *Among Cannibals*, was convinced that some of the aboriginals with whom he lived along the Herbert River were enthusiastic cannibals who sometimes set out to kill people and to eat human flesh. During his time amongst them they killed two aboriginal men and ate parts of the flesh, especially the fat around the kidneys. Cannibals, he gravely warned his readers in 1889, could be outwardly quiet and charming. 'It is a mistake', he announced, 'to suppose that the cannibals have an uglier look than other savages.'

V

Abortions, warfare, the killing of unwanted babies, and the inability to care for the old were persistent obstacles to the rapid rise of Australia's population. Other obstacles were sporadic. When about 20,000 years ago the rising seas began to lick the coastal plains, food there became scarcer. It is easy to suppose that in many regions the population declined during parts of that epoch in which perhaps one-seventh of the continent's soil disappeared slowly beneath the sea. Similarly epidemics, now and then, probably scythed the aboriginal camps. Even one major epidemic occurring, on average, once in every 5,000 or 6,000 years could reshape the population graph. It is even possible that the population lost in such an epidemic might not have been recovered for many centuries.

In enquiring how population fluctuated in a nomadic society we instinctively tend to see it in terms of our own experience of a specialist and sedentary society. That experience, however, is irrelevant. We easily imagine a population of nomads recovering quickly after a disaster, but such a society was so structured that its population could not quickly revive after a setback. Only when the next stage occurred in economic activity, and herds and gardens were kept, could a population recover quickly from natural disasters. Once women stayed immobile near their house and no longer had to wander daily to gather food, they could care for a larger number of infants. By using milk from sheep, goats, or cows in their own herds they weaned their own children earlier. The spacing of children could be narrower. Infanticide and abortion were no longer so essential. Thus a rapid increase in infants was at last possible, though hazards might kill many of those infants in unfortunate years.

Compared to the aboriginals' Australia the Asian settlements which pioneered the keeping of herds and the planting of crops had an unprecedented capacity to increase their population rapidly in favourable eras. Their new population ledger, however, had debits. As they obtained their food from a few specialized animals and crops, they were unusually vulnerable to natural disasters, to swine fever, insect plagues, grain diseases. A natural catastrophe—the kind of freak happening that might occur only once in a millennium—could cut their population even more drastically than a similar event could hurt a nomadic, unspecialized society. Perhaps, too, those crowded riverside settlements on the Nile, Euphrates or Indus were more liable, being compact, to lose a high part of their population through sudden plague or epidemic; but this supposition is open to dispute.

Generally these farming and herding economies were more prone than nomads to serious setbacks, but their capacity to increase their population after setbacks was also remarkable. Moreover, after the population recovered to its pre-disaster level, it could possibly continue to rise through the people's skill in using new land intensively.

The nomadic peoples of Australia probably were incapable of increasing population quickly. Many curbs on the growth of population—infanticide, abortion and warfare—were cultural and could not be turned off like the twist of a key. These restraints on the fast growth of population were ingrained in the culture and needs of a nomadic life. They

114

operated indiscriminately, or relatively so, in lean and fat years.

If natural disaster had killed many of the people living within seventy miles of Cape Leeuwin (W.A.), and in the space of one generation had reduced the population from say 1,000 to 500, the recovery of population to the former level might have taken two or three centuries. Even if many aboriginals in that region had wished to increase the population quickly—and in that event they must have had in mind an ideal family-size rather than an optimum tribal population—they could do little to achieve their wish. Abortions were still necessary: babies born too close after sisters or brothers perhaps had to be killed. A mother in a wandering group could carry and breast-feed only one child at a time. Admittedly if food were plentiful her breasts would yield more milk, so reducing slightly the rate of infant mortality. But a succession of lush seasons and abundant food did not probably lead, as in some western countries, to earlier marriages and to mothers bearing their first child at a younger age. Nor did a lush season necessarily quell the desire to move camp, for the desire for a change of diet often seems to have been as strong as hunger in motivating the movements of nomads.

It could be argued that the recovery of population was aided by a decline in deaths from warfare. That hypothesis would be attractive to those who believe that population pressures are a major cause of war and that therefore in a diminished population warfare would be less frequent. It is hard, however, to find compelling evidence that a decline of population pressure actually promotes peace in either nomadic or highly industrial societies. From these surmises, then, a plain conclusion offers itself. Whenever population fell sharply in any region of aboriginal Australia the subsequent revival was of a slowness inconceivable, after a similar crisis, in a society of herdsmen, peasants, or city dwellers.

If we had to draw a graph of the population history of Australia, perhaps the shape would resemble a slightly sloping saw-tooth roof. A gentle rise in population would often be followed by a dramatic fall, and the fall would usually be followed by another long, slow rise which would sometimes pass the previous peak before another fall or levelling out of population took place.

The circumstantial evidence that population could only rise slowly in aboriginal Australia had vital implications for any attempt to tell the history of how the continent was populated. This evidence runs against the valuable pioneering study of Australia's population made by the American anthropologist, J. B. Birdsell. He had argued that the aboriginals could have rapidly reached their maximum population. Professor Birdsell's graph of Australia's population— leaving out the smaller dints and bubbles—tended to imply a rapid rise followed by a long plateau. He pointed out that a tiny band of migrants to Australia could have multiplied quickly, for an aboriginal generation could be counted as only sixteen years. As mothers gave birth to their first child at an early age, the population in favourable conditions could grow rapidly in the space even of half a century. The tempo of reproduction meant that many women were great-grandmothers at the age of 50. Even an initial stock of twenty-five migrants, he explained, could have grown to a population of 300,000 in the space of only 2,204 years.

Professor Birdsell's interpretation assumes that there were few cultured curbs against rapid growth of population. On the contrary the curbs were probably strong and moreover were probably present from the first aboriginal migrations. As the first settlers were hunters and gatherers their women must have had to kill many of their offspring, before or after birth. Such restraints would have retarded the fast growth of population even if Australia's northern plains during the first millennia had been vast bowls of meat and honey. As the first migrants had originally been nomadic gatherers and fishermen in their own homeland, they would presumably have practised, even before their migration, those restraints on population which were common to pre-agricultural societies. Migrants do not easily forget old habits and customs even if the new land is different.

There is another curious facet of theories which describe a fast growth of population in Australia and then a long period of stagnation. Those theories suggest that the supply of food provided an unchanging ceiling beyond which the population could not rise. They assume that the maximum supply of food in the average year did not differ much between say 35,000 B.C. and 2,000 B.C. Thus in the early period of aboriginal settlement the supply of food was abundant, even prodigal, but eventually the rapid growth of population approached the level of food supply. Thereafter population could rise no more, except the temporary rise in a cluster of good seasons. The belief in a static food potential fits, like a key in a lock, the idea of a static population, but this neat-fitting argument is dubious.

The food supply of Australia was not static because knowledge of foods was not static. Within each of the numerous regions of Australia, Tasmania, and New Guinea the food resources must have altered greatly. In some areas they could have declined through changes in climate. Perhaps winter sunshine had diminished, thus choking a staple food plant; or the summer rain had become less reliable, thus lowering the level of lagoons; or on inland plains the higher winds and heavier scouring rain could have blown away the topsoil which yielded summer grain for pounding into flour. But even if the food potential had neither increased nor decreased, the effective supply of food would have been altered by the activities and preferences of men and women. Some of the alterations were quick, some probably took place over thousands of years.

117

The food supply depended on man as well as nature. It depended on a knowledge of what was edible, and on a willingness to acquire a taste for fruits or bulbs which might previously have been wasted. The food available to aboriginals depended partly on their hunting equipment, and that changed. The Water Whistle-Ducks might dive in their thousands in waterholes in the Kimberleys—offering enough meat for a daily banquet for a thousand people in season—but ducks were not food unless they were efficiently caught by aboriginal weapons or techniques. The food resources often depended on the aboriginals slowly learning about the feeding and breeding habits of hundreds of animals, insects, birds, fishes, reptiles. Many of these creatures must have been unfamiliar to the pioneer aboriginals. The traditional hunting and fowling methods must often have failed, but ultimately came new methods.

Millions of aboriginals owed their life to innovations which increased the supply of food. Australia today commemorates those white breeders of wheat and merinos, devisers of ploughs and harvesting machinery, clearers of forest, and planners of irrigation, all of whom increased the land's capacity to yield food; and yet the additional white people who were thereby fed were probably fewer than the millions who centuries previously had been fed because of simple innovations made by unknown aboriginals. It was the essence of aboriginal culture to give all credit to remote ancestors, and so it would not have honoured contemporaries who added to the food resources. Probably no lasting honour was given to the inventor or a more efficient fish trap, the finder of a new method of sharpening stone axes, or an inventive stalker of emus or wombats.

There is no reason for believing that the first migrants in each Australian region came with all their botanical and zoological knowledge, their hunting and fishing skills and weapons so perfected and poised that they could quickly use the new foods with full efficiency. Why should a slow chain

118

of migrations which began on tropical islands and eventually reached the parched bushland near the Great Australian Bight be seen as a series of smooth transitions? If many migrants reached the coast of the Southern Ocean after their ancestors had spent a dozen generations on the grasslands of the interior, their grasslands' background was hardly an apprenticeship for winning most of their food from the sea. Nor would they have been consoled by a reminder, as they made heavy work of catching a few bream from a canoe designed for the mirror-flat waters of inland lagoons, that two thousand years ago their ancestors had been fishers of renown on the Timor Sea.

Aboriginals were not stubbornly opposed to the very idea of change. By the standards of the twentieth century, when novelty is an obsession, aboriginals resisted change but they appear to have been sympathetic to those innovations which seemed useful and which could be accommodated within their traditional way of living. In the nineteenth century they eagerly adopted iron and copper when they became available for cutting and hammering instruments. In the Cape York Peninsula in 1879 and 1880 the explorer Robert Logan Jack saw how the tribal aboriginals had scavenged metals from shipwrecks or from the debris discarded by the diggers who had made a lightning visit to the most northerly gold rush in Australia. He saw aboriginal women carrying old jam tins and saw men using implements and weapons which they had shaped from bits of telegraph wire, the iron bolts of a ship or the discarded iron tyres of a digger's cart. One night, dozing in his tent, Robert Jack was given further evidence when he was speared in the neck by a long spear, 'barbed with seven inches of quarter-inch iron rod beautifully pointed at both ends.' The iron rod may have been made in Birmingham but the sharp points were the work of stone-age men who were skilled in adapting themselves— without any lessons and without an instruction manual—to the age of iron. These events do not support the idea that

119

aboriginals were innately opposed to changes which might ease their life or increase their skill in gathering foods.

Over thousands of years the food resources of aboriginals were probably altered by new techniques and by the unintended effects of their own activities. Some fruits and vegetables must have been spread inadvertently through the wanderings of aboriginals who carried seeds and roots in baskets or bowls. Some edible animals, it would appear, were extinguished partly through the hunting activities of aboriginals; other animals were probably multiplied through the effects of aboriginals on predators or the natural vegetation. Undoubtedly the fire carried by the aboriginals increased the potential food supply by diminishing the area of forest and expanding the grasslands in many parts of the continent; forest is rarely a generous producer of food for man. The taboo which aboriginals placed on the eating of certain edible foods must have had varying effects on food resources, sometimes increasing them by protecting them from excessive hunting and sometimes reducing them. Of course, a taboo on a plentiful item of food, for instance the boned fish in Tasmanian beaches and estuaries, decreased the available food resources. An animal or plant is not a food resource if it is shunned.

VII

We will probably remain ignorant of many of the important phases in the history of population in Australia. In some phases knowledge may increase considerably as a result of archaeological work or the reinterpreting of earlier information. But at present the circumstantial evidence throws heavy doubt upon the theories that the population in 1788 was necessarily at its prehistoric peak, or that food resources probably had long been static. Likewise, the evidence makes one doubt the contemporary theories that nomadic societies were relatively free from deadly warfare and deadly epidemics—both of which were strong curbs on population in settled societies.

It is tempting to praise or condemn the practices and restraints used by aboriginals. The nomadic life of aboriginals, however, was so different that to apply there the system of values culled from a society of settlements would be irrelevant. Their values and our values—whether on abortion, infanticide, the treatment of the old, killing in battle, the eating of human flesh—are not eternal and therefore not to be indiscriminately imposed but are in part ephemeral because they arise from the necessities and background of different societies.

PART THREE

Reign of the Wanderers

CHAPTER EIGHT

The Hunters

Aboriginals travelled lightly, carrying few possessions, but our luggage is full of objects. Accordingly we tend to visualize the daily life of aboriginals mainly through the familiar objects which they manufactured. As curators of museums naturally prefer to display objects, and as a weapon is more likely to catch the imagination of spectators, weapons often typify our view of aboriginal society. Moreover they match our idea of a 'savage society'.

The most curious and symbolic of their weapons, in our eyes, is the boomerang, and we easily imagine them killing kangaroos and low-flying birds with boomerangs, carrying boomerangs wherever they wandered, and relying for their daily catch of food more on boomerangs than we rely on any single machine or instrument. But this picture of the meat-eating, boomerang-throwing aboriginals is more a mirror of our own mind than of their societies.

II

Boomerangs aroused wonder in the first Europeans who saw them somersaulting through space. One summer Sunday morning in 1804 at Farm Cove, in Sydney Harbour, some Britons witnessed a fight between aboriginals and recorded in print the flight of a boomerang. According to the *Sydney Gazette* they 'were justly astonished at the dexterity and incredible force with which a bent, edged waddy resembling

125

slightly a turkish scymetar was thrown by *Bungary*, a native distinguished by his remarkable courtesy.' They marvelled at the velocity with which the weapon twirled in the air, the way in which it bruised the right arm of one of Bungary's enemies and then, on the rebound, hurtled perhaps another seventy yards. The aeronautics of a weapon which could travel far before returning obediently to the thrower were surprising to those who thought that the aboriginals were unskilled in manufacturing. And it seemed reasonable to expect that such a remarkable weapon would be vital during those hunts on which aboriginals seemed to depend for their food.

Boomerangs were often seen in hunts as well as fights in the first years of contact. A flock of cockatoos might be roosting high in the gum trees on the banks of a billabong. An aboriginal carrying a boomerang would be seen creeping towards them. Almost at the instant when the flock took fright and flew above the water he jumped forward and, raising the boomerang over his shoulder, hurled it towards the still water. When it seemed about to strike the water it suddenly changed course and spun upwards. 'In vain', wrote the explorer Sir George Grey in reminiscences of Western Australia, 'the terrified cockatoos strive to avoid it; it sweeps wildly and uncertainly through the air, and so eccentric are its motions, that it requires but a slight stretch of the imagination to fancy it endowed with life.' It also takes no imagination to see one or two cockatoos falling into the water.

Boomerangs, however, were not indispensible in Australia. They were not used in hunting or warfare in Arnhem Land at the time of European contact, though they were used to clap the rhythm during ceremonies. They were known but not used in the Gibson Desert, where instead the hunters threw a simpler, curved stick which did not return to the thrower. Boomerangs were not thrown by at least one coastal

126

people, the Wonunda Meening tribe near the Great Australian Bight. They were not used, or used so sparingly as to be inconspicuous, in some northern regions of South Australia. And they were unknown in Tasmania when the first Europeans arrived. Admittedly it is possible that in some parts of Australia the boomerang had once been used in hunting but had been discarded in the far past. Whether it was an Australian invention or an import is not known.

In Australia the name 'boomerang' was given by Englishmen to any throwing stick which was shaped like a scimitar. The same name was given to the heavier, longer, flatter stick which did not return to the thrower. Though boomerangs and a variety of straight short throwing-sticks were widely used, it is doubtful whether they were the main hunting weapon of any nomadic group. If we could compile statistics of all food eaten in the continent on the eve of the white invasion, it is improbable that as much as one per cent of food was gathered by the boomerangs and allied throwing sticks. It is likely that the pointed digging-stick carried by women provided more food in a day than boomerangs provided in an average month.

Of the hunting weapons used on land the spear seems to have been the most important at the time of the white invasion. Heavy spears—used for warfare and occasionally for killing emus—could be as long as nine feet and perhaps four or five pounds in weight. Some had wooden points and others a stone spearhead, serrated at the edges. Usually the spears which were carried on hunting forays were lighter, with a spearhead into which were adjusted wooden barbs. The shape and sharpness of the barbs varied greatly. While some spears held no barbs, others had a row of perhaps twelve or twenty barbs like the cutting edge of a carpenter's saw.

The effectiveness of a spear was aided by the use of a spear-thrower or woomera. That wooden instrument was usually about twenty-five to thirty inches long, about four inches wide, about one pound in weight and slightly scooped in shape. It was an ingenious launching pad, held high in the throwing hand. Spear and woomera were held aloft by an arrangement of fingers which was slightly like a first attempt to use chopsticks. The rear end of the spear rested on a small hook or peg at the front of the woomera, and the hunter clutched the woomera which in turn largely supported, with the aid of his fingers, the spear itself. At the instant when the hunter hurled the spear he continued to clasp the woomera, for the woomera in effect guided the spear into flight. The woomera was virtually an elongation of the hunter's arm, giving the spear more thrust and range at the expense of a slight loss in accuracy.

The woomera or spearthrower was not used everywhere. It was unknown in Tasmania when the first whites landed: it was not used by Queensland tribes on the Nogoa River, in the vicinity of what is now the town of Emerald; and it was apparently not used on the Yorke Peninsula of South Australia or along some reaches of the River Darling and its tributaries, or in the Clarence and Richmond valleys of northern New South Wales. Why an instrument should generally have been so effective and yet be ignored in many districts is mysterious. The mystery is probably more tantalizing than the question of where the woomera originated. It was not uniquely Australian, for it had been employed in many versions by peoples as far apart as stone-age Europeans and recent Eskimos.

Of aboriginals' accuracy with the spear the evidence is variable. Spear-throwing as a skill varied from native to native, and region to region. In the Gibson Desert some spearsmen using the woomera could spear a standing kangaroo from forty yards, but at a distance of one hundred yards the kangaroo was very unlucky if he were hit. In contrast those aboriginals from western Victoria who toured England as cricketers in 1868 sometimes gave uncanny demonstrations of spear-throwing.* Aided perhaps by their physique—they were stronger than hunters of the desert—they hurled a spear eighty or ninety yards with such accuracy that their kinsmen on the playing field of The Oval in London had to leap aside to avoid being felled. At Rochdale in Lancashire their accuracy with a woomera even at one hundred yards was impressive.

Bows and arrows were used in New Guinea but if they ever crossed Torres Strait into northern Queensland they apparently did not extend far south. As hunting weapons the arrows generally were superior to spears. They were more accurate and more portable: assets to wandering hunters. At the same time the velocity of the arrow depended partly on how far the bow could be drawn; and a bow was more likely to be stretched to its limit by a shortish hunter with well-developed chest, shoulders, and arm-muscles. Indeed the bow was more prevalent amongst races of short people, according to an anthropologist and anatomist, Alice M. Brues. Her valuable observation may be one clue to the refusal of aboriginals to adopt the bow and arrow. They tended to be long-armed and rangy rather than stocky and deep-chested, and so would have gained less by adopting the bow and arrow. Aboriginals had a more appropriate physique for throwing spears. The use of the woomera increased this advantage.

In addition to spears, woomeras, and a variety of boomerangs and throwing sticks, hunters used other weapons. Heavy waddies and clubs often killed bandicoots, goannas and wallabies. The axe, often with a sharply-ground edge and a stumpy wooden handle attached with resin, was valuable in extracting possums from hiding places and in raiding beehives. Once an animal was killed, a variety of stone or

---

* They could also throw a cricket ball long distances. Dick-a-Dick, proudly wearing his bright yellow cap, reputedly threw a ball 114 yards, only six yards less than the best throw of the famous bowler, 'Demon' Spofforth, a decade later.

bone blades and knives and scrapers removed the skin or cut the meat.

With this simple armoury the aboriginals were capable of killing virtually every walking creature from emu to rat, virtually every reptile from snake to goanna, and hundreds of species of birds.

III

The weapons were perhaps weak but the hunters' instinctive and intellectual equipment was powerful. As our civilization tends to enthrone technology, we place too much emphasis on the instruments and weapons and not enough on the techniques and tricks with which the game was tracked and snared. For the act of killing—an act which glamourizes the physical weapons—is only the last stage of the chase.

Many aboriginal hunters had sharp hearing and an ability to reproduce sounds which they had heard. European explorers and settlers in Australia often observed this gift for mimicry without comprehending its advantages in the hunt. Thus a white man who was speared in the calf of the leg by Tasmanian aboriginals called out again and again, 'Oh, my leg', and his cries were faithfully mimicked by the aboriginals who began to chant 'Omyleg'. Their mimicry was sometimes macabre, sometimes charming. When Major Thomas Mitchell in the spring of 1836 was leading his exploring party homewards across central Victoria, he thought he heard in camp one morning the voice of a woman, indeed a Scotswoman. As no white woman probably was to be found within fifty or even one hundred miles of his camp Mitchell was astonished, and yet the accent and lilt were unmistakable. A Scot himself, he was not likely to mistake the accent. To his surprise he learned that the speaker was an aboriginal, Tommy Came-last. Tommy was casually mimicking a Scottish woman whom he had heard at Portland Bay, on the distant coast.

Mimicry could be an accurate bullet in the chase for food. A skilful click of the tongue decoyed crabs from the holes in the mud of the mangrove swamp; a whistling sound could entice a hermit crab from its shell; a snake-like hiss could drive a bandicoot from a hollow log; and an imitation of the call of a hawk often halted a fleeing goanna so that he stiffened and stood still, becoming an easy target for a huntsman. When the season arrived for geese to flock to waterholes on the plains in northern Australia, hunters climbed paperbark trees and in the high branches they parroted the cry 'Honk, honk-honk'; and geese would settle in the branches, honk-honking in reply until suddenly they were attacked with missiles and poles. 'Down the crippled geese would fall, crying for their mates,' we are told, 'and we children would delight in imitating the goose call as the slaughter went on.' It would not be surprising if the tricks of these ventriloquists were sometimes more a ritual of the hunt than a noose designed for animals and birds, but their noose was often intended and deadly.

Aboriginals played tricks on the hearing of the hunted creatures; they also played tricks on animals' and birds' sense of smell, their sight, their rigid habits, and their curiosity. An emu could run faster than a hunter but an emu was also inquisitive and could be diverted by a strange object or antic. A kangaroo grazing on a windy day was unlikely to catch the scent of a hunter who smeared his body with earth and quietly approached into the headwind. Likewise an aboriginal setting out to spear fish in a creek usually waded upstream so that the water made muddy by his movements did not disturb the fish or cloud the patch of water which he was approaching. If two or more men were hunting together they preserved silence and yet kept in touch by means of an elaborate language of hand signals and gestures.

W. E. Roth, a surgeon in north-western Queensland in the mid 1890s, was one of the code-breakers who penetrated this sign language. He first noticed it when travelling on horseback on the Upper Georgina. The aboriginal with whom he was riding suddenly asked him to halt, adding that a friend about 150 yards ahead had just signalled that he had seen an emu hen and her young and was giving chase. As Roth had seen no sign, heard no voice, and seen no emu he was flabbergasted and told the aboriginal he was a liar. A little later he was shown the slaughtered emu and some of her young. So he was led, he recalled, 'step by step to making a study of what I subsequently discovered to be an actual well-defined sign-language, extending throughout the entire North-West-Central districts of Queensland.'

Aboriginals were remarkably observant of the habits of animals. Many 'discoveries' announced by European natural-scientists were mainly their gathering of knowledge which had long been known to aboriginals. For decades one of the open questions in zoology was whether the most primitive mammals—the platypus and echidna—laid eggs. Many aboriginals insisted that these mammals did lay eggs, but as late as 1868 the English anatomist Sir Richard Owen thought otherwise; to him the evidence suggested that the baby platypus was 'brought forth alive'. Sixteen years later, on the Burnett River in north Queensland, the dissection of a female platypus revealed an egg, fertilized and about to be laid, thus confirming what aboriginals had long believed. As observers of nature the aboriginals, however, were not infallible; moreover some of their knowledge was colourfully concealed, like an easter egg, in the wrappings of their own mythology.

They are said to have sharper eyesight than Europeans: it is almost a stereotype drawing of an aboriginal to depict him standing on a ledge of rock and—with his eyes set deeply beneath the jutting eyebrows—gazing towards the horizon. The eyesight of Western Australian aboriginals was surveyed in the 1950s by Dr Ida Mann, and she concluded that aboriginals were less likely to be colour-blind or short-sighted than Europeans. She found, however, no evidence of sharper vision. Instead their vision had been trained by the demands of survival. Looking for the tracks of humans and animals, the portents of the flights of birds, or signs of weather and water, their motivation was probably more important than their sight.

IV

For many tribes the sea was the main source of food. For the aboriginals as a whole, the sea might have been more important than for the Europeans who, in 1800, believed themselves to be masters of the sea. While European fishermen had the advantage of large vessels, strong trawling lines, iron hooks and tough nets, and their ships could venture with some safety into deep seas, they were not necessarily more successful than aboriginals in living off the food of the sea.

It may well be that on most days of 1788 the aboriginals ate a greater number of fresh fish than the thirteen million Australians eat today. Whereas fresh fish was a common food for most aboriginals who lived on the coast or along inland rivers, it is not a common food for white Australians who live in coastal cities today. When it is common it is not very fresh. Only in a few weeks of summer, when tens of thousands of people fish for pleasure, are as many fresh fish now likely to be eaten as in ancient Australia.

On the eve of the European coming the fishing techniques around Australia probably were as diverse as in Europe itself. Even in the same region of Australia the ways of fishing varied. In some bays of the south-east the line and hook were used but in other bays they were unknown or at least unrecorded. Fish were caught with hook and line near the present site of Sydney but not near Melbourne. The lines were invariably made from a fibre, and a hook of horse-shoe shape was sometimes cut from a piece of sea shell. Spears were probably used more often than hook and line in the catching of fish. In scattered strips of coast stretching from the sandy beaches of New South Wales to the muddy estuaries of northern Australia, wooden spears were tipped with bone prongs for the spearing of fish. The four-pronged spear was common near Sydney, but some of the wooden spears in coastal Arnhem Land were pointed with about fifty spikes of the sting-ray so that they resembled more a pin cushion than a spear.

The phrase 'stone age' is often used in describing the techniques of aboriginals, but in the craft of fishing and in many of the techniques of food-gathering the phrase is misleading. Wood, bone and the fibres of plants were the essence of their fishing methods. Bone was vital for the barbs and points of fishing spears, and in the last few centuries of aboriginal life the practice was increasingly to use bone rather than stone for a variety of implements. An excavation near the shore at Batemans Bay (N.S.W.) revealed that within the last five centuries even the bones of birds were being shaped into tips and barbs for the wooden spears. An excavation further down the coast, in aboriginal rock shelters at Glen Aire near Cape Otway (V.), disclosed a slightly fresher layer of ash and debris containing at least 66 artifacts of bone—mostly of marsupial bones—and only four trimmed implements of stone. The discoverer, John Mulvaney, was inclined to conclude from the evidence of different Australian regions that craftsmanship in stone was waning and the making of implements from bone and other organic materials was increasing on the eve of the European coming.

Aboriginals fishing on the Pacific coast supplemented their bone-pointed spears with large nets made skilfully from fibre. Even in heavy surf the aboriginals could net fish successfully, as the Scottish naturalist MacGillivray found to his surprise. Camping with aboriginals one cold night in 1849 on Moreton Island, not far from Brisbane, he watched the men gorging themselves with hot roasted mullet which they had netted in the surf on the previous day. In the first light of morning the aboriginals showed him how simply they could catch fish. The breakers were rolling in, and in some curling waves a shoal of mullet was held aloft for all ashore to see. As the waves carried the fish towards the beach the porpoises pursued them, even herding them, and aboriginal men almost encircled the shoal with their scoop nets while boys were quick to spear mullet that darted clear of the circle of nets. Many of the mullet trapped in the nets were each a meal.

Far around the coast, on the islands at the western edge of the Gulf of Carpentaria, canoeists hunted turtles and used a woomera to launch their spears or harpoons. As the turtles arrived with the south-east monsoon, swimming to sandy beaches to lay their eggs, their arrival was easily predicted; and at the expected time the canoeists patiently rode the choppy sea, waiting for turtles to swim into sight. When a turtle swam within shooting range they set a rope-tailed spear in the woomera, took aim, and hurled. As the spear trailed a long rope a turtle which was struck could not easily swim out of danger, for the canoeist could clutch the rope and allow his canoe to be pulled along by the swimming turtle. When the heavy turtle became exhausted, the hunter tugged his canoe closer to the turtle until he could grasp it by a flipper and club it to death.

On the opposite side of the continent some of the most prized catches were seals or whales which had been washed ashore. There survives an account of a small seal stranded on a sandbank in King George's Sound (W.A.) by the retreating tide on Christmas Day 1821. As the seal tried to waddle to the safety of deep water, an aboriginal cautiously approached and, halting ten or twelve yards away, fitted his spear in his woomera and neatly speared the neck of the seal. Another aboriginal ran forward, also speared the seal, and then hammered it on the head. Everyone in the vicinity hurried over to share in the plunder. They dragged the seal ashore, splashed it with water to clean away the sand, and carried it to a fire on the edge of the grass. Before the seal was even

135

singed, before it was even dead, strips of flesh were hacked from the warm body and eaten raw. Soon the seal oil was mixed with a reddish earth to form a paint with which the feasters smeared themselves from head to toe. Nothing so churned the stomachs of European settlers as the sight of aboriginals emerging from a dead whale, their bodies covered with blubber, and a strip of uncooked whalemeat in their hands.

There must have been few stretches of Australian coast on which molluscs or shellfish were not eaten. On many sandy beaches of southern Australia the chance erosion of the sand dunes at the rim of a beach often reveals the thin seams of charcoal enclosing mussel shells or limpet shells—remains of fires where aboriginals had camped. Shellfish were eaten in larger quantities in Tasmania than in most other parts of the south seas; and at one period most Tasmanian groups along the coast shunned the eating of scale fish. The ear-shell or *haliotis* was one of the most favoured molluscs in Tasmania and was also collected along rocky fringes of the Victorian shallows. Tasmanian women dived for ear-shell at low tide, suspending from their left shoulders neat baskets which they had plaited from grass. As the creature inside the ear-shell clung to the rock with its sucker-like feet, a wooden chisel was usually needed to prise away the shell. A swimmer's ability to stay beneath the cold water for long periods, and the frequency with which she harvested a full basket in her first dive, surprised many Europeans; for around the year 1800 few European men, and even fewer women, were capable of swimming. The flesh inside the ear-shell was large and rather tough, and was usually roasted or heated on the embers or ashes. Known as mutton-fish a century ago, at a time when mutton was the food of everyman, it is now known as abalone and is gathered professionally by skindivers and sold at high prices to gourmets.

On the coast of South Australia many aboriginals probably ate a wider variety of shellfish than the united menus of all the restaurants and fish-shops of Adelaide display today. The debris in the aboriginal sites suggest that at least twenty-nine different marine shellfish were eaten. Even in the same bay perhaps as many as twenty of those varieties could be prised from rocks or scrabbled from the sand. In South Australia four species of mutton-fish were eaten: the smooth-shelled, round-backed, corded, and common mutton-fish. From rocks or beaches were gathered dog whelks and sand snails, tulip shells and helmet shells, ridged limpets and large shield limpets, the common warrener or periwinkle, and that kind of nerita which, with its white apex on a black shell, is called a black crow. Scattered points from the sandy beaches of the Coorong to the bays of the Great Australian Bight yielded mussels, scallops, the multi-valve chitons, the long narrow razor shell, and the Port Lincoln oyster. And there were platoons of cockles:

White Cockle,	Goolwa Cockle,
Wheel Cockle,	Sand Cockle,
Southern Cockle,	Mud Cockle,
Common Heart Cockle,	Red Stained Cockle.

Amidst the abundance of molluscs the aboriginals in different areas had their own preferences which were influenced presumably by taste, tradition, and taboos as well as ease or scarcity of supply. Recent excavations of camp sites on the narrow isthmus leading to Wilson's Promontory (V.) reveal that 3,000 to 6,000 years ago the most favoured shellfish were those harvested at low tide on the rock platforms and carried to the shrublands where the aboriginals camped. But 1,200 years ago changes of diet were clearly visible. The traditional shellfish of the rock ledges were eaten less frequently, most shellfish were collected from the sand and for reasons unknown, the menu of shellfish was not so varied.

The millions of meals of shellfish had one strange effect on the landscape. Whereas our highest monuments to economic activity are probably skyscrapers, television masts and chim-

ney stacks, the highest monuments built during the aboriginal epoch were heaps of empty shells. Large mounds of shells
littered points of the Victorian coast. In the north-west of
Australia, at Hanover Bay, one hill of broken shells was ten
feet high and covered nearly half an acre. At Port Essington
in northern Australia a shell heap resembling a witch's hat
was about five times the height of the tallest European sailor
who saw it. At Weipa, on Cape York Peninsula, heaps of
empty shells rose about thirty feet above the mangrove
swamps, and aboriginals' huts and fireplaces stood on the
summits. Radio-carbon tests of one of the smaller mounds at
Weipa revealed that the bottom layers were about 800 years
old; thus, when the second European crusade to Jerusalem
was about to begin, the cockle-eaters of Weipa were tossing
aside those empty shells. That was in the twelfth century
A.D., but a surviving mound at Milingimbi, on the other
side of the Gulf of Carpentaria, was rising shell by shell as
long ago as the seventh century. Some of these shell heaps
represented the remains of tens of thousands of meals.

Why the mounds should have been built to such heights
is a mystery. What was the advantage in carrying the marine
molluscs up the steep slopes of a shell mound simply in
order to eat the fish and discard the shell? One anthropologist suggested that the aboriginals did not build the high
conical heaps: they did not fit in with the known behaviour
of the race. Excavations, however, in some of the shell heaps
at Weipa disclosed the kind of ground-bone points which
even recently had been used by aboriginals as barbs and as
spear-tips. Why then did they build the mounds? When a
naval explorer saw shell mounds in 1818, he thought they
might be 'a burying-place of the Indians', as the aboriginals
were quaintly called. So far, however, no human bones have
been found at the foot of the mounds. Alternatively the
mounds could have been designed as a lookout on the flat
ground, but surely it was quicker to climb a tree? Again the
mounds could have represented a retreat from the floods on

138

the flat shores, but why build such mounds when higher ground lay not far away? An archaeologist, R. V. S. Wright, recently examined some of these hypotheses and decided that none fitted the evidence. Even the suggestion that the mounds were towers, to which inhabitants in the wet season could retreat from sandflies and mosquitoes, did not make sense. Wright himself spent some time at the top of the shell heaps of Weipa and was pestered by biting insects. He could only conclude that an unknown reason made the aboriginals build high mounds rather than litter the mud-flats with broken shells.

V

In the interior many peoples who had never seen the sea, and presumably did not even know that there was a sea, practised their distinctive skills as fishermen. In reaches of the Darling River on winter days men could be seen in flimsy canoes, a tiny fire burning slowly on a clay hearth on the bark bottom, warming themselves while they awaited the chance to spear a passing fish. Or two groups of men with short spears in hand could be seen swimming and diving towards one another, spearing the fish or driving them into the shallows where they were caught between gaps in the reeds. When the swimmers began to shiver they scrambled from the water and warmed themselves in the centre of a circle of small fires stoked by women. In winter, women were not spared the cold river, and they waded in the shallows, the mud oozing through their feet as they scrabbled with their toes for crawfish or mussels. 'These savages', wrote an explorer in the 1830s, 'have a power of manipulating with their toes, so as to do many things surprising to men who wear shoes.'

Holding the ends of the long nets people would walk slowly through the lagoons in the Riverina, and sometimes they hauled 300 or 400 pounds of fish in the one sagging net.

To trap the small crawfish or yabbies, nets with a mesh of a quarter of an inch were also carried through the water: from a variety of flax-like fibres, nets of many meshes were woven with wooden needles near hundreds of billabongs, swamps and river-reaches from the Georgina to the mouth of the Murray. One of the most cumbersome of all the aboriginal possessions was the big fishing or fowling net. The heaviest nets were probably to be seen in those favoured regions where permanent freshwater and plentiful food sometimes enabled groups to camp in the one place for several months on end.

The word 'trapper' usually denotes someone who sets traps to catch wild animals, but amongst aboriginals the art of trapping was practised more by fishermen. An ideal spot for a fish trap was in those narrow channels where swamp waters, at the end of a flood, flowed back to the main river. There, in openings only seven or eight feet wide, men built their snares and weirs. Along the River Darling many traps consisted of tall wooden stakes, planted close together, so that the fatter fish were held in the fast-drying swamp, an easy target for the canoeists' spears. When the swamp was almost empty, fish lay in thousands near the fish trap—more fish than any tribe could eat. Near The Grampians, fish traps were seen along the swampy fringes of the Wimmera River when the first Europeans arrived with their sheep. Strange traps woven from rushes, they were shaped like a wind sock on an airfield, and the fish which swam with the ebbing waters into the socks did not easily escape. More than a thousand miles to the north, on the dry plains of the Boulia region, the fish traps on the rivers were often permanent weirs of stone which funnelled the escaping water onto platforms covered with grass and boughs. When the water fell through the platform the fish were stranded on the grass and boughs.

Of all the fish traps, one of the most ingenious was set in the valley of the Glyde River, a tropical tidal stream which drained a wide summer swamp in Arnhem Land. This trap was used by only two small groups of people and was virtually recognized by neighbours as their distinctive patent. At the end of the wet season the peculiar trap was laboriously erected: the level of the stream was raised by a mud-plastered weir; one or two large funnels or snouts were made of eucalypt bark and inserted in the top of the weir; and the water flowing downstream was funnelled through the bark snouts. From the spout the water poured on to a platform of grass and sticks where any fish were stranded. They could not jump back into the bark snout above them. Unless they were tiny and inedible they could not fall through the grating of grass and sticks of the platform into the stream below. They could not escape sideways because a circular wall of bark trapped them. Known as the *gorl* the trap caught many barramundi, cat-fish, and archer-fish which were moving to the tidal estuary as the inland swamp receded. As the fish migrated during the brief season when long grass concealed wallabies and bandicoots, and plagues of mosquitoes made hunting insufferable, the ordeal of searching for game could be largely avoided if the fish traps were effective.

Except in a few corners of northern Australia hardly a sign remains of the fish traps which stood in all their variety. The knowledge of how to make them had been passed many times from generation to generation, but now that knowledge was handed on no more. While white men recorded how many traps and nets were built, in most areas they recorded only a few of those fishing skills, hints, and observations which were at least as important as the fishermen's hardware. Nothing is really known about the ways in which the aboriginals fished in rocky sounds near the Timor Sea at the time of Christ nor how they caught the Murray cod 10,000 years ago. We can see the bones of a fat golden perch which, perhaps 30,000 years ago, swam in the fresh waters of Lake Mungo—and was caught, cooked, and eaten—but how that fish was caught remains a guess. The sheer variety of fishing techniques within Australia around the year 1800 A.D. indicates that local conditions must have had a vital part in the evolution of fishing techniques, but when and how that shaping took place will mostly remain mysterious.

VI

In most regions the aboriginals fished or travelled in frail vessels. These flimsy craft, however, had at least one strong advantage; they were quickly built and were thus appropriate for nomads who carried few possessions.

The simplest vessel was a floating log which men pushed slowly ahead as they dog-paddled. It was often the safest way of crossing flooded rivers or narrow straits. From the coast of central Queensland aboriginals often crossed the six miles of sheltered water to Great Keppel Island by alternatively pushing along and resting on a long pandanus log. In many inlets of the Indian, Pacific and Southern Oceans a row of wooden stakes was lashed together with vines or fastened with pegs to form catamarans for fishing or travelling. Captain King, sailing into Hanover Bay in north-western Australia in 1821, saw the tiny catamarans afloat: 'five mangrove stems lashed together' to form a buoyant mat on which two fishermen could sit with knees drawn. As many as nine parallel poles were used to construct catamarans on that coast. A sizeable craft measured ten feet by four and was propelled by a double-bladed paddle.

The bark canoes of the inland rivers and sheltered bays of south-eastern Australia seemed as hazardous as the catamarans. Along the quiet swamps and cliff-protected reaches of the River Murray, bark canoes appeared so precarious, so likely to be swamped by five-inch waves or so likely to capsize when boarded, that they called for a man with the bodily poise of a tight-rope walker. Indeed, the canoeist

142

usually stood rather than sat as he poled his craft through the water.

Even in those parts of the south-east where a century has passed since the last bark canoe was launched, the scars of the ancient boat-making industry can still be seen on gnarled living trees. In Melbourne suburbs a few canoe trees stand, the trunk still revealing the long rounded tongue of bark which had been neatly cut away by the boat-builder. An aboriginal building a canoe tried to select a straight tree close to the water's edge. Sometimes he cut the bark high up the trunk—perhaps thirty feet from the ground—if the shape or texture of the lower part of the trunk was unsuitable. Using a stone axe or a wooden chisel he cut around the edge of a long strip of thick bark, and by levering and chiselling he removed the bark in one oval piece. With the aid of fire and moisture he turned and twisted the piece of bark into the shape of a low sided craft. By applying heat and a caulking of clay the ends of the bark could be joined together. In many bay canoes along the New South Wales coast the bark ends were tied together, and further north they were skilfully sewn.

Robert Edwards, in his *Aboriginal Bark Canoes of the Murray Valley,* suggests that an aboriginal, with luck and energy, could make a small bark canoe in half an hour but the canoe was likely to be more durable if the bark could be seasoned for a fortnight before it was carried down to the shallows. A canoeist who occasionally greased the bark of the canoe and carefully plugged any crevices with clay might use his canoe on and off for two years before the bark finally became waterlogged.

On some lakes and lagoons the mutilated trunks of fat river-gums must have resembled colonnades of high arched doorways along the water's edge. The part of the trunk from which the bark had been peeled did not heal itself even if the tree continued to live for another 100 years. Moreover the short life of each canoe and the large number of canoes afloat in any year contributed to the mutilation of the massive tree trunks. Major Mitchell, exploring the Murray near Lake Boga in the winter of 1836, counted on one small lake a total of twenty-four canoes fleeing in surprise to the safety of a reedy island. To keep afloat that small bark fleet would, in the space of one decade, call for the scarring of perhaps 200 big river gums. In the entire Murray-Darling Basin, with its thousands of miles of river, several thousand canoes might have been built each year for fishing and the hunting of birds and eggs; and the tally of canoes was notched by the oval doorways on the trunks of the river-gums.

Before the Europeans arrived, two strips of Australian coastline used relatively sophisticated vessels. Parts of Arnhem Land had the strong dug-out canoes known as *lippa-lippa*, which were recently introduced by Indonesian fishermen who sailed south annually from the Dutch Celebes to fish for trepang. On the opposite side of the Gulf of Carpentaria the aboriginals often fished from dug-out canoes equipped with outriggers. These craft must have been copied from the Torres Strait Islands and Papua, and they could have been made and sailed in north Queensland as long ago as 1,000 years, perhaps much longer. The outrigger canoes were made by hollowing out the tree-trunks of tropical softwoods, and were launched as far south as Cape Grafton, near the present Cairns, where they supplemented rather than replaced the popular sewn-bark canoes*.

VII

In many parts of the continent the aboriginals were clever pursuers of birds, snaring or netting or spearing them. They were egg-collectors on a large scale. In the top third of the Northern Territory they ate hundreds of thousands of eggs

* The deficiency of suitable hardwoods in the temperate south was one important reason why the dug-out canoe was confined to parts of tropical Australia.

each year and the poultry they killed annually in swamps and lagoons—if strung and stretched on a long line—would have extended for miles.

Close to the coast of Arnhem Land is a swampy basin scattered with melaleuca trees and surrounded by hills. In the long dry season the Glyde River flows through the basin, but when the north-west monsoon brings torrents of rain the river overflows and the basin becomes a breeding swamp for magpie geese. Known as the Arafura Swamp it covers an area almost as large as suburban Melbourne. Like a city it can swallow strangers. It was also like a city in the way it once supported a specialization of economic activity not to be expected in a hunting society.

Towards the end of the wet season, when the Arafura Swamp was in flood, the magpie geese flocked in to build nests in clumps of tall grass. In February or March, in lagoons and still waterways at scattered points around the tropical coast, these large birds with their black and white feathers and elegant black necks announced their coming by loud resonant honks. On the hills overlooking the Arafura Swamp the aboriginals did not need to hear the honking to know that the goose-hunting season was about to begin. As soon as the swamp was high, a spy had set out in a canoe to see whether the magpie geese were laying.

Aboriginals whose territory touched the swamp arrived to build huts. In the eucalypt forest on higher ground above the swamp the aboriginals cut stringy-bark for the canoes, and with a single sheet of bark each man built his own canoe. The canoe was about ten feet long and distinctive in design, resembling no canoes of the rivers or estuary. The bow of the canoe was shaped like a shoe except that it sloped up rather than down towards the toe. The shoe-shaped bow and flattish bottom enabled the craft to slide more easily over the swamp grass or to pass over submerged logs. Hidden snags or stakes often penetrated the bark canoes, and rarely did they last more than about fifteen days on the water.

145

As the canoe was likely to ship water, a bailing spoon of bark was carried. The swamp-grass and submerged obstacles often impeded the craft and the hunter normally used a long pole—as long as the canoe—to propel the canoe through the swamp. When he stood like a gondolier in the stern, his own weight accentuated the upwards slope of the shoe-shaped bow. It is not known whether the unusual canoe had been invented in the Arafura Swamp or whether it was a version of a canoe which had been used in the swamps of a pre-Australian homeland; undoubtedly it was an efficient and ingenious way of navigating a short-lived swamp.

While the geese were laying eggs in hidden nests just above the water, the hunters carried their canoes to the edge of the swamp. Their families moved too, and near the swamp they built huts in the shape of a beehive. They were tightly cocooned to keep in smoke and keep out mosquitoes. Grass as well as bark clad the hut: when the aboriginals had crawled inside, the entrances were stuffed with grass; and from the small fire which burned inside during the night only a faint thread of smoke escaped through the hole in the roof. Women and children remained in the hut while the men entered the swamp in hunting expeditions that often lasted seven or eight days.

In Arnhem Land the magpie geese usually nested in clumps of the tough-stemmed spike-rush though some preferred the wild rice or knife grass. They liked to nest in a moderately-dense clump of vegetation and rarely made a nest where the water was either very shallow or deeper than three feet. A careful count of nests on Tommy Policeman Plain, near the Adelaide River, disclosed four nests to every three acres; and the scattering of concealed nests across the wide swamp aggravated the task of hunters. Moreover aboriginals were not the only hunters. The scattered nests of magpie geese were closely observed during an experiment conducted by two wildlife scientists, Frith and Davies, in an area where aboriginals had largely ceased to hunt the geese.

146

The nests which the scientists regularly surveyed held 304 eggs, and 220 of them were eaten by birds and other raiders. In one nest they saw a black snake trying to swallow an egg; most of the other missing eggs, they suspected, had been stolen by crows, small eagles, water rats, goannas and dingoes. Aboriginal hunters had difficulty in locating the hidden nests and in vying with other egg-hunters but they were also thwarted by floods. In some wet seasons the waters in the swamp would rise unexpectedly and the geese would fly away and the eggs would disappear beneath brown waters.

Donald Thomson was one of the first white men to enter the Arafura Swamp and take part in the hunt for the magpie geese. Ten canoes set out on the first expedition which he accompanied and twelve canoes in the second. The hunters soon scattered, vanishing from sight behind a screen of reeds or the light foliage of the melaleuca trees, but keeping in contact with the cry, *hee-ee hee-ee*, which travelled far across the silent swamp. On a successful day a hunter might spear six or seven geese, and he stood in a carnage of black and white feathers as he poled his canoe in the late afternoon towards the camping site. The common clutch of eggs was six to ten, and if two geese had laid in the same nest the aboriginals' catch might be slightly larger. The white eggs were usually piled in the shoe-shaped bow: shell against shell with nothing to prevent breakages if the canoe hit a hidden log.

The canoeists, out of sight of each other for much of the day, came together in the late afternoon. A secure camp was needed before sunset, when the mosquitoes in the middle of the swamp became unbearable. The ideal camping site was a clump of melaleuca trees, each with branches forking out at about the same height. Leaving the canoes floating at the foot of the tree the men climbed up the trunk and carefully cut straight boughs and wedged them into the forks of the trees to form the outline of a platform. Smaller boughs and strips of paper-bark completed the platform. No rope, no vine, was used in the building of this fragile stage high above the water: one careless step, one clumsy lunge of the body, and the hunter or half the platform fell into the swamp.

In the trees the evening meal was cooked. A pile of swamp grass, plastered with blue mud, was the hearth on the fragile platform; and on a small fire the plucked geese were roasted and the eggs were baked in the ashes. Night after night the geese and the eggs were the hunters' meal; the remainder was put aside, to be carried across to the shore at the end of the expedition. Often the party of hunters also built a stronger sleeping platform in another clump of trees across the water. Six or eight men might spend the night on that platform, waving their fans of goosewing-feathers across the face, huddled together in the smoke of a slow-burning fire, exhausted by their day's work but unable to sleep long because of the bites from mosquitoes and leeches. To a naked body the smoke of the fire did not offer sufficient protection. Moreover the dry wood was scarce in the swamp, and during the middle of a night—when the fire was low—one of the men had to shin down the trunk and push his canoe to another tree in search of a dead branch which, torn from the trunk, could be ferried back in the darkness. The aromatic smell of the fire, the greasy touch of the cooked goose, the whine of mosquitoes, the heaviness of the hot air, the faint noises of the swamp or the night—they were mainly forgotten by the time Donald Thomson sat down to record his two expeditions into the Arafura Swamp. But, rare amongst anthropologists, he retained the sense of wonder he felt at sunrise and evening in the presence of these tree-dwellers:

> It was an unforgettable experience to sit looking across the park-like expanse of the swamp and see from one's sleeping platform the sun rise or set over the water, or watch the long file of canoes converge at dusk on the prearranged camping place, bringing in their spoils. Unforgettable too the scene at night; the glimmer of camp fires high up in the trees, or reflected in the dark waters of the swamp below, and the talk

of the natives as they plucked and cooked the geese. They recounted and lived over again the day's adventures recalling critical moments in the stalking of the quarry they had killed or lost.

And in the morning they set out again, poling their canoes, alert for the honking of geese or the sights which to sharp eyes could indicate a nearby nest. When finally they returned to shore, their bark canoes laden with eggs and half-cooked geese, they craved for vegetables and other food as much as the women on shore craved for a taste of cooked goose.

After a spell on land and a long sleep in the smoke-filled hut they often built another canoe before venturing into the swamp again. The hunting season could last almost two months, and by then the last of the unhatched goslings were big in the eggs: those eggs tasted sweet and were valued more than the fresh-laid eggs. Thomson noted the cry of *cheep, cheep* that preceded the hatching, and on 2 May he jotted in his notebook that he had seen the first baby goose of the season.

He wrote the comment in his notebook, which is still unpublished, in 1937. Observing a hunt that might have been enacted in many swamps almost annually for several thousand years, he had happened to voyage in those strangely-elegant canoes in the year that the jet engine was invented in England. His aboriginals were sitting in their tree platforms, sweltering, in the year that the Russians established a scientific observatory on an ice floe near the North Pole. In 1937, when that refinement of clothing—the nylon stocking —was first manufactured on the other side of the world, the goose-hunters went naked day and night. These contrasts, however, were certainly not all in favour of European society, because 1937 was also the year of George Orwell's book *The Road to Wigan Pier,* and Orwell's average coal-miner in Lancashire could not afford to buy in a month as many pounds of cooked poultry and as many eggs as these primitive hunters were eating in a day.

The Arafura goose-hunters were unusual in the economic history of the aboriginals. Their ingenuity in coping with the mosquitoes and in navigating the swamps deserves admiration but similar examples of regional ingenuity are easy to find. What was unusual was their concentration on one kind of food-raising: it dominated their life for weeks, excluding all else and even compelling them to spend nights away from the women and family. The goose-hunters, in their single-minded pursuit of the one form of bread-winning or flesh-winning, resembled shepherds of other lands who guarded sheep all day or men who dug the soil all day. The sustained goose-hunt therefore had some resemblance to agriculture and herding—that later stage of economic activity. The goose-hunt in the Arafura Swamp also embraced the short-term hoarding of food: and hoarding was part of the great economic change that came with permanent agriculture and herding. To hoard seeds and livestock was the essence of that agricultural or neolithic revolution which so altered human history.

Within living memory the magpie geese laid their eggs and incubated their young in many parts of Australia. As late as 1900 they bred regularly in shallow swamps and lakes in the south east of Australia—at the Western Port Bay, the mouth of the Murray, the Riverina, and the western plains of Victoria where the last of their natural breeding grounds was near the one-pub town of Darlington—but the spread of farmlands to the edge of the swamps cut out their southern breeding grounds and confined them to the tropics where in very wet seasons they blackened the sky above the swamps. They fed on seeds and on blades of grass and with their hooked bills they rooted up bulbs, and when rice and other tropical crops were planted at Humpty Doo and the Ord they descended like a plague of locusts.

The magpie goose was only one of the many species of water birds which were dispersed widely across the continent and were hunted and snared, but perhaps we know very little

150

about the silent canoes which approached them and the weapons which killed them and the zoological knowledge with which aboriginals directed the hunt. Fortunately the methods of the fowlers on the Arafura Swamp have been skilfully recorded but we do not know whether their methods were applied in many tropical swamps from the Kimberleys to the Pacific or, being peculiar to Arnhem Land, were shaped by local needs or adapted from ways long ago imported from Indonesian islands.

VIII

Near the Murrumbidgee wide swamps were filled by the cold overflow during the Spring, and ducks and other waterbirds bred in reedbeds in their thousands. The aboriginals simply set out in their small canoes—consisting of one sheet of bark from a red gum—and made short journeys into the reed beds which, to European settlers, seemed as prolific as a poultry farm:

> 'during the breeding season of these birds they got eggs innumerable, the canoes arriving at the camps in the evenings then are literally laden down to the water's edge with no other cargo but eggs; they are heaped up at both ends until there is hardly room for the native to stand and paddle.'

The largest catches of waterbirds in the mid-Murray were probably made when the swamps had dried and the rivers were narrower and the birds were concentrated onto shrinking expanses of water. There the bird-catching was ingenious. A long net was carried to a narrow point of the favoured lagoon or river. Some of these nets were wide enough to cover a cricket pitch and many were almost five times as long as a pitch. A net 100 yards in length and two yards in width required considerable skills in fibre-making and weaving, and the fine duck-nets surprised the early European explorers in the inland. Major Thomas Mitchell, finding a long duck-net tied to two high trees and suspended

151

across a tributary of the Murray River, realized that here was an object which could be placed alongside the manufactures for which the north of England was famous:

> Among the few specimens of art manufactured by the primitive inhabitants of these wilds, none come so near our own as the net, which, even in quality, as well as in the mode of knotting, can scarcely be distinguished from those made in Europe.

While the duck net was suspended across a river or a narrow pond by four or more older men, the young men went along the watercourse towards the place where ducks were feeding. Some of the youths climbed trees overhanging the river and waited there, holding a round disc made of bark. Another of the aboriginals walked ahead until he reached the feeding ducks, crept slowly round to the far side of them, and suddenly disturbed them so that they flew away in fright, following as always the course of the river.

If the ducks began to fly higher and showed signs of leaving the river to reach a lagoon across country, an aboriginal hiding in the tree threw the bark disc into the air and gave a shrill whistle like a hawk. The ducks, presumably seeing the swooping disc or hearing the feigned call of the hawk, returned to the protection of the tree-lined river and continued their flight along its course. When the ducks were tempted again to leave the river, another aboriginal in a tree threw his disc and gave his hawk-call. Planned like a military operation in which the exact placing of the disc-throwers was crucial, the stratagem drove the ducks towards the suspended net and the hunters concealed nearby. And suddenly the ducks hit the net. Stunned or flapping in terror, they were soon captured. 'Hundreds and hundreds of ducks', wrote one of the early sheep-owners of the Riverina, 'are captured in this manner during the months when the waters are confined to the rivers' beds.'

In different parts of the continent, birds were trapped,

netted, snared, boomeranged, lassooed, strangled and clubbed after being detected or enticed or approached by many ingenious ways. A hunter would conceal his face and shoulders with leaves and twigs and wait by a log in the middle of a waterhole: when a corella or cockatoo alighted on the log the hunter would grab its legs, pull it under the water, and wring its neck. A pelican asleep on the bank of a river would be approached quietly by men who had greased themselves with ashes to disguise their smell and had covered their heads with shrubbery to camouflage their shape. Nets were placed on the water's edge where birds alighted to drink, and a sudden twist or tug of the net entangled them. Men would lie inside grass huts, on the roof of which they had laid bait for the birds, and if a duck or crow happened to alight to peck at the bait its legs were grabbed and its neck wrung.

The annual coming of swarms of bees, moths or beetles often ushered in pilgrimages. When the Bogong Moth migrated to the Australian Alps each spring to feed on the blossoms, the aboriginals followed them from the lower ground and easily caught them in clusters in caves and crevices. As more than sixty per cent of the dry weight of the bodies of the heavy moths was yellow fat, and as the fat tasted like a sweet nut when roasted, the aboriginals feasted on them day after day and grew fat. These annual festivals of the moth-eaters were as regular as the snow-skiing seasons of the Europeans who later occupied the region. On the plains several hundred miles to the west, aboriginals who had never seen a snow-capped mountain had their own insect festival when millions of green beetles excreted their larva on the young shoots of the mallee scrub. In taste the white substance was sweet with a slight tang. It was deposited in such profusion in a dry summer that an aboriginal could gather forty or fifty pounds of it in a day. And it was so nutritious that the aboriginals who daily walked a long way to reach patches of mallee scrub to eat the *laarp* became fat and sleek in the space of six weeks. The craving for sweet food goes some way towards explaining the ease with which their descendants were snared by the ration of sugar and flour offered to them by European sheep-owners, missionaries, and government-guardians.

CHAPTER NINE

Harvest of the Unploughed Plains

For several generations most European settlers who had opportunities of observing the traditional life of aboriginals came to clear conclusions about their diet. Aboriginals, they decided, were mainly flesh-eaters who occasionally ate fruit and vegetables. Thus the first European explorer in western Victoria, finding a bag in which aboriginal women carried food, looked inside and saw three snakes, three rats, some yabbies, about two pounds of a tiny freshwater fish resembling whitebait, and many small roots of a dandelion or chicory which was then specking the plains with yellow flowers. The explorer saw no evidence in the spring of 1836 to suggest that vegetables were more than a small supplement to a diet of fish and meat. He was inclined to conclude that the main food was opossum. Caught in the trees and lightly toasted, it had the flavour of singed wool.

Wherever the British explorers went they tended to decide that flesh dominated native diet. Many early pastoralists, moving inland with sheep or cattle, saw little evidence to minimize the dominance of flesh in the diet. When in 1860 the Victorian Government sent an expedition north in the hope of crossing the continent they included packets of seeds in the packs of the camels and instructed the explorers to plant seeds along their route; they could not imagine that in the dry centre of Australia plants were a vital part of aboriginal diet and indeed would keep alive the expedition's only survivor.

155

An old Queensland pastoralist, Edward Palmer, must have been one of the first to stress that the aboriginals depended on an astonishing variety of berries, seeds, roots, pods, fruits, bulbs, and greens. In 1883 he sent a paper to the Royal Society of New South Wales, vowing from his long experience with aboriginals in the Gulf country that 'nearly half of their daily food' consists of roots and fruits. He listed 106 plants which were used for food or medicine. He could have added another fifty, he said, if he had known how to classify them. Surprisingly little attention was paid to Palmer's writings. How the aboriginals made their living interested scholars much less than which deity they believed in, whom they married and how they structured their society. Only in relatively recent years were many attempts made to investigate the traditional diet of aboriginals.

The recent field work has confirmed the importance of plant foods, at least in tropical Australia. According to the anthropologist, Mervyn Meggitt, perhaps seventy to eighty per cent of the bulk of the food eaten in tropical Australia had been vegetables. In Arnhem Land perhaps six of every ten pounds of food eaten by nomadic groups were estimated to have come from plants. In most parts of the Cape York Peninsula plants probably provided at least half of the food though fish dominated the diet of aboriginals at Princess Charlotte Bay, north of Cooktown. Wherever bays and rivers were a rich source of fish the plant foods probably did not constitute as much as half the diet, whether in bulk or in calories. Thus plants probably were not the most important food along most reaches of the Murray River and in many sheltered bays of Tasmania and New South Wales where fish were plentiful.

On the grassy plains of northern Victoria plant foods were probably as important as in many parts of the tropics. South of the Murray the Bangerang people lived 'in great measure' on wild roots and vegetables. On the plains beyond Geelong vegetables were a large part of the diet; and a man who spent half a lifetime with aboriginals recalled long periods when roots were the main food and meat was almost a luxury. In Western Australia, on a plain near the Hutt River, grew a yam root about as thick as a man's thumb, and the yam was so prolific in the loamy soil that the plain resembled a great potato garden. It supported a dense population each harvest —'the most thickly-populated district of Australia that I had yet observed', wrote explorer Grey. He found the ground so perforated with the holes dug by women foragers that for a distance of $3\frac{1}{2}$ miles the walking was difficult.

II

In a normal year the aboriginals in many parts of the continent ate a variety of plant foods such as no present green-grocer or fruiterer in an Australian city could hope to display. His shop, even with those foods which had been refrigerated or air-freighted, could not match the variety of plant foods eaten in a typical year by wandering aboriginals. In the Cape York region at least 141 species of plants were known to yield food to aboriginals. In that region 73 different fruits and 46 different roots were eaten. Add 19 kinds of nuts and seeds, 11 varieties of green leaves and shoots and the list is probably not complete. Compared to the favoured parts of Cape York Peninsula, Arnhem Land was not a paradise of plant foods but it yielded at least 35 different fruits and 34 vegetables to wandering aboriginals. As these varieties did not all grow along the same wander-route, no aboriginal family would taste every kind of seed or berry in the course of a normal year. In some months, moreover, their choice must have been meagre. The sheer variety of plant foods they used was partly a sign that nomads—unlike a society of gardeners and herdsmen—lacked a sure supply of two or three staple foods.

In the south-eastern corner of the continent, near Wilson's Promontory, an adult who today wandered from the car

157

park and became lost in the bush would be unlikely, even when hunger became painful, to detect one plant which could be eaten with confidence. And yet in a relatively small area between the sandy beaches and the forest about 120 edible species of plants exist, and all but a dozen are known to have been eaten at one time or other by aboriginals. Moreover most of the plants required no cooking before they were eaten. The most abundant were in freshwater swamps not far from the coast; there the starch-filled tubers and yams were dug with ease. The forests of tall eucalypts on the high spine of Wilson's Promontory offered little food but the adjacent zones of vegetation—swamps, the banksia-studded woodland, the sandy shrubland and the seashore—were sufficiently contrasting to produce in all a greater diversity of edible plants than most parts of tropical Arnhem Land.

In Victoria the aboriginals ate the small roots of a variety of orchids in spring and autumn. They ate roots of bulrushes and the shining blisters of gum exuded from the trunks and branches of wattles. They dug a kind of yam which tasted like a radish and grew in many creeks now flanked by tiled roofs and paling fences; the yam grew on the banks of the Moonee Ponds Creek long before the bulbs of European gladiolii multiplied. Victorian aboriginals ate the heart and young fronds of tree-ferns and the pith of the grass tree, and its shoots when tender. They ate sow thistles, a kind of nasturtium leaf, leaves of clover-sorrel, water grasses, the fruits of the Lilly Pilli, wild raspberries, kangaroo apples, native cherries, and the fruit of the colourful pig-face. They gathered mushrooms, prizing a small native truffle which was somewhat like 'unbaked brown bread'.

Of the plants eaten by aboriginals in the south-east of the continent the ground-roots were probably the most important, though the favourite differed from region to region. 'The root most sought after', noted a guidebook on the Adelaide district in 1839, 'is a highly nutritious oxalis, resembling a small carrot, and tasting like cocoa-nut'. Women with long digging sticks looked for the leaf of the plant and then prodded the ground and levered up the carrot. In most parts of Australia root-vegetables were cooked in a scooped hole into which a cover of hot ashes, coals and sand were pushed.

As virtually every piece of fruit sold now in Australian shops belonging to a species whose seeds were imported to the continent in recent times, it is understandable that we imagine that aboriginals had no fruits worthy of the name. Australia, so far as is known, provided aboriginals with no apples, peaches, strawberries, apricots, pineapples, oranges, lemons and pears, of a kind that we would recognize; Australia did not even provide edible bananas though on the northern side of Torres Strait banana trees were plentiful. And yet the continent had its own diversity of fruits—mostly small, some acidic, some sweet, and nearly all eaten raw.

Northern Australia produced a wide variety of edible fruits, and many of them still ripen within an apple's throw of diamond-drillers' camps or roadmakers' caravans where nothing but canned or refrigerated fruits are eaten. On stony ridges near Cloncurry (Q.) a glossy-leaved shrub produces dark red fruit, acidic to taste. In sandy forest near the Saxby River shady trees produce small yellow stone-fruits which when ripe attracted emus and aboriginals. In sandy ground on the Upper Cloncurry a low bushy annual yields a light-yellow fruit like a Cape gooseberry. On the island of Groote Eylandt (N.T.) a wild grape was eaten in the wet season. Tropical Australia had many variations of figs, plums, and berries; and the knowledge of where they grew and when they ripened was passed on from generation to generation. Many were tiny berries which only a hungry or patient woman would bother to collect in her netted bag, wooden coolamon or bark dish.

Even in the dryness of central Australia, explorers wondering where to find their next water, came across wild fruit-trees. W. C. Gosse, travelling with camels in August 1873 in the expedition during which he discovered Ayers Rock, saw the banks of a dry watercourse, vivid with the red fruit of the quandong. Some of the fruit was almost as large as a golf ball. 'It is the prettiest fruit I have seen growing', he noted in his journal; 'the rich red contrasts so well with the green leaves.' In hot ranges, hundreds of miles from the nearest farm or orchard, he prized the wild peaches which he found miraculously growing in country that had only sparse patches of feed for his camels and horses. Filling a big billy-can with peaches he boiled them into a sweet jam and served it daily to his men, believing that it kept away the scurvy and the festering skin sores. In central Australia at least thirty edible fruits were known to aboriginals, but that area was so vast that no aboriginal probably encountered every one of those fruits in the space of a year.

On the Pacific coast, about seventy miles north of Brisbane, one fruit was so abundant and delicious that its ripening marked one of the festivals of the aboriginal calendar. To the west of what now are the seaside resorts of Maroochydore and Alexandra Headland, tall pines topped many of the ridges. The trunk of the Bunya Bunya Pine was as straight as a mast, grew to twenty feet in circumference, and supported an umbrella of foliage. Ludwig Leichhardt, who visited the ranges for the Bunya Pine feast at the end of 1843, quietly marvelled at the grandeur of the trees with the curving green branches and the massive trunk which resembled 'a pillar supporting the vault of Heaven.' He was reminded, nostalgically, of the pines of Germany though the Bunya was really closer to the Norfolk Island pine or the 'Monkey Puzzle' tree of Chile. In the hot humid days of summer he watched the aboriginals climb the trees, using a brush vine as climbing rope. From the swaying heights where they could sometimes see faraway plains on one side and the Pacific Ocean on the other, they tugged at

160

the prickly pine-cones and dropped them to the ground. The cones whistled as they fell through the air—a useful warning because they were heavy enough to knock a child unconscious. Between the scales of each cone were sweet, floury kernels which—raw or toasted—had a delicious taste. Once people began eating them they usually stopped only when their stomachs began to stretch. The kernels were rich and fattening. Young men often broke out in boils during the feasting. Such was the craving for the fruit that when the crop was prolific—and every third year was said to be prolific—aboriginals came from as far away as one hundred miles and camped near the Bunya Bunya pines for two or three months, so that in all several hundred people congregated, forming one of the biggest gatherings of the Pacific coast. So valuable was the food supply to aboriginals that when pastoralists moved flocks and herds into the surrounding grasslands the government banned grazing in the forest where the Bunya pines towered.

III

Central Australia does not at first sight seem likely to offer many plant foods to aboriginals, but in the course of a year it could yield a surprising diversity of foodstuffs. An irrigated market-garden at Alice Springs today would not grow a fraction of the variety of plants visible to sharp eyes in the desert where perhaps twenty kinds of greens and about forty-five species of seeds, nuts and kernels were eaten by aboriginals.

Seeds were a more important food on the dry inland plains than in the coastal areas. Grinding stones were used to crush seed into meal as long ago as 15,000 years in parts of the interior, but were probably not used in Tasmania at the time of the European's coming, a sign that seeds there were not a vital food. The heavy consumption of grass seeds, tree seeds and various nuts in central Australia possibly reflected

161

the lack of other foods in certain seasons but this is only a hypothesis. In the emergence of eating habits perhaps the tastes and preferences of people were almost as influential as the local resources of plant foods.

One of the favoured seeds in central Australia was nardoo, the seed in the spore case of the clover fern. Growing in dry places as far apart as Southern Asia and North Africa, the clover usually grew in dry tracts liable to flooding, and after the water subsided the plant grew rapidly to a height of a foot or more. When the plants were eventually withered by the hot sun and parched soil, aboriginals harvested them in netting bags and sometimes roasted the spore cases before they began the tedious process of milling the imprisoned seeds. Inside the spore case the seeds were grey and hard like watermelon seeds; but on the grinding stone they were reduced to a mixture of flour and husks. When the mixture was shaken in a wooden bowl, the light wind—or a puff from the miller—carried the husks away. The coarse seed-meal was mixed with water and eaten raw, or was baked in the ashes of a fire, and it served as the staple food for many months of the year for the aboriginals near the border of Queensland and South Australia. There the nardoo was also the main food eaten by the exhausted explorers, Burke and Wills, when their exploring ceased in 1861.

IV

Plants supplied so much of the food eaten in many parts of Australia that the digging stick rather than the spear was the vital implement. As the gathering of plant foods was a female occupation, women rather than men were the main breadwinners in many regions. And yet it is unlikely that women spent abnormally long hours in gathering plants and preparing and cooking them. Their working day would rarely have exceeded eight hours, and in the season when vegetables were very abundant their effective working day

162

might have been only two, three or four hours. Peasant women of eastern Europe two or three centuries ago must have spent far more time than aboriginal women of Australia in tilling, harvesting, preparing and cooking food.

The first attempt to measure the work hours of aboriginal women in a nomadic background was made in Western Arnhem Land in October 1948. It was the time, on the other side of the world, of the Berlin Blockade; and the food that was flown daily into Berlin was weighed with no greater accuracy than were the vegetables and carcases which aboriginals brought home to their camp on the dry creek-bed at Fish Creek.

The observations of women's work, it is fair to say, provide a useful rather than a typical record. In the camps of gatherers and hunters there was no typical working day, for there was no typical climatic season. Moreover, in a continent as large as Australia, and as diverse in its resources of food, no district could be called typical; and so the daily quest for food in Arnhem Land differed as much from the daily quest for food in a cold Tasmanian bay as does the economic life of modern Sydney from that of Calcutta. In nomadic Australia the hours spent in the quest for food varied according to the time of the year, the kind of terrain, the daily weather, the age and fitness and skills of the food collectors, the numbers of mouths to be fed, and the tribal tastes and preferences.

Even the charting, in 1948, of the working day of that small group in the patch of monsoon forest in Arnhem Land was not necessarily typical of the October activities of aboriginals in that area one year earlier or a century earlier. The aboriginals had been touched by European civilization; several had worked in an outback tin mine; all had learned the taste of European foods; and when they returned briefly to self-sufficient nomadic life at Fish Creek they carried European objects. The women had an iron digging stick and men had an iron point on their hunting spears, and while these

163

were minor advantages in the circumstance of that terrain and season they were advantages. Moreover, as McCarthy and McArthur, the scientific investigators at Fish Creek, knew only too clearly, the mere entry of white people into an isolated aboriginal area disrupted the very life which the newcomers were trying to analyze. News of visitors attracted aboriginals from some distance away, and the inquisitive aboriginals were inclined to stay so long as the inquisitive white newcomers stayed, and so the hunters and gatherers which were now the subject of study might not be quite a normal team. And yet, even with these asides and doubts, there emerged from the patient diary of food-gathering at Fish Creek a revealing outline of an activity which was pursued during every day of the human history of Australia but was rarely watched and recorded until that activity had virtually ceased.

The seventh of October 1948 was the first recorded day and as close as any of the fourteen to a typical day. The four adult women set out from the camp on the creekbed at 8.30. They carried receptacles but few possessions. They also carried an iron digging stick, but it was probably less useful than four traditional wooden sticks.

Not far from camp their dog caught the scent of a bandicoot in a hollow log, and the women prodded the bandicoot from its hiding place, caught it, and killed it by swinging its head against the log. Later they saw a goanna on a tree trunk and they grabbed and killed it in the same way. About two miles from camp they began to look for yams in the burned-out country but signs of yams were few; grass fires had destroyed the leaves and stems which pointed to the roots below and the soil was parched, for the dry season was at its peak. The women caught two small fish with their hands in a pool and dug a hive of honey from an ant hill before they found their first edible roots beneath creepers and vines on the banks of a shaded creek. They dug out roots weighing three or four pounds and then returned to the main camp, arriving at 12.45 pm.

While the men were away hunting—they returned at 2 p.m. with a slaughtered kangaroo—the women cooked and ate the bandicoot, goanna, and all the yams of one variety. The other yams were poisonous and had to be sliced, peeled, and left to soak overnight in a fish net in a waterhole before they were safe to eat.* The preparing of the poisonous yams took three women about one hour of leisurely work. Apart from a small time spent in collecting firewood for the cooking of the kangaroo, the women's work was done. In all they had spent just over five hours in gathering and preparing vegetables and that proved to be their second busiest day during the fortnight.

On most of the days when women set out to dig for vegetables, they were back in camp in less than four hours. As this was the dry season the women spent part of the time in futile search; in moister months more time was spent in gathering plant foods. Plant foods at the end of the dry season were so rare at Fish Creek, and the people so craved for some variation in their diet of meat, that on the fifth day of the survey two aboriginals—unobserved by the anthropologists—set out for the mission station at Oenpelli to procure flour and rice. On their return they were intercepted, told about the purpose of the survey, and presumably persuaded by some offer of reward to eat none of the imported foods until the survey was completed.

In addition to recording the food-gathering of the women an attempt was made to count their siestas. The siesta was

---

*It is easier to find evidence of the effects of poisonous yams on white men than on brown men; aboriginals were saved by their botanical knowledge. About 1873 a police trooper near the East Alligator River in Arnhem Land decided to taste an edible yam near a lagoon. He did not know that the yam needed careful leaching. After one bite his tongue began to swell. It became about four times its normal size and could scarcely fit in his mouth. He was far from the nearest medical man and for a time his mates thought he would die.

normal for men and women though it did not always occur in the heat of the day. At Fish Creek the shortest daytime sleep was fifty minutes but on some days most of the daylight hours were spent in sleep, the men and women lying flat on their backs. The daytime fatigue was caused partly by the tropical climate, but another cause operated in cold as well as hot months. Sleep at night was often disturbed by insect pests, occasionally a shower of rain, the lack of suitable garments or blankets, or the need in cold weather to fetch wood to keep the fires alight.

In the same year the food-gathering at Hemple Bay, on Groote Eylandt, was briefly recorded. There three families were camped behind flimsy wind-breaks of leafy branches, a shield against the south-easterlies blowing on to the long, exposed beach. The rainy season was over, and the vegetable harvest was at its height, so the women were more successful than those of Fish Creek in digging plant foods.

Behind the sand dunes of the beach was a fresh-water lagoon, where the women spent much of their day gathering plant foods in the water or eating or warming themselves by their fire on the shore. There the most abundant food was the rhizome of the small blue water-lily. The women waded into the water and wherever a water-lily was afloat they traced the stalk under-water and gathered the roots. If the water was shallow they squatted as they dug the roots with wooden sticks. In deep water, however, they dived and stayed down while they prised out the roots. Placing the lily roots in bark baskets which floated on the water, they periodically waded ashore and roasted some for themselves and their playing children, taking the remainder back to the camp when their work was over.

The gathering of the roots of the water-lilies tended to take place in leisurely passages of an hour or two, after which the women would come ashore and warm themselves by the fire, cook and eat, sit and gossip, or walk short distances in search of other fruit or yams. The harvest of the roots of water-lilies at Hemple Bay was remarkably large. In four days the women gathered sixty-six pounds, and that equalled half of the gross weight of the fish caught by the men in their dug-out canoes. To gather these roots and other yams and fruit, the women spent more time at or near their work than the women at the inland camp of Fish Creek. In the week in which their work was timed, their shortest working day was four and a half hours. Curiously, at both the inland camp and the beach camp the weekly hours spent by the men in hunting, fishing, or making or repairing equipment did not vary much from the hours spent by women in collecting and preparing plant foods.

The survey in 1948 of the way in which aboriginals gathered food in Arnhem Land suggested that no group had to put herculean efforts into the task. 'The quantity of food gathered in one day by any of the groups could in every instance have been increased', wrote Margaret McArthur of the Australian Institute of Anatomy. Both the men and the women preferred to hunt and gather on nearly every day rather than hoard food. Often they could have collected, if they wished, enough yams or fish to last for several days but the food expeditions were also social outings in which much time was passed in talking and resting. Miss McArthur, observing the women, saw no sign that they disliked their work, no sign that the walking and digging and carrying was seen 'as either monotonous or as drudgery'. Moreover they had first call on the plants and fruits which they gathered, just as the men had first choice of the meat and fish which they captured.

V

Australia had such differences in food resources from district to district and such a diversity of food preferences and taboos amongst the diverse peoples that any conclusion has to be offered with caution. One can confidently affirm, however,

167

the importance of vegetables in the diet of most aboriginals. It is probable that in most regions of Australia the people in a normal year gained at least half of their energy from plant foods. Whether they depended so heavily on plant foods 10,000 or 20,000 years earlier is impossible to tell.

Several anthropologists, however, would dispute the suggestion that in the colder parts of the continent the plant foods were a large part of diet. In the 1960s an influential school of opinion argued that nomadic peoples ate smaller amounts of vegetables and grain if they lived in colder climates. Thus nomads in central Africa were said to have relied far more on plant foods than the nomadic Eskimos, who relied on meat and fish. This opinion was reinforced not only by the abundance of plant foods in tropical regions but by the digestive advantages of greens, fruits, grains and yams in a warm climate; in a warm climate a meal of meat was said to be less suitable, because the digesting of it absorbed a lot of energy.

In 1967 an anthropologist, Betty Hiatt, applied this theory to Australia. She argued that Tasmania, being cold, was an appropriate laboratory in which to test the theory; and she made a painstaking study of the early writings on the Tasmanian aboriginals and their eating habits. She concluded that Tasmanians—compared to tropical Australians—ate fish and meat more often and tended to rely on vegetables.

Naturally her study relied heavily on the memoirs and diaries and journals of the white men who first saw the aboriginals doing their daily tasks; and those pages disclose more even than archaeological work about the meals once eaten by aboriginals. But the written accounts of shell-fish eaten or wallabies killed are only part of the story. The silences and omissions in the journals of explorers and reports of archaeologists are also revealing. One may suggest that the surviving records of Tasmanian diets are like a court case in which many of the key witnesses failed to appear;

168

most of those absent witnesses, moreover, belonged to one side of the controversy.

The records of the diet of Tasmanian and Victorian aboriginals are often silent about plant foods. The reasons for the silence are curious. Firstly, as the brilliant American anthropologist Carl Sauer argued of nomadic societies, archaeological work was more likely to dig up hunting implements and the bones of animals and fish than the debris of a vegetable diet. Even for a tribe which fed mostly on plant foods, the archaeological evidence might point only to their hunting habits. Secondly, the white migrants who witnessed the last phase of a nomadic society were more inclined to notice the hunters than the vegetable gatherers; the men's spears were obviously more frightening than the women's digging sticks and more likely to be watched closely and later reported in memoirs, travel books and letters. Thirdly, whenever Europeans decided to employ aboriginals as guides, trackers, interpreters or stockmen they chose men, and so they unknowingly gathered knowledge more centred on male methods of food-gathering. Fourthly, tribal society collapsed swiftly in Victoria and Tasmania, robbing many observant Europeans of the opportunity there to observe quietly the traditional food-collecting habits of aboriginals.

In Victoria and Tasmania a ration of flour and sugar was handed to a high proportion of the surviving aboriginals in the first decade of European settlement; and the flour, being accepted as a welcome substitute for many of the old plant foods, probably hastened the decline of plant gathering even more than it hastened the decline of hunting; in contrast a ration of meat was not often given to aboriginals. Furthermore the sheep imported to Australia's south-east were perhaps more destructive of native plant foods than were the cattle imported to the tropical north: if that were so, gatherers of plant foods would perhaps be less successful and therefore less visible in the south after the arrival of sheep. Likewise, Tasmanian aboriginals quickly adopted

169

European dogs and used them skilfully for hunting; accordingly one prehistorian wondered whether Tasmanian aboriginals in their last years might have come to depend far more on meat than they had depended when they owned no dogs. At the same time the rapid abduction of Tasmanian women, traditionally the collectors of plant foods, could also have accelerated a new reliance on meat by the surviving men. If these observations are true the evidence of the nineteenth century would not be reflecting the traditional but the recent and crumbling Tasmanian society.

At least eight arguments can thus be found to explain how the importance of plant foods might have been masked in Tasmania, Victoria, and other areas of south-eastern Australia. In essence, vital evidence about aboriginals' food has either vanished or been misconstrued. The elusive evidence has unexpected implications. For instance it suggests that the food resources of parts of Australia were possibly greater than is realized and that therefore the peak population of prehistoric Australia is perhaps under-estimated. The slanted surviving evidence also warns us that we could easily minimize the horticultural skills of aboriginals: they were not gardeners but many perhaps possessed attitudes and knowledge which, elsewhere, were amongst the prerequisites for the cultivation of plants. The slanted evidence also deprives them of adequate recognition of one of their achievements; for botany, as the following chapter suggests, was perhaps the pinnacle of aboriginal learning and one secret of their remarkable ability to tame wild terrain.

CHAPTER TEN

Medicines and Drugs, Liquids and Cosmetics

The average Australian, adult and child, knew more about botany one thousand years ago than they know today. Knowledge of botany supplied them not only with much of their food but also with drugs and cosmetics and—in a drought—with water.

II

As medicine is seen as a hallmark of civilization, and as aboriginals in the nineteenth century were mostly seen as uncivilized, it was widely assumed that they were simpletons in medicine. Their high death rate, and the extinction of many tribes, probably heightened the impression that they could not cope with any kind of sickness. In fact they had many effective remedies.

A belated survey in the late 1960s found that at least 124 different species of native plants were believed by aboriginals to have medicinal qualities. As medicine based on herbs is essentially regional, and as a continent as huge as Australia consists of many botanical regions, the statistic did not mean that a skilled aboriginal knew all these plants. Nor were the plants necessarily as curative as the aboriginals believed: there were mountebanks long before the patent-medicine and toothpaste proprietors of our era. Nevertheless Dr L. J. Webb's recent survey suggested that many aboriginal medicines were valid. Thus some of their intoxicants, poisonous sedatives, sore ointments, diarrhoea remedies, cough and cold palliatives, and even an oral contraceptive fit in with present pharmaceutical knowledge. Many of their other medicines, like ours, probably depended on the faith of the swallower.

It would be difficult to envisage an aboriginal walking more than a mile without recognizing a grass, shrub, flower or tree which was valued as a medicine or poison. Many of the plants which overhang the fences in Australian suburbs today—pittosporum, melaleuca, grevillea, acacia and euca-lypt—were once prized for healing rather than ornamental qualities. At least four species of acacia were used as a cure for coughs, colds, and laryngitis, the common method being to mash and soak the roots to make a syrup. The warmed leaves of a species of pittosporum were held against the breast of a mother to induce the first flow of milk for a new child. The inner bark of the custard apple was pressed against an aching tooth in the hope of killing the pain. The leaves or bark of at least eight species of eucalyptus were prepared for a variety of ailments ranging from gastro-intestinal illnesses to heart troubles; the eucalyptus oil was one aboriginal potion which was widely imitated by white Australians, and the aroma of handkerchiefs soaked in euca-lyptus or footballers' limbs rubbed with the same liniment oil became one of the most familiar smells of winter in Australian cities. In preparing eucalyptus oil the aboriginals lacked the advantage of the boiling process—they were un-able to boil any liquid—but by rubbing and bruising and squeezing the young gum leaves and soaking them in a wooden coolamon of water they could produce a green liquid which, once swallowed, was said to cure any cold or headache.

Herbal remedies were part of aboriginal surgery. The Reverend T. T. Webb, writing in a learned journal in 1933 on 'Aboriginal Medical Practice in East Arnhem Land', described sympathetically the surgery he had seen during long experience in that region. If a man were so wounded that his intestines protruded, the first test was to see whether the intestines leaked. The wounded man sat down and allowed a mate to ease out as much as possible of his viscera, which were then arranged spaghetti-like on the sand. While the wounded man drank water the spectators crowded around, closely watching the exposed viscera to observe the effect. If the water leaked out, that was bad news. If no water was seen to leak, the viscera were washed and eased back into the body. Now was the time for herbal medicine. A small carrot-like root and a kind of grass were pounded between stones, and the resultant mash was stuffed inside the abdominal cavity 'in order to keep the organs in position'. The outer wound was then painted with white clay, dressed with a concoction from the bulb of the white lily, and finally bandaged with strips of paper-bark. One conclusion can be safely drawn. The recuperation, or death, of the wounded man was quick.

III

Aboriginals had no knowledge of alcoholic fermentation. They did not attempt to convert grain or fruit into alcohol. Nomadic people are unlikely to learn how to make alcohol because they do not own the necessary vats and vessels in which fermentation takes place: moreover they frequently travel and they travel too lightly to be bothered with the carrying of food and liquids. In a few places, however, fermentation occurred naturally and the aboriginals drank the liquor which nature preserved.

In Tasmania a cider eucalypt in season yielded a stimulating drink. Rather like a blue-gum in appearance, the tree grew in the bracing climate of the central plateau, flourishing mostly where forest met open country. It was apparently not a common tree; George Robinson had been travelling with Tasmanian aboriginals for almost two years before he saw them tap a cider tree in the early summer of 1831. Quickly the aboriginals who were with him chopped a hole in the trunk not far above the ground, and from the wound the sap or honey flowed down to a hollow which they cut at the foot of the trunk. The sap was no sooner flowing than aboriginals began to suck it. If they allowed it to flow without interruption, more than a quart of liquid could sometimes be collected at the foot, though cockatoos and possums and ants raided juice which stood unguarded. In taste the sap was rather like sweet cider. If it was allowed to dry into a kind of manna it tasted like and resembled a bruised apple. 'The natives are very fond of the juice', wrote Robinson, 'and I am told it frequently makes them drunk.' Robinson spent more time than any other white man in the company of Tasmanian aboriginals, and during all his wanderings with them he noticed only one other plant that seemed to have a whiff of alcohol. Once on Bruny Island he saw aboriginals sucking the flower of the honeysuckle in order, he thought, to draw up the juice. Across the straits in Victoria aboriginals had also been seen to suck honey-rich plants and to immerse the opaque manna of the peppermint gum in water and greedily drink the mixture. In South Australia the flowers of species of banksia and hakea possibly produced a little alcohol in damp weather. Such alcohol would have been 'quite insufficient to produce even merriment,' Professor J. B. Cleland commented soberly, 'though enough to intoxicate honeyeating birds.'

The virtual absence of alcohol until the European invasion may be part of the explanation for the savage effects of alcohol on the first generation of aboriginal drinkers. Alcohol had been virtually unknown in their society. Equally relevant was perhaps the tendency, in aboriginal society, to gorge food when a windfall came: the gorging of food is understandable in a society where the hoarding was impracticable and where the supply of some prized foodstuffs was erratic.

174

Tobacco, in many stretches of Australian coast, arrived with the Europeans but in huge areas of the interior it long preceded the Europeans. Native tobacco was chewed, not smoked. It was usually known as *pituri,* or by a variation of that name.* The first printed record of this narcotic is probably in the diary of W. J. Wills who with Burke lost his life while crossing central Australia in 1861. Wills had received a little of the tobacco from an aboriginal and, after chewing it, said it was 'highly intoxicating'. Later that year the explorer William Howitt, travelling in the same area in search of Wills, received 'a small ball of what seemed to be chewed grass as a token of friendship'. The usual ball of 'chewed grass' was about the size of a man's thumb. It was sucked within the lower lip and rolled around with the tongue: at meal time it was squeezed behind the ear. Tobacco was so valued as a stimulant or narcotic that it constituted the main traffic of long trade routes in central Australia.

The most celebrated species of native tobacco was not the leaves of the *Nicotania* shrub but rather the true pituri which came from a scrub in the sandhills of south-eastern Queensland, especially around the dry banks and bed of the Upper Mulligan River. The shrub, a species of *Duboisia,* was a twiggy wheaten-yellow plant which a white man, craving for tobacco, would have walked past without realizing its punch. By what accident or experiments its narcotic qualities were discovered by aboriginals will never be known, but it was one of the hundreds of useful botanical discoveries which they made—discoveries which in utilitarian value surpassed those made by outstanding European botanists in Australia. The plant flowered about August, and the flowers and thin

*The most common species of native tobacco was *Duboisia hopwoodii,* named by the botanist Baron von Mueller after Henry Hopwood, who ran a ferry and built, in 1856, a pontoon bridge across the Murray at Echuca. It was perhaps appropriate that Australia's most famous narcotic should have been named after a publican and ex-convict.

leaves and dry stems were harvested and dried. They were carried in netted bags about the size of a woman's small handbag. The mixture consisted mostly of yellow twigs, not unlike the 'wood' one sometimes finds in a packet of coarse ready-rubbed tobacco. Whether the *Duboisia* was chewed on its own or was mainly blended with other leaves and wood ashes is not clear. In 1933 it was closely studied by two medical professors of the University of Adelaide, T. Harvey Johnston and J. B. Cleland, who concluded that it was highly poisonous and therefore not likely to have been chewed persistently on its own.

Narcotics were not only for chewing. They were widely used for hunting and fishing in central Australia. The immersing of leaves of *Duboisia* in a waterhole poisoned the water, and emus which drank it were stupefied and were easily caught. (In areas where the plant was used as a hunting poison it waš, apparently, not chewed.) Another variety of the *Duboisia* was used along the Shoalhaven River, near the coast of New South Wales: a branch soaked in a pool so affected the water that eels were intoxicated and easily caught. How many varieties of bark, leaves, vines, and roots were used to poison fishponds will never be known, but probably there were many. In the rivers flowing into the Gulf of Carpentaria the coolibah or flooded box tree (*Eucalyptus microtheca*) grew up to thirty feet high; and its leaves or bark were pounded and then immersed in the ponds in the hope of stupefying fish. A freshwater mangrove near the Laura and Mitchell Rivers in north Queensland (*Barringtonia racemosa*) yielded a bark which, pulverised with a stone, was used to poison waterholes. Near Geelong (V.) the bark of a willow was used, while small lagoons and waterholes of the Cloncurry River (Q.) were poisoned with the tiny pods and thin leaves of the *Tephrosia,* a small bluish shrub. In some parts of Queensland a poisonous bark was placed in a dilly bag which was lowered into the creeks like a tea-bag.

Fish-poisoning had been practised by many primitive societies scattered across the globe. The Ssabela of the Upper Amazon knew no other way of catching fish. A leap in the technology of man, the knowledge of fish poisons probably came—in the opinion of the distinguished American scholar Carl Sauer—through intelligent accident. Perhaps a man on the water's edge was using a stone weapon to mash the stalk of a plant in order to make fibres for fishing line or bow strings. A piece of the mashed fibre might have fallen in the pond, and before long the stunned fish might have been floating on the surface. The crucial test was to eat the stunned fish and await the consequences. As many of the poisonous plants in the Malay Peninsula were also used for making fibre, Sauer's theory is feasible.

It seems likely that when the first aboriginals reached Australia they carried knowledge that certain leaves or barks could be used to poison fish; and that they applied their knowledge when they found the poisonous plants growing in Australia. By experiment, observation, or the harnessing of accidents their repertoire of poisons was probably much increased as they occupied more and more of the continent. In this accumulating of knowledge, however, there must have been unintended casualties, human and animal.

Likewise the aboriginals' knowledge of how to extract glues and adhesives was augmented as they occupied each new Australian region. The adhesives and cements with which they assembled their weapons and implements came ultimately from a wide range of Australian plants. In southern Australia the gum of the wattle trees was widely used for fastening points to spears and handles to axes. In parts of Queensland they took resin from the roots of the young ironwood tree, and in the western deserts they used the black resin exuded from the leaf sheafs of the porcupine grass or spinifex. In the tropics the wax of the wild bees was a favourite glue, and in countless ceremonial grounds the blood drawn from the human elbow made ornamental

177

feathers adhere to the body, but plants were the main source of those sticky substances used in making knives, axes, spears, and woomeras.

IV

A knowledge of plants and animals also guided aboriginals towards water in places which, to European eyes, were water- less. Their ability to find water was one of their remarkable skills. Without that skill they could not have remained in occupation of most of that dry, oval-shaped region embracing more than one third of the continent. Running from the cliffs edging the Great Australian Bight in the south to the tropical zone of the Northern Territory, and running from a strip of the western coast to the Darling River (N.S.W.) is an oval-shaped region receiving less than 10 inches of rain in an average year. As most of that dry area has intense heat and an annual evaporation rate of more than 100 inches, the supply of water is precarious. The land around Lake Eyre (S.A.) is even drier, and the average rainfall in an area as big as Spain is only 4 to 6 inches. As rain fell on few days in the average year most of the creeks which collected the rainwater soon ceased to flow and were parted into a chain of waterholes which in turn became sun-cracked mud. For much of the year the aboriginals here came to rely on small waterholes in the great granite outcrops, and soaks which yielded a little shallow water to those who scratched or dug at appropriate places in the sandy beds of creeks. Here and there a native well went down perhaps fifteen or twenty feet and held—if rarely used—a little water which sometimes was putrid with the bodies of birds and small animals. On some mornings a light dew covered the scattered clumps of grass and the foliage of bushes, and that moisture could keep parched aboriginals alive when travelling. Near the Great Australian Bight the explorer John Eyre once shook and brushed the spangles of dew from grasses and leaves in imitation of aboriginals, and in an hour he caught a quart of drinking water.

In a faraway time aboriginals in the dry plains had learned much about the kinds of trees which, in a year of heat-waves, could yield water. When moving camp or making long journeys, they tapped water from trees and bushes. The South Australian explorer, William H. Tietkens, was once travelling with camels not far from where the transcontinental railway now crosses the eastern part of the Nullarbor Plain. The afternoon heat was intense, their waterbags were dry, the camels still had to travel fifteen miles to reach water. Tietkens was accompanied by a small aboriginal boy, and both were gasping for water when suddenly the boy jumped from his camel and ran towards a desert-oak or casuarina and began to claw the hot sand near the trunk of the tree. He reached one of the horizontal roots, snapped it, and then moved slowly away from the trunk, tugging at the root as he walked. After he had ripped about eight feet of root from the soil he broke off a slender piece and drained it into his dry mouth. Tietkens copied the boy, and was delighted to feel the cool drops of water falling on his tongue. 'We did not take any more than the one root', he reminisced, 'and I think there were eight or ten more such roots—enough in abundance for a dozen men.'

Aboriginals identified certain kinds of mallee scrub as the precious givers of water. One species, with snowy-coloured bark and an umbrella of oily leaves that glistened in the sun, grew to a height of only about fifteen feet, but its roots often stretched—an inch or two below the dry soil—for a horizontal distance of forty or eighty feet. The roots were really thin, porous water-pipes. They were first probed with a yam stick, ripped from the ground, cut into strips, and held vertically so that the water dripped into a waiting mouth or a wooden coolamon. Classified as *Eucalyptus transcontinentalis* in botanical textbooks, its water-holding roots were possibly known to aboriginals long before the

179

Roman empire rose and fell. As clumps of that Mallee scrub grew in many dry parts of Australia they were more useful as an emergency reservoir than the currajong tree, the needle bush, and other shrubs whose shallow roots could also be tapped for water.

Cavities in the trunks or forked branches of desert-oaks or mallee-oaks sometimes yielded clear fresh water. The water could be sucked out by a hollow reed or soaked up by tediously lowering a spear-point, padded with a wad of dry grass which served as sponge. Sometimes the scurrying of a march of ants or the flight of flocks of zebra finches pointed to the presence of water in holes in trees or roots.

In the deserts two species of bloated frogs were reservoirs which, if excavated from their hiding place in hard mud, yielded safe water. In central Australia a small green and yellow 'aestivating frog' could survive in a tight burrow a foot or so below the surface when a waterhole was baked into hard mud. Bloated with the water which it stored, it could sleep for months through a dry spell. It could be tricked, however, by an aboriginal who stamped his feet on the ground above. The noise, perhaps sounding like the thunder which preceded rain, sometimes provoked hidden frogs into croaking, thus revealing their presence. Unearthed by the probes of a digging stick, they were snatched up and squeezed like a lemon, so that their water ran into a waiting bowl or mouth.

Many of the white teams which explored the dry interior in the second half of the nineteenth century engaged aboriginals as water-finders. But the string of pack horses, the riding horses or the camels which made up these gluttonous expeditions, consumed so many gallons of water on any day in which water could be found that the real water-seeking skills of the desert aboriginals were naturally irrelevant.

If we had a detailed knowledge of aboriginal history we would probably mark the development of these water-finding skills as one of the important economic achievements of aboriginals.* Undoubtedly the discovery that the thin buried roots or trunk cavities of certain kinds of trees yielded water must have been made by Australian aboriginals. And in economic importance that innovation must have matched those ideas which enabled a few Europeans to settle in the dry parts of Australia. It must have been as important as the later discovery of artesian water, the use of windmills for pumping, the importance of camels and the building of railways—innovations that enabled a few Australians to run sheep and cattle in dry regions which the aboriginals had long occupied.

In the eyes of aboriginals their own ability to find water was far surpassed by older men's ability to make rain. Even in desert in the dry months aboriginals believed they were protected by benevolent ancestors who, courted with the charms and rituals, would hasten the coming of rain. They believed that ancestors roamed central Australia, ruling the rainclouds. In virtually all the songs of Central Australia, writes Professor Strehlow, 'the country is described as it would look at the height of a good season'. In essence the arid, harsh landscape was seen as fundamentally benign, for the rainmakers in each tribe had deep faith that songs, rites, charms and the lavish spilling of ceremonial blood could invoke those ancestral rain-makers who still commanded the rainclouds which spasmodically sailed across the blue sky.

V

Aboriginals could almost wring water from a stone. They were less capable, however, of extracting a mineral. They did not enter the Bronze Age or the Iron Age. They used mostly

*This knowledge would not have been carried to Australia by early migrants, for there is no evidence that the springboard islands to the north-west had such dry conditions as to promote knowledge of out-of-way sources of water. Moreover the eastern islands of the Indonesian Archipelago lacked mallee scrub and many other arid-zone trees which yielded water in Australian deserts.

the stone which came cold from the surface of the earth—slabs of sandstone for pummelling and crushing seeds into meal, and fragments of harder stone for making spear-heads, tomahawks, scrapers and knives. Presumably they learned by trial and error which deposits of quartzite, diabase and greywacke were the most appropriate for the making of cutting tools, and the quarries—once begun—were worked generation after generation. The favoured stones were carried long distances to tribes which lacked a quarry of suitable stone.

Minerals were also the basis of a cosmetics industry which, across Australia, must have made thousands of gallons of body paints each year. The most popular source of paint, the ochres, were often made by exposing iron oxide to the heat of fires; and some deposits of iron ore served the needs of people hundreds of miles away. Red ochre from the hematite deposit at Wilgie Mia, east of Geraldton (W.A.), is said to have been carried as far away as Queensland. In a gorge to the south of Ulverstone (T.) the fine ochre attracted aboriginal visitors from as far away as Oyster Bay on the east coast and Cape Grim to the west. The same area yielded a dark ore—perhaps lead or perhaps antimony—which, after simple treatment, became eye shadow or black lines above the eye. Not far to the east, behind Mount Roland, another celebrated mine yielded red ochre with which men smeared themselves from head to toe.

Cosmetics gave a wonderful amount of pleasure. The very thought of them seemed to excite aboriginals. The Englishman, George Robinson, was taken to the mine near Mount Roland by aboriginals in the winter of 1834 and he observed how enthusiastically they began to mine the rock as soon as they arrived, 'being quite overjoyed at the sight' of the quarry. The women were usually the miners, at least in the twilight of Tasmanian life, and they levered out the iron ore by gripping a stone in their hand and using it to strike a sharp-pointed stick into the rock. Robinson was amazed to

182

see the signs of strenuous working—the old excavations, the heaps of stone discarded on the slopes, and narrow holes with collapsed sides. He watched the way in which women squeezed themselves down narrow excavations—one became stuck in the crevice and had to be pulled out by the legs. When the ochre had been packed in the kangaroo skins kept for that purpose, the women set out slowly, some carrying large loads which would have tested the strength of a man. With the ocean visible below them, and to the right the blue hills standing out across the Tamar, the women walked slowly along a well-trodden track with enough iron ore on their backs to furnish cosmetics—if used frugally—for ten thousand faces. As always they squandered the red ochre with the extravagance of millionaires.

Ochres of red, brown, orange and yellow and the pipeclay or kaolin of white and grey were—along with the black of charcoal—the foundations of their paint and cosmetics.* One colour was seen rarely on the painted men and women. The colour blue, wrote Baldwin Spencer, was 'never used by any Australian savage' though he had seen the Arunta of central Australia using blue-grey tint from manganese ore.

Mineral specimens of unusual colour, shape or sheen were valued as ornaments or charms. In 1904 in the Victorian mallee a boy found a nugget of gold at an aboriginal camp which had long been deserted. The 'Watchem Nugget' weighed forty ounces—worth about $5,000 at the 1974 price of gold—and must have been carried there by man rather than deposited by nature; the nearest known source of nuggetty gold was far to the south, requiring a walk of several days. Rare mineral specimens were believed by certain tribes to have the power of implanting sickness in enemies or healing sickness or wounds in friends. Quartz

*There were regional variations. In the Gibson Desert, for example, dry kangaroo-dung yielded a darkish yellow-green colour for paintings on rock surfaces.

crystals or the smooth black australites—buttons of volcanic glass—were revered with the superstition reserved for famous precious stones in Paris and Johannesburg; they were revered for similar reasons, being lucky charms and rarities as well as objects of beauty.

CHAPTER ELEVEN

The Logic of Unending Travel

Aboriginals cocooned their landscape and daily life and human relationships with myth and make-believe, and for a long time that attitude fascinated the more tolerant scholars and disillusioned others. Aboriginals also had a deep understanding of so many conditions which affected their daily life.

Nothing in the traditional life of aboriginals was more impressive than their practical knowledge. They were masters of their environment even though they could do little to change it. Their wide knowledge enabled them to harvest food without strenuous effort. Indeed the frequency with which they moved camp—and the exact timing of their movements—reflected their understanding of climate, winds, marine life, insect life, the maturing of plants and the habits of wild animals.

II

The Wik Monkan tribe occupied part of the Cape York Peninsula, about sixty miles to the south of the present bauxite mines at Weipa. As the tropical seasons changed, they moved to the inland ranges, the tidal reaches of the Archer River, or the sandy beaches to the west. Their movements each season were watched by the anthropologist Donald Thomson, who in 1939 wrote a short article which is now recognized as a bold searchlight on nomadic economies in many lands. He called his article 'The Seasonal

Factor in Human Culture'; in a dozen pages, marked by a disdain of academic jargon and a sense of wonder at the life he had observed, he showed how the Wik Monkan people were able to classify the contrasting landscapes and swampscapes within their tribal area 'as accurately and as scientifically as any ecologist'. As the seasons changed, the aboriginals altered their way of life so that they could exploit the peculiarities and products of each season to the full.

Near the tip of Queensland the wet season usually begins in December. It is ushered in by lightning and sharp thunderstorms, and soon much of the low country is flooded. The grass grows miraculously, and within a few months the Blady Grass is six or seven feet high. The flooded ground and the rising rivers and creeks naturally curb the movements of the Wik Monkan people, and during the three or four months of the rainy season they rarely travelled far.

After the first heavy rainstorms the sap ran freely again in those eucalyptuses known as stringy-bark and the bark could be stripped away and used as building material. With the stringy bark the aboriginals often built more permanent camps on the high ground. To ward off the mosquitoes, smoky fires burned in the huts. With stringy bark they built canoes and set out on hunting expeditions over the new swamplands. In the swamps the birds built nests or incubating mounds; and aboriginals robbed the big yolk-rich eggs from the nests of brush turkeys, jungle fowl and other megapodes. The eggs of turtles and the crocodile's white egg—the size of a duck egg—provided essential protein during the wet season. In swamps and creeks, fish and crabs and other shellfish were strenuously sought. In the grasslands the wallabies and smaller game were protected from hunters by moat-like sheets of water and the concealing green grass whereas the larger kangaroos were particularly vulnerable to hunters in these first stormy weeks of the wet season. The big red and grey kangaroos, wrote Donald Thomson, 'become more approachable, for they may now be stalked under

186

cover of the noise of the great winds.' As the wet season dragged on the craving for vegetable foods grew and grew, but was rarely satisfied. As slight compensation a few fruits were plentiful—small sweet currants, native figs, and the 'Lady Apple'.

The passing of the wet season, usually in March but sometimes in April, altered their way of life—their movements, daily work, diet and housing. The sky became clearer, and a bark-roofed hut became unnecessary. Protection from the stinging mosquitoes, however, was needed more than ever, and so the camps were now located on exposed beaches, plateaux, and river spits where the new south-easterly wind could blow mosquitoes away. Aboriginals moved more often, at first in their bark canoes and then overland as the grass dried and mosquitoes dispersed. As the ground dried out a great harvest of vegetables was made, the women returning to camp in the afternoon with dilly bags full of water-lily tubers, arrowroot, the large seeds of the white mangrove, and yams in all their variety. Set out in baskets on the ground, a display of these vegetables might disappoint a modern shopper, for most species were relatively small in size, but they offered bulk and a diversity of tastes to people who were tired of eggs, meat and fish.

As the months became colder, and the swamps were drained into the receding rivers, fish-fences and fish-traps were built at strategic places. A haul of fish was very welcome at that season, for meat was often scarce so long as the high grasslands swallowed a hunter and retarded his movements.

The wet season and the ensuing season of the vegetable harvest usually covered about eight months in the territory of the Wik Monkan. Then from the last part of July until October ran a third season, embracing the heart of the dry period. In that cool dry weather the vegetable foods were at first plentiful but became scarce as the ground hardened. The women returned often with their dilly bags half empty or only a few shrivelled roots to show for the day's search. A large round yam could still be dug in many places but the yam required careful preparation and leaching to remove the soluble poison within. The 'sugar bag' honey from the small native bee and the Nonda plum were now more plentiful. Fresh plums were eaten raw, and desiccated plums were pounded with stones and soaked in water; resembling pummelled, soaked prunes, they were a favourite with the old, almost toothless, women.

This was a time of frequent moving of camps. The habitations were now flimsy because there was no rain, no cold winds and few mosquitoes. To dig enough vegetables required movement. and sufficient deep waterholes remained to make travel relatively easy. Moreover the long grass was now dry and could be burned systematically in hunting drives, thus trapping wallabies, goannas and snakes.

The fourth distinct season or phase usually ran from October to early December. The sun became hotter, the ground dryer, and usually vegetables were more difficult to find though the bulbs of a spike rush (resembling a hazelnut in size and taste) and a few yams and Nonda plums were accessible. The movement of people became more cautious, and they often stayed for long periods near a permanent waterhole which was within walking distance of a food supply. By burning the remaining grass they could ambush wallabies and capture small creatures. As most waterholes shrank, the methods of fish-poisoning became more practicable; and the branches of poisonous bushes were dropped in the water, stunning the fish, which floated to the surface. Nearly every liability had its corresponding asset in an alert nomadic society; the poisoning of fish would have been a herculean, frustrating task when swamps and lagoons covered a wide area, but in the hot dry months it was practicable. Now, as December approached, the weather began to run again from the north-west: the humidity increased; lightning flickered and flashed in the heavy sky at night; the wily rain-makers set to work to call down the rains and the full cycle of the seasons was almost completed.*

Far to the west in Arnhem Land, another seasonal cycle was outlined by Donald Thomson. Most of Arnhem Land was affected by the same monsoons as the Wik Monkan country, and its aboriginals applied similar knowledge and skills to wring the best living out of the succession of contrasting seasons. Indeed Donald Thomson found that the aboriginals in the north-east of Arnhem Land had themselves classified the year into six seasons, each season having its name, its distinctive climate and food supply, its special type of hut or shelter, and its peculiar supply of woods and fibres and resins for manufacturing purposes. The six seasons ran in this order, beginning with late December:

1. The north-west wind and the first rain-storms
2. The wet season
3. End of the wet season
4. The cool season
5. The hot dry season
6. The time of thunder or 'the nose of the wet season'.

Thomson insisted that this classifying of the seasons was not artificial: 'It is entirely that of the natives themselves, and shows a critical almost scientific appreciation of the environment and its resources.'

Every part of Australia had its seasonal cycle of movements and activities and diet. The fluctuations of that cycle—and the resulting change in nomadic life—were probably most gentle along those coasts with a warm climate and plentiful

---

* Thomson argued that an archaeologist who made a successful excavation on the site of several of these seasonal camps could easily be induced into thinking that each camp represented a different way of life and therefore must have represented different populations. He also observed that an archaeologist who had not seen living nomadic societies would have little chance of fathoming the complexity and material success of this nomadic life.

supplies of seafood. The contrasts were probably sharpest in the central deserts, especially in drought or after deluge.

III

By moving about the countryside in small groups, the aboriginals could efficiently harvest the foods of scattered places. There were limits, however, to the territory which they could exploit. The limits were formally set down by tribal boundaries though these boundaries were not a barrier to everyone. But the tribal boundaries themselves had probably been drawn over a long stretch of time by the facts of geography and economics. In essence a small group of people with no transport other than their feet, and with their own children and implements to carry, could travel effectively only over a moderately-sized area. Moreover they could know the varied resources in detail only if the area was not too large. Even the groups who in the course of twelve months moved camp over a large territory, which might be 100 miles long and 60 miles wide, did not always have access to ample food in every month of the year. Even if their tribal territory embraced sea coast, plains, fresh-water lakes and high mountains, the diversity of foods which they gained from differing altitude and terrain could still leave them with two or three lean months when a lot of energy was spent in finding enough to eat.

Winter was the lean season in many parts of Australia. No matter how often people moved camp, winter went with them. Most aboriginals did not see a fall of snow as long as they lived, and even in Tasmania snow rarely fell on those plains, estuaries and low-lying forests inhabited by the people in winter; but the southern winter was still cold enough to restrict the supply of plant foods. Unfortunately the evidence of how aboriginals coped with scarcity in an abnormally severe winter is meagre. Knowledge of the tribal life in the colder parts of Australia is sparse because, soon after the arrival of Europeans and their sheep, aboriginals there died out or the old way of living was quickly shattered.

South of the tropics only a handful of whites actually lived with aboriginals when tribal life was still unaltered, and only four or five left behind reliable recollections of what daily life was like. One observer was a British seaman named Bob Darge who was shipwrecked in the winter of 1836 on Fraser Island and lived with aboriginals for two months on the adjacent mainland until he escaped them and pushed south towards Brisbane. Darge was calm and alert, not given to dramatizing or exaggerating experiences which he found extremely distasteful and bewildering. Cross-examined after his return to London he recalled that the aboriginals near the beaches had to work hard to find food in winter and the men needed all their skill with fishing nets and as spear-fishermen to make a catch. To his surprise he came across two Englishmen wandering with aboriginal groups. They were convicts who five and ten years ago had escaped from the guarded prison settlement at Brisbane. Physically, said Darge, they were like walking skeletons. They assured him, however, that when warmer weather came they would go with the blacks to the mountains for 'the honey and the kangaroo' and all would grow fat on the good food.

At first sight this is strong evidence that the aboriginals north of the Sunshine Coast lived on the fat of the land in the warm months but that in the mild winter they struggled to make a living by the sea. The contrast between summer in the mountains and winter on the beach is irrefutable. More elusive is how insecure were the living conditions of those aboriginals in winter. Bob Darge himself worked hard while with the aboriginals—he said he worked harder than his masters—but was thrown only the scraps and bones of the more nutritious food. He admitted that a palatable vegetable, a fern root, was prolific but that he himself could not eat a large quantity of it because of its effects on his digestion.

It is likely that aboriginals had physiological thermostats

which enabled them to cope more efficiently with cold weather, thus requiring less food than a European in order to keep warm. J. B. Cleland confirmed, in medical experiments, the capacity of naked aboriginals to absorb radiant heat from the tiny personal fires near which they slept. Aboriginals seemed, he added, to have a more efficient blood circulation. In the part of the body exposed to cold air the circulation of blood was diminished, and that in turn minimized the loss of heat. Unlike Europeans, aboriginals did not require more food in winter; their intake of food was not needlessly wasted in order to provide warmth. If Cleland's observations are valid, the fate of a European thrown amongst tribal aboriginals in winter, and given less food than his hosts, was hardly a measure of the welfare of the aboriginals in winter.

The days which really disrupted aboriginals were wet and cold. Several days of driving rain and chill winds were enough to paralyse their activities more completely than a general strike dislocates a city today. For aboriginals the paralysis was more complete for they usually had no food to fall back on, no clothes to wear, and no waterproof roof over their heads. If the rain was drenching it doused the only fires in the camp. So the people shivered and waited, having no way of lighting a fire until the rain halted, the bush dried out a little, and they could search for dry bark and tinderwood. Even if the fire stayed alight during the rain-storm they had to walk from their windbreak or brushwood shelter every few hours to find firewood. There was no thought of hunting or fishing or digging for yams. They preferred the camp—fire or no fire—to the search for food in wind and rain. Faced with the alternatives of being cold or hungry they preferred to be hungry.

On cold, stormy days an inertia, a numbed helplessness, enclosed an aboriginal camp. William Buckley, during his thirty years with the aboriginals of western Victoria, was often deprived of fire on cold days. Then, he recalled, the people 'suffer greatly from hunger and cold'. A Norwegian anthropologist in the mountains of coastal Queensland in the 1880s observed the same willingness to be hungry rather than be cold and drenched. An alert pioneer observed it in the Riverina. And an explorer noticed that aboriginals near the coast of Western Australia preferred to sit, without food, for two successive days by the fire in their humpy rather than journey out into the cold and rain. In summer a short heat-wave fostered the same inertia. We are so accustomed to stressing the material merits of the sedentary life that we can easily overlook the fact that the aboriginals often suffered when they were anchored to the one spot.

In coping with cold the fire was their main support, as it was in most activities. The primitive humpies, windbreaks and brushwood shelters were more useful in keeping in the heat and smoke of the fire than in keeping out steady rain; oddly, the most elaborate Australian houses were in the tropics and were designed to keep in the smoke of fires as a deterrent to mosquitoes. In the cold of South Australia, and especially in Tasmania, the fat of animals and the oil and grease of seals and fish were smeared on some bodies to keep out the cold. In the south the skins of kangaroos and possums were sometimes worn as cloaks in cold weather though they were more often shoulder capes, worn by women as cradles for their babies. In Victoria the sewing of skins into rugs or cloaks was perhaps the most skilled of all the crafts. One rug contained eighty-one possum skins and resembled a one-man tent. It must have been so heavy when wet that it weighed down the wearer, suggesting that perhaps it had been made to meet the specifications of one of the first white settlers. But in most parts of the continent—even when the ground was whitened with frost or sand was lifted by the freezing wind—the only cloak or rug at night was a tiny elongated fire.

IV

The aboriginals generally had a higher standard of living than the European invaders realized. At the same time they did not exploit those foods to the full; every society has its restraints. The astonishing knowledge of plants, animals, birds and fish could not always be exploited because of institutional and religious restraints; and the abundance of food was often wasted because of the limitations of nomadic life.

Aboriginals could eat only a fraction of the foods available during the prolific time of the year, and usually had no way of conserving any of the surplus yams and greens, nuts and berries. A few annual gluts of food were not altogether wasted. The migrations of the nutritious Bogong moth to the Snowy Mountains and the oozing of palatable gum from acacia trees in Western Australian swamps provided so much food in such a small area that for a few weeks hundreds of aboriginals could gather to eat, gossip, barter and fight. The ripening of a kind of wild raspberry on the sandhills of the Glenelg River (V.) provided feasts which—like the Bunya Bunya pine—drew large annual gatherings. For people who lacked the herds and gardens which normally facilitate the feeding of large assemblies these seasonal gluts were vital.

Normally no attempt was made to preserve and hoard the surplus food of a lavish season. Here and there, however, was practised the kind of housekeeping which we associate with sophisticated economic life. In the Cape York Peninsula round yams and the tubers of water-lilies were occasionally stored at the height of the vegetable harvest. Far to the west, near the East Alligator River, yams were occasionally dug and placed in 'great stacks' in readiness for the winter when food was less plentiful. These yams remained poisonous until treated by hot ashes and hot sun, and perhaps the poison guarded them from attacks by rats and other predators.

In scattered places on the continent a few fruits ranging

194

from wild peaches to wild plums were hoarded at the height of the season and desiccated. Nonda plums, picked by the Wik Monkan on the eastern shores of the Gulf of Carpentaria, were stored in holes sunk deep into dry sand. On the other side of the wide gulf another fruit was spread on the hot ground and allowed to shrivel until the fragments became as wrinkled as prunes. Greased with red ochre, dried again until they became brittle, the prunes were stored in parcels made of that universal packaging strip, the soft bark of the tea-tree. Much later, when fruit was a luxury, the parcel was unpacked, the dried fruit was prepared by steady pummelling with a stone held in the hand and, after being soaked in water, the pulped fruit was eaten. The dried-fruits industry in the continent was probably ancient and certainly widespread. In the western desert in recent times at least three fruits were preserved, and one method was to pound them into a reddish-brown paste which could then be shaped neatly into a loaf almost as big as a basketball. Dried hard by the sun, the ball could be stored in a hollow or cleft of a tree.

A few seeds and nuts were conserved by some aboriginal tribes. Sometimes seeds of the Bunya Bunya pine were said to be buried, and eaten later. In parts of northern Australia the sliced nuts of the Cycad palm were wrapped in paper-bark and the packages were placed in a grass-lined trench which could be as long as twenty feet. The trench was then filled with earth. Those trenches were probably the largest storehouses so far recorded in aboriginal Australia.

Near the border of Queensland and South Australia it is recorded that the seeds of portulac—which tasted like linseed meal—were hoarded. A granary containing perhaps 100 pounds of the seeds was once discovered by explorers near Lake Lipson. The larder was cleverly concealed and was preserved by an inner wrapping of grass and an outer wrapping of an oblong of clay. As edible seeds were a vital part of the diet in the dry centre, and as annual rains were not always annual, this granary marked a significant attempt to cope with scarcity. While I have found no other instance of the storing of grain, that does not necessarily mean that the practice was unusual. Hoards of food were always hidden and so were usually invisible to European explorers. Locked away in manuscripts and old diaries is probably more evidence about the practice of conserving food in aboriginal Australia than has yet been gathered.

Aboriginals appear to have had no knowledge of how to preserve foods by smoking. As far as is known they did not know how to preserve meat and fish with salt: sun-dried salt lay on the shores or the dry beds of many inland lakes but the salt does not appear to have been gathered and used. In contrast almost within sight of the tip of North Queensland, the Torres Strait islanders were able to smoke fish and to preserve meat; they sliced up turtles, boiled the slices in a melon shell, and then stuck them on skewers and allowed them to dry in the hot sun. The preserved meat was carried in the canoes embarking on long voyages and could last up to several weeks. This method of curing the meat of green turtles was not practised on the Australian mainland where the technique of boiling had not been adopted.

A startling discovery in a sand dune near the River Murray suggests that some aboriginals had their own method of preserving fresh shellfish. Near Lake Victoria (N.S.W.) a buried heap of freshwater mussels was exposed by the wind erosion, and an examination of the mussels in 1968 revealed that they had been alive when buried, that they had been neatly stacked in a dozen or more layers, and that at least 360 edible mussels had been carefully hoarded in the one place. Would the mussels have remained fresh for long? Buried deeply in moist sand, mussels apparently can live for weeks and even months.

Water as well as food was occasionally conserved. Clay dams built by aboriginals were observed by the explorer Ernest Giles in the Great Victoria Desert (S.A.). The embankment of one dam in the sandhill country was five feet high and sixty feet long. A curved embankment about six times as long has been recorded on the dry Bulloo River, east of Tibooburra (N.S.W.); and if that dam—as the evidence hints—was built by aboriginals the embankment would have required the movement of about 150 cubic yards of clay and stones. That project would have been, therefore, one of the boldest carried out by aboriginals.

It seems likely that hoarding was not widely practised by Australian aboriginals. The incentive to accumulate a hoard of seeds, grain or shellfish was probably strongest in the first good year after a drought or famine; then the memory of recent privation was sharp. Such a store of nuts or yams would accordingly have represented no great amount of labour because it would have been undertaken in a time of overflowing abundance. While the incentive to set aside plentiful and preservable foods must have been strengthened by recent hunger, it was diminished by a knowledge that the hoard might be discovered and robbed in the following weeks. In a land of many burrowing animals the ground was not always a safe place of storage.

The hoarding of food is most successful when the people settle in one place and can therefore protect their hoard from human or animal intruders. As the aboriginals were wanderers, the rewards for conserving and hoarding food were smaller. Likewise because they could not hoard effectively, they had no alternative but to wander systematically to obtain their food.

V

If one region of Australia had a glut of food and a region across the ranges was suffering from drought, there was no sure way of sharing the surplus. Even peoples who shared adjacent territories could not always co-operate if a scarcity of food in one territory called for co-operation. Though many of the adults in adjacent territories were related to one another, only certain people had—through kinship—

the privilege of hunting outside their own territory when they so desired; a son, for instance, was often permitted to hunt in the territory from which his mother had come at the time of her marriage.

The intimate knowledge of edible foods and how to find them was also affected by human idiosyncracies and fads. In some districts everyone preferred to go hungry rather than to eat certain meats or plants; and their shunning of those foods was dictated by customs which had the force of religious edict.

If it were possible to list all the prohibitions imposed on the eating of specific foods in Australia two or three centuries ago, the printed list would probably have made a large statute book. Many societies overseas imposed a taboo on certain foods—the word *taboo* comes from Tonga—but the multitude of distinct societies within Australia and Tasmania multiplied the number of taboos and the kinds of people on whom they were imposed. One fish or marsupial might be the subject of total prohibition as a food in one part of Australia and eaten freely by everyone in another district. Pregnant women might be prohibited—on pain of death or punishment by supernatural forces—from eating fish, and the father as well as mother might be affected by the taboo; but only a few miles away a pregnant woman in another aboriginal group might eat fish freely. In one group certain prized foods—perhaps the flesh of the emu— might be reserved primarily for the old men but in other groups no such privilege belonged to the old. On the contrary the young were often privileged; and some groups accepted taboos on the food which children could give their parents but none on foods received by children from their father and mother. In many groups in Australia a taboo on the eating or giving of certain foods was often linked with pregnancy, menstruation, and circumcision. Indeed a recent study by a Londoner in the land of the Wik Monkan, that green hunting ground of anthropologists, suggests that certain foods were sex symbols and therefore taboo. For instance geese eggs were like a man's testicles and so were not eaten by certain people or on certain occasions. A taboo was often linked tightly to a fertility rite, to the need to woo those spirits who alone could ensure an abundance of food.

Some taboos may have originated partly as a preventive to illness. Two fascinating prohibitions—and they embraced every woman, man and child—were imposed on the eating of scale fish in north-west Tasmania and on the eating of freshwater mussels in much of the south-west corner of Western Australia. It is likely that in a past time mussels were contaminated in rivers or pools of Western Australia and that people who ate them were violently sick and that many died from food poisoning. Indeed a local tradition hinted strongly at such a happening. Long ago aboriginals had eaten freshwater mussels and had died; and their death, said the tradition, had been willed by the sorcerers to whom that species of shellfish belonged.

In contrast, the Tasmanian taboo on fish other than shellfish cannot be explained in terms of present medical knowledge. For a time I had wondered whether, thousands of years ago, the barracouta or other species of boned fish in Tasmanian waters had briefly been carriers of a contagious disease, which led to the death of aboriginals and promptly inspired a prohibition on the eating of all boned fish. This hypothesis, put to a marine biologist, was quickly filleted. He explained that in relatively cold seas the fish were unlikely to carry the kind of disease which could be transmitted to those who ate the fish. One plausible way of explaining, medically, a ban on the eating of boned fish is to argue that in a far-away summer a group of aboriginals had caught a shoal of fish, had neglected to eat them for thirty-six hours, and had then been fatally poisoned by a meal of now-putrid flesh. While food-poisoning could explain a temporary ban on the eating of one species of fish it could not easily explain a ban, century after century, on the eating of all boned fish. For a taboo to reign so long, a powerful cultural reason, a support-ing myth, is needed.

At present archaeological evidence—not yet conclusive—suggests that the north-west Tasmanians ceased to eat scale fish about 3,500 years ago. One can only marvel at the tenacity of a taboo which for thousands of years deprived a large population—most of whom lived near the sea—of one of the most abundant and nutritious foods. One conclusion is clear. In several coastal regions of Tasmania the aboriginals must have had relative abundance in order to survive with-out using a food of such importance.

While in some societies a taboo warned everyone against eating a special food, another form of taboo affected a minority group—young men or pregnant women—and allowed everyone else to eat it freely. This partial taboo in effect served to redistribute, or regulate the apportioning of, duck eggs or wallabies' viscera or other foods within a camp. Such taboos could indirectly have fulfilled an economic function similar to the price mechanism of capitalist societies. Just as scarce foods today are usually sold at high prices, thus restricting the demand for them, so the demand for certain scarce foods in an aboriginal society was restricted by a taboo. Whereas our economic rituals prevent us from eating caviar or crayfish if we lack sufficient money—money being the right to acquire these foods—aboriginal societies based the right to eat certain foods, not on money and not even on the hunters' right to what they had slain, but more on sexual and spiritual rituals.*

---

* It would be a mistake to see them as simply ways in which men exploited women. Their effects were often complicated. Thus a woman who for some reason was temporarily unable to eat kangaroo or wallaby could be more inclined to eat a larger daily share of the vegetables she gathered and of the lizards, bandicoots and smaller women-snared game which she caught. In consequence she might bring home to the camp fire less food than normal. Her husband might be deprived more by a scarcity of yams than his wife suffered through a scarcity of meat.

The taboo on foodstuffs probably did not originate as rationing devices though that was one of their effects. If they had been designed to limit the consumption of scarce foods, or to ensure that favoured people monopolized those foods, they would have been applied primarily to scarce foods. And yet, while scarce foods were often taboo to the young—for instance turtles—plentiful foods could also be the subject of taboos.

While aboriginals had wide knowledge about plant and animal foods, the complicated variety of taboos numbed the usefulness of parts of that knowledge. Of the specific effects of taboos, however, one can only speculate. Whenever they lasted only a few weeks, they probably did no damage. If they affected trifling items of diet—items for which substitutes were available—they did no harm. If they severely curtailed the right to eat certain totem animals then their effects—as the famous explorer George Grey observed in Western Australia—sometimes resembled those of the contemporary English 'game laws': they protected animals which otherwise might be in danger of extinction through over-hunting. On the other hand several taboos might have harmed the health of pregnant women and unborn children. To deprive women at Groote Eylandt of fish during their pregnancy was possibly to deprive them of an irreplaceable source of protein. The birth rate and infant mortality in some aboriginal societies could have been strongly affected by these food taboos on pregnant women. If so, the taboo would have to be classed as one of those variables which curbed the growth of population and thereby helped to explain the way in which, in the last ten thousand years, the human history of Australia diverged sharply from that of Asia and Europe and the Americas.

VI

We usually condemn nomads as reckless or improvident, perhaps because in our society the nomads traditionally are poor people: the swagmen, gypsies, fossickers, hawkers, seasonal workers, surfies, drop-outs and indeed, in recent times, uprooted aboriginals. But the traditional aboriginal societies would have been reckless if they had rejected the opportunity to be nomads. To live in the one place is still a measure of worth with us, perhaps because the settled person accumulates property which in our eyes is a sign of material success. To nomadic aboriginals, however, possessions were a burden; they were hobbles. That aboriginals moved frequently to new sites was a sign of their knowledge and skill. In moving camp and winning a living from a variety of botanical environments they faced reality rather than evaded it. In moving around they were not creatures of whim but of purpose; their wanderings were systematic, not aimless. Our present picture of a hunting society is dominated by the idea that it was improvident and deficient in foresight; but in fact nomadic societies in Australia were characterised by an intimate sense of the future and by seasonal planning that was almost rigid. Their people were nomadic because they understood the future, because season after season they could predict the intimate relationship between climate, the maturing of plant foods, the breeding and migrating habits of birds and reptiles and insects and marsupials.

Their knowledge of the land and all which it grew was supplemented by a spiritual belief that the earth would not continue to be productive unless they obeyed its rules and its deities. One aim of their religious ceremonies and many of their taboos was to maintain the fertility of the land and its creatures. Individuals and groups believed that they had a religious relationship with particular species—perhaps a grey kangaroo or certain birds or plants—and that through religious ceremonies those species could be increased or multiplied. The land itself was their chapel, and their shrines were hills and creeks and their religious relics were animals, plants and birds. Thus the migrations of aboriginals, though spurred by economic need, were also pilgrimages.

CHAPTER TWELVE

Trade Routes and Rituals

Trade between distant people is often seen as a mark of a more advanced economic life. If this insight is valid, many groups of aboriginals must have been far from backward because their raw materials and manufactures were traded to people hundreds of miles away. It is probable that every tribe in Australia traded with its neighbours, and a few commodities were involved in such a sequence of transactions that they crossed from the tropical coast almost to the Southern Ocean.

Pearl shell travelled further perhaps than any other item. In Western Australia an explorer saw an aboriginal wearing, as a sporran, pearly oyster-shell which had travelled at least 500 miles from its point of origin. Some of the pearl shells were as wide as a bread-and-butter plate, and their silvery-white surface was engraved with a simple pattern. Many shells were neatly perforated at the top so that they could be worn as a pendant. They could be seen, suspended from the neck of aboriginals, near the Great Australian Bight, which was about one thousand miles overland from their home seabed. Similarly, Kimberley pearl-shells were found as far away as the Mallee scrub lying between Adelaide and the Victorian border. Baler shell from tropical beaches near Cape York were picked up far to the west of Alice Springs and as far away as Leonora (W.A.). Many hands must have fondled those ocean shells in the course of their long journey to the interior. Their journey consisted of many transactions between neighbouring groups, most of which did not even know of the existence of an ocean. If sea shells could travel so far into the interior, it is likely that spears or ochres from the interior were traded in the opposite direction, eventually reaching the hands of people who did not even know that the world held sweeping plains and deserts.

In eastern Australia the axe-stone also moved over a wide area. In a quarry on the smooth slopes of Mount William, about forty miles north of Melbourne, stone axes were intermittently mined and shaped by Billi-Billeri at the time when the first Europeans arrived with their sheep. The stone was volcanic, ranging in colour from black to lightish green, and perhaps was prized in its own hinterland even more than high grade axe-steel was to be prized there a century later. For generations, stone axes from that quarry cut wooden canoes for the rivers flowing south to the Murray, and the axes reached aboriginals as far away as Swan Hill, nearly 200 miles to the north.

A quarry which provided stone fit for stronger, sharper axes was likely to supply trade routes stretching in every direction. As many quarries were worked for generations, yielding thousands of tons of rock, they eventually scarred a considerable expanse of ground. At Melton Mowbray in southern Tasmania the chips and debris of a chert quarry covered about one acre. At Moore Creek, near Tamworth in New South Wales, an outcrop of greywacke running along the crest of a saddle-back ridge was mined prolifically; the axe-stone was quarried by aboriginals for a length of three hundred feet and to a maximum width of twelve feet. On countless still days the noise of the chipping, the patient chipping, must have carried across the slopes.

As the written records were thin in tracing the trade in stone axes from the Tamworth district, other ways of re-constructing the extent of the trade were needed. Petro-logical analysis was one promising technique. It has been applied as long ago as 1923 to reveal that the so-called bluestone used in building Stonehenge in southern England had been carried all the way from Pembrokshire in Wales. With this technique in mind an enterprising archaeologist, Isabel McBryde, examined a total of 517 edge-ground axes which had been found scattered over a large part of New South Wales. She mapped the places where each stone axe had originally been collected—old aboriginal camping grounds, trade routes, or simply places where an aboriginal had lost or broken his axe or had bartered it away to a European pioneer. In the laboratory a thin sliver of stone was sawn from each available axe. Each specimen of stone was then ground down to a transparent thinness and examined under the microscope of the geologist, R. A. Binns. Once the minute characteristics of the stone had been identified, the search for its place of origin could be concentrated on those regions or even specific hills or valleys which were known to contain that type of stone. In those areas which had been mapped with intensity the exact quarry which produced some axes could even be located. Binns and McBryde were able to name one quarry which had originally produced the stone for sixty-five of the axes that were found in scattered parts of New South Wales.

This kind of archaeological jigsaw—the exact matching of axe and quarry—can be solved only when every likely source of stone has been discovered and described. In a sparsely-peopled territory the mapping is slow and the geological knowledge is not easily gathered. Nonetheless Binns and McBryde were able to gauge the extent of territory or market which was supplied with stone axes quarried from the long ridge of Moore Creek or from similar rock formations to the north of Tamworth. They found that axes had gone overland through a chain of tribal territories to Cobar, Bourke, Wilcannia, and other points on the plains as remote as 500 miles from the home quarries. The longest of these routes, transposed on to a map of western Europe, was almost equal to a walk overland from the English Channel to the Mediterranean.

II

Stone was probably the heaviest item in overland commerce in Australia. But a lot of the stone was carried in small neat packages. Thus each spearhead from Blue Mud Bay in Arnhem Land was wrapped in bark and about a dozen spearheads was then arranged in a parcel of melaleuca bark, which was as soft as suede to the touch but durable as a wrapping. The bark parcel was then tied with native string. Each parcel was light, perhaps weighing no more than three pounds. In some parts of Australia the rough-shaped stone intended for axes varied in weight but could be as heavy as fourteen pounds. Such stone was tough and needed no packaging. The heaviest stones to be carried a long way were the slabs used as millstones on the inland plains where edible seeds were an essential part of diet but accessible stones for grinding were scarce. The millstones were irregular in shape but their surface was flat. In north-west Queensland some of the sandstone slabs were carried a distance of at least 200 miles to many tribes, and perhaps 300 miles in order to reach the plains along the Middle Diamantina where suitable stone for grinding seeds was scarce. The millstones and the smaller hand-held grinding stones moved in stages as part of a chain of transactions. The burden of carrying them was shared by a slow relay of carriers. To the outback physician who in the 1890s pieced together the pattern of this dying traffic, the carrying of stones across the hot dry country was an impressive feat. 'It seems almost incredible that some of these large slabs should be carried such immense distances: but then, the poor women of course are the beasts of burden.' In some tribes on the plains the young men were the carriers and made long trips with the specific purpose of procuring millstones which they carried home, balanced on their heads like a flat hat.

Much of the ancient Australian trade was in raw materials —in stone, the coloured ochres and clays, shells, fibres and furs, and special timbers used for the making of weapons. The exchange of raw materials was the vital part of commerce, because it provided regions with raw materials which they lacked. Most of the exchanges, however, seem to have been in manufactured goods.

Manufacturing and handcrafts were often the work of specialists, and each locality tended to make certain objects with a skill or flair which was admired in other localities. The specialization was the basis of the trade. Thus in the north-west of Australia a tribe near Cape Leveque often sent softwood spears and the non-returning kind of boomerangs to the peoples in the south, receiving in return spears of hard wood as well as yellow ochre, pipe clay and other items. In central Australia groups living in the west of Alice Springs were recognized for their skill in making the wooden bowls or *pitchi* used as receptacles for liquids. The finest spears were made near Alice Springs, the finest boomerangs to the east and north-east, the best spear-throwers in the south-west, and the best shields—cut from the light softwood of Sturt's bean tree—were made in the north. The scarcity or abundance of particular timbers may help to explain why one region specialized in spears and another in pitchis. Often, however, there was no such correlation. Much of the specialization had existed for generations, and its origin was even the theme of tribal myths.

In foodstuffs the trade between tribes was not large. No food appears amongst the articles exchanged in the two parts of the Northern Territory—the Daly River and eastern Arnhem Land—in which trade was studied closely by anthropologists. Between some of the islands of Torres Strait, however, yams and other vegetables were traded. There the large canoes provided that cheap transport lacking in every over-

207

land route of the mainland. As the root vegetables were not as perishable as meat and fish, nor fragile like eggs and soft fruits, they formed a suitable commodity for trade in those few places linked by big canoes. Above all several islands had gardens and, at times, surpluses of vegetables.

Any trade in meat or fish or perishables required quick communications—a rarity in Australia—or a very cold climate. In the cooler parts of Victoria there is evidence that fish and meat were sometimes traded. In the twilight of tribal life, meetings for the exchange of food were periodically arranged near the lakes and timbered hills to the southwest of Port Phillip Bay. Big Buckley, while living with aboriginals on the banks of Lake Modewarre near Geelong, saw a messenger arrive to negotiate one of these meetings. The messenger, on behalf of his tribe, offered to exchange vegetables in return for the large freshwater eels on which Buckley's tribe was feasting. The messenger's arms were striped, and the stripes apparently signified the number of days required for the journey to the bartering place on the upper reaches of the Barwon River.* The invitation was accepted. Eventually the eel-carriers set out, carrying their fish in a wrapping of kangaroo skins. At the chosen site near the river they ceremoniously delivered the eels on long sheets of bark. The other tribe likewise placed their vegetable roots on bark sheets, which two men carried on their head. Some time later, by arrangement, the two tribes met again at a lake near Colac where roots were exchanged for kangaroo meat. Such meetings were prolonged—often for days after the exchange was over—by the staging of corroborees, by gossip,

---

* Buckley recalled that the messengers' stripes signified a journey of fourteen days. It is impossible to see how fourteen days could be spent in a short journey of perhaps fifty miles. It is impossible even to imagine the stench of eels, which by then would have been at least a fortnight old. As Buckley spoke his recollections of this event to a journalist the detail could have been blurred in the transposing. The 'fourteen days' probably referred to the time when the exchange of foodstuffs was to take place.

and by the parading of 'their very elegant, amiable, marriage-
able daughters.'

These fascinating snatches from the memoirs of the wild
white man veil much which we would like to know. Nonetheless they depict a commerce which was very different to
that recorded in northern Australia where implements and
ornaments rather than food dominated the deals. Moreover,
there is a hint, in the trading of the yams and eels, that this
was indirectly a way of feeding an unusually large population
for a few days on a common site. Here in effect was the
biblical pooling of the loaves and fishes.

III

The Australian trade, about which most is known, linked
coastal and inland areas in Arnhem Land. Christened the
'Ceremonial Exchange Cycle', it was studied by the anthropologist Donald Thomson not long before flint spearheads
were supplanted by transistor radios as prized objects.
Thomson had been making a long patrol on foot across
Arnhem Land in 1935 in order to investigate tribal fighting
which perturbed the government in remote Canberra. Far
inland on the wall of a rock shelter, Thomson was surprised
to see a drawing of an iron axe of the type imported to the
coast by Indonesian fishermen in the nineteenth century. At
first he wondered whether iron axes had travelled inland
simply as the result of irregular barter. Later he decided
that another explanation was needed for the kind of exchanges which were busily made in that part of Arnhem
Land.

He found that each area specialized in producing certain
goods and in receiving others. Thus a man on the Lower
Glyde River, near the Arafura Sea, would receive a different
range of goods from each neighbouring region. From the
coastal north-east he received a few prized goods of foreign
manufacture—calico, blankets, tobacco, tomahawks, glass

and knives: many of them he later traded away. From the east he received, amongst other items, black pounding stones which had been quarried in islands near the north-eastern tip of Arnhem Land. From the south-east he received items of possum fur, dilly bags and, above all, the spearheads shaped from stone which was mined in a famous quarry near Blue Mud Bay. Most boomerangs which arrived—for the people of the Glyde River did not make boomerangs or even hunt with them—originated from the south-west, along with hooked spears, ceremonial belts made of human hair, and pieces of wire and iron from cattle stations. And from a fifth direction, from the north-west, came such goods as forehead fillets and heavy fighting clubs.

'Each individual in Arnhem Land', wrote Donald Thomson, 'is the centre of a great ceremonial exchange cycle'. So long as he lived he was under a social obligation to send gifts to partners in remote areas. Generally the individual did not long retain most of the gifts given to him. After a time he sent a gift in a different direction to that by which it had come to him, but always forwarding it to a relative or friend with whom he was firmly linked in the cycle of gifts. Between giver and receiver was a solemn obligation: 'All time, till die, we two people'. Under the power of this social obligation he had to keep on providing gifts for his distant kinsmen: and by giving he gained self esteem just as by slowness in repaying gifts he earned disapproval, perhaps social ostracism, or even illness. He could even die through the combination of his own guilt and the psychological power of sorcery used against him by a disillusioned trading partner.

On the Daly River, about 400 miles to the west, a similar commerce between tribes and within tribes had been observed even earlier by another gifted anthropologist, W. E. H. Stanner. The essence of the transactions, he said, was in the giving. Both males and females took part in the trade and the partners in the transactions were always friends and some-times relatives. Journeys were not made specifically to exchange goods or repay gifts but the goods changed hands when tribes from the Daly River came together for initiations or communal gatherings during the dry season when travel was unimpeded. In the great assemblies in the open air the goods appeared—the red and yellow ochres, the kaolin, the spears, boomerangs, stone axes and stone knives, dilly bags, the beeswax and resin which served as adhesives, the hair belts, the pubic coverings of pearl-shell and other decorative objects. By the time Stanner saw the exchanges between members of the Mulluk Mulluk and the Madngella, those being two of the scores of tribes near the Daly River, items of European manufacture or design had intruded. Blankets, coloured wool, small tools of iron and steel, and beads and dresses changed hands and were given a valuation which often made the locally-made spear or dilly bag seem a third-rate gift. Even the appearance of these exotic goods, however, could not save the traffic in *merbok* fading as the ties of tribal life fell apart and the traditional weapons and ornaments were depreciated.

There are several puzzles about the exchange of goods in northern Australia. Firstly, was it a traditional trade or was it recently spurred by the Indonesian fishermen who, about two centuries ago, began to come regularly to the coast with gifts of glass and iron? Thomson argued—and his argument can neither be refuted nor reaffirmed—that it was a traditional practice, quickened by the recent intrusion of glamorous goods from the world outside. Secondly, what was the motivation behind the merry-go-round of giving and taking? On this point Thomson sometimes wavered but in most passages of his argument he insisted that the exchange of goods was in aim more social than economic, of more importance as a ceremonial ritual than as a type of trade, and usually more useful in linking remote groups than in apportioning scarce commodities. In that web of relationships, he said, it was more praiseworthy to give than to receive. Stanner agreed, suggesting that to aboriginals the

211

act of giving was more important than the object which was given. So the exchange of goods at the tropical end of the Northern Territory, it seems, was more like a family Christmas tree than a street stall.

Such a sharp distinction between the social and the economic, between ceremonial exchange and economic exchange, is perhaps invalid. The contrast belongs very much to the mid-twentieth century, when specialism was acute and when economists and others believed that the boundaries of economics could clearly be marked with white paint, enabling one activity to be labelled economic and another social. Every exchange of goods is partly social and partly economic. Economics pervade social relationships just as social links pervade economics.

Reading between the lines of the fascinating evidence which Donald Thomson set out in his small red book we begin to see that it was much closer to barter and trade than he realized. The traded articles tended to move from places of plenty to places of scarcity where they had strong utilitarian value. While Thomson stressed that it was more blessed to give than to possess, most of the precious iron axes which had come from Indonesia remained with the people of the coast and did not reach the inland people who craved for them. Both Stanner and Thomson argued that the ceremonial, ritual nature of the exchange could be shown by the way in which the traditional traffic in certain articles continued even when the economic need for them had passed. More conspicuous, however, was the way in which the traditional traffic was re-routed or disrupted by the rise of a strong demand for such utilitarian commodities as pieces of imported glass and iron. While the prestige was said to come more through giving, many aboriginals who received goods did not send something in return. 'Defections', noted Dr Stanner of the Daly River, 'were not uncommon'.

When aboriginal commerce is dissected it no longer appears so different from modern commerce. Dr Stanner for instance argued that the exchanges on the Daly River were not essentially utilitarian because so often they involved gifts 'which can easily be duplicated by the craftsmen any tribe possesses'. If, however, that same argument were applied to the world in the 1970s, large segments of international trade in the hands of big corporations or profit-seeking merchants should also be classified as ceremonial and social rather than economic. A great volume of trade today is in commodities which any craftsman can duplicate, but the buyers have been persuaded that in some way the item is different: in subtlety of design, in the presence of a supposedly-secret ingredient, or simply because it was made in a workshop or a land which has long had a reputation for excellence. Paris perfume, Scotch whisky, Czechoslovakian glass, Manchester textiles, Swedish cars and scores of hand-made or machine-made products have owed at one time or other a considerable part of their commercial success as exports to social as much as economic considerations. Studies of the tribal trade in northern Australia were valuable but they suffered perhaps because the anthropologists did not realize that the social component which they saw admiringly in primitive exchange was also present in the cities from which they came. In that mistake they were in good company, because most of the influential economic theorists of the 1930s asserted that trade and other 'economic' activities could be understood solely in terms of narrow economic needs.

The exchange of goods in several near-coastal regions on the Northern Territory was not only trade but a vital expression of social solidarity. We can accept the importance of the trading side without in any way minimizing the social contact. The economic links and social obligations were intertwined and it is unnecessary to follow the anthropologists who thought they could stress the social role of the cycle of exchange only by playing down the economic role. The need to trade and to honour relatives could be satisfied simultaneously. Indeed it is difficult to see how else trade could have been carried on in a nomadic society where groups might meet only once a year and therefore had to delay the completion of a transaction exchanging goods. An unwritten contract was necessary for commerce to take place. Credit or trust was necessary when the gift of, say, a spear, was not likely to be repaid with a lump of red ochre until at least a year had elapsed or, if drought intervened, two or three years. The merits of trading mainly with people who are related by marriage or by totemic bonds—in short, with those who seemed most creditworthy—must have been as obvious to a naked man from Blue Mud Bay as to an immaculate man from Wall Street. Seen in this context trade was both a way of distributing useful goods and raw materials and a way of honouring distant relatives by conferring on them goods which were economically useful and productive of prestige to giver and receiver.

The social and economic were lock and key. Without the social bonds the trade would have been difficult to carry out, and the incentive to trade would have been smaller. Without the economic relationships, the social bonds could not have been expressed so satisfactorily nor maintained so firmly.

IV

Not every tribe engaged in trade. Tasmanians, for example, appear to have had little trade. Though the boundaries between tribes appear to have been defined, the tribes sometimes moved far outside their own territory to gather eggs or ochre. Freedom of movement lessened the need for trade. If a group were freely permitted to enter alien territory it could gather the raw materials and carry them home, thus removing the need to acquire those items through formal exchange. Of course the tribe might regularly have had to give presents in order to win permission for such journeys. If this were so, the gifts could perhaps be interpreted as

214

part-payment for a trading concession—namely the right to take away raw materials.

In many regions of Australia the economic effects of trade must have been strong. Through trade, some techniques and skills were probably diffused at times, though trade does not necessarily have to be invoked to explain the spread of manufacturing skills. Through trade, many specialized weapons were exported to areas where they enabled animals to be hunted with more success or the expending of less energy. Trade supplied distant tribes with many of the ornaments and cosmetics which gave pleasure and enriched tribal life. But the main economic effect of the exchange of goods was to raise the standard of living in some areas which lacked essential raw materials. The traffic in axe stone and the stone for spearheads was vital to some regions which relied heavily on hunting; without those imports the level of population which the area could support might have been lower. Perhaps more vital was the long-distance traffic in grinding stones to the hot inland plains where seeds provided one quarter to one half of the food in many months of the year. Those plains were mostly covered with soil and sand and lacked accessible stone for grinding, and yet their way of life depended heavily on the grinding of hard seeds into flour. It may not have been previously observed that the importing of grinding stones to the near-desert plains was probably essential for the continued populating of a vast part of central Australia.

Understandably there were limits to the expansion of commerce. Property was for the most part a burden, and so it was foolish to indulge in the accumulation of possessions. Wanderers, moreover, usually moved to the site of the foods and raw materials which they needed, thus lowering the need for trade. Furthermore, trade could progress beyond a certain stage only if transport became cheap; but when that stage was reached with the invention of the wheel, the domesticating of bullocks and horses into beasts of burden, and the building of large watercraft, the nomadic life itself was obviously endangered. For, indisputably, a nomad existence was logical only so long as there was no cheap way of carrying food and raw materials to fixed settlements.

CHAPTER THIRTEEN

The Prosperous Nomads

Aboriginals in most parts of Australia appear to have had an impressive standard of living at the time of the European invasion. But the window through which we see them is so smoky or misted that only with difficulty can we recognize the kind of abundance in which they lived.

We often judge the material success of ancient empires by their surviving monuments and the remains of their temples and city walls, and by that test the aboriginals failed. But elegant, long-standing buildings were essentially a sign of a sedentary society, and often those buildings reflected the extreme contrast between the wealth of the rulers and the poverty of their subjects; and indeed some stately palaces in ancient societies were built only by sacrificing the standard of living of ordinary subjects whose daily food even in good years was probably less in volume and variety than that of aboriginals. Similarly the aboriginals were usually naked; and to Europeans, especially in the nineteenth century, nakedness was seen as evidence of material poverty. This bias was understandable in cold lands, but clothing was an irrelevent criteria of well-being for people in a warm climate. It was also easy to overlook how often the aboriginals were extravagantly dressed. Their ceremonial dress, however, took the form of body paints, gaudy feathers from birds, and ornamental scars and coverings which provided decoration and not unwanted warmth. As the aboriginals were nomads they had few possessions, and that also lowered them in the eyes of a civilization which believed that well-being and possessions were identical. In essence the contrast between nomadic and settled peoples was so vast that neither could easily understand or assess the standard of living of the other.

The later Australians were unable to believe that the aboriginals usually found plenty of food. The disbelief was understandable. The vital role of aboriginal women as food-gatherers was not understood. Moreover aboriginals seemed to live from hand to mouth, and such a habit is associated more with the poor in a settled society. Likewise many foods favoured by aboriginals seemed unappetizing to later Australians, and so the myth arose that aboriginals had to rely on the land's second-rate foods which Europeans ignored. Aboriginals of course relied on those foods because they preferred them to many other foods which they could have caught or picked. The astonishing range of foods which grew in Australia before the coming of potatoes, cattle and wheat has been forgotten. Almost everything eaten in Australia today* belongs to species of flora and fauna introduced to the continent within the last 200 years. Accordingly the plentiful foods available to aboriginals slowly slipped from common knowledge.

While one achievement of aboriginals was their ability to survive in vast arid regions where white settlement was to fail, the fact that aboriginals survived there spread the idea that they normally had lived on the meagre crumbs of the desert. Almost everywhere their knowledge and their economic skills were not understood; abundance seemed beyond their reach.

II

Several famous episodes amplified the mistaken message that aboriginals lived on the brink of starvation. The death in

---

* Two minor exceptions are the Macadamia nut and the so-called New Zealand spinach *(Terragonia expansa).* Other exceptions are seafoods.

1861 of Burke and Wills, on the return leg of the first crossing of the continent ever made, emphasised the harshness of living conditions in central Australia. One of the lessons of their death was simple: since they had died virtually of malnutrition, how frugal and perilous must have been the living conditions of the aboriginals inhabiting that region. The impression that aboriginals there lived close to famine was deepened by the fact that Burke and Wills for weeks had tried to live off the land, eating mainly the foods which the aboriginals ate. But when the last days of Burke and Wills are examined more closely, it becomes difficult to interpret their experiences as a rough index of the standard of living of the aboriginals living in the region.

The explorers had reached Cooper's Creek, near the border of South Australia and Queensland, in May 1861. During the previous four months they had walked long distances on nearly every day and were close to exhaustion. One explorer had died and now only three remained—Burke, Wills and King. They had lost most of their pack animals and the two survivors were weak and skinny. They had a small store of flour, rice, sugar and a potential supply of dried camel meat but that food could not be expected to last long. Their digestion was not ready for the change from soft foods to the roughage of native grains; and when they began to make their own flour from native seeds and to bake flour-cakes in the ashes they were not readily able to digest the roughage and also the sand and grit accumulated during the pounding, winnowing and baking of the seeds. Arriving from the tropics with ragged clothes they shivered during the bitter nights; firewood was often scarce and the three explorers lacked the experience of the aboriginals in making tiny camp fires and nestling into their warmth. Above all, the morale of the explorers was low, and their energy was sapped by the scurvy which a deficient diet had fostered.

The three men remained near Cooper's Creek, and as their own supply of groceries dwindled they began to eat one of the many native seeds. The nardoo or clover fern was plentiful and they collected the seed spores and used the native grinding stones to mill the seeds. The daily harvesting of the seeds required more energy than they now possessed, and the leader Burke could no longer take part. On some days he remained in an aboriginal shelter and pounded the nardoo which the other two men gathered. In the end Wills also became too weak to gather the seeds, and Burke became too weak to clean and pound more than a handful of seeds. So King gathered nardoo as best he could in the cold winds, and pounded the seed and winnowed the husks when he returned to the hut. The wholemeal was rolled into cakes and baked in hot ashes, and mainly on nardoo the three men lived.

Wills kept his journal until a day or two before his death. The son of a physician he was a quietly-alert observer and he noted the effects of nardoo on his health. He had recently suffered from constipation, and at first he had trouble digesting the bread loaves baked from nardoo seeds, and when he crouched down to relieve himself he was in pain as the hard excreta or (to use the Elizabethan word he preferred) 'stools' inched towards the ground. 'I cannot understand', he wrote on 20 June 1861, 'this nardoo at all; it certainly will not agree with me in any form. We are now reduced to it alone, and we manage to get from four to five pounds per day between us. The stools it causes are enormous, and seem greatly to exceed the quantity of bread consumed.' A few days later he found the diet of nardoo more digestible though he felt weaker and his legs and arms were now mere bones. His appetite remained and he was even relishing the nardoo, and the last entry in his journal noted that 'starvation on nardoo is by no means very unpleasant, but for the weakness one feels, and the utter inability to move oneself.'

It is reasonable to infer that the volume and variety of food which Burke and Wills ate during their last two months at Cooper's Creek was less than that eaten by aboriginals living in the vicinity. Undoubtedly they were not as skilled as aboriginals in harvesting and grinding nardoo. They lacked the nimbleness, the manual dexterity of the aboriginal women who normally gathered and pounded the nardoo seeds. Wills regretted in his journal that the explorers' attempts to harvest the dark seeds were 'a slower and more troublesome process than could be desired.' In contrast, when they made contact with the aboriginals, they often received presents of nardoo cakes and nardoo flour in such amounts as to suggest that the aboriginals had an abundant supply.

Nor did the aboriginals in that area depend solely on nardoo. They must have also eaten roots, greens and many other plants of which the marooned Europeans had scant knowledge. One day Wills was unable to find nardoo seeds but found plenty of large beans which the aboriginals called 'padlu'. Wills boiled them and shelled them and said that they tasted like a kind of French chestnut. Perhaps the beans had adverse effects for they are not mentioned again in Wills' journal. Apart from a little herbal tea, brewed from the leafy portulac plant as a preventive against scurvy, the explorers seem to have consumed no other plant foods. They apparently believed, almost to the very end, that they would survive on nardoo cakes until search parties found them.

In gathering meat the Europeans were even less successful. They had revolvers but shot only a few crows. They snared no birds, caught no reptiles, and the only rats they tasted were gifts from kind aboriginals; a fat rat baked in its skin tasted delicious, wrote Wills. Only once in their last two months did they record a small meal of freshwater mussels; perhaps they were not skilled in scrabbling mussels from the muddy shallows of the waterholes of Cooper's Creek. Although their expedition had left Melbourne with four dozen fishing lines and scores of fish hooks in its mountain of baggage, the hooks were said to be too large for the species of fish which swam in the waterholes. Wills, according to his journal, caught only two fish along the creek and both virtually fell into his waiting frying pan. Once at the duck-holes he had heard crows fighting over a prize and he was delighted to find, near the water's edge, a fresh fish from which meat had been torn by the crows. He took the fish and that night it augmented what he called 'my otherwise scanty supper of nardoo porridge.' On the following Sunday he had more luck, and wandering past a waterhole he saw a large fish choking in its attempt to swallow a smaller fish. He pulled them ashore, lit a fire, and quickly cooked and ate them. Ironically, when the weak-legged Europeans occasionally made contact with the wandering aboriginals they observed beside their camp-fires the piles of fresh fish which had been caught in their nets.

If Burke and Wills and King, in their last weeks, had contrived to attach themselves to one of the small groups which migrated up and down the creek, the three would have survived; the aboriginals in their few encounters were generous in giving them nardoo and fishes. But for the last three weeks in which the three Europeans were together they met no aboriginals. King, finally left alone, was more fortunate. He fell in with aboriginals and was fed fish and gruel until the arrival of a relief expedition two months later.

Whenever the last days of Burke and Wills were recalled —and in a land with no military heroes the dead explorers were dressed and buried as heroes—there appeared a mental picture of a wilderness where only a miracle enabled men to survive. Certainly by the standards of vegetation in Europe or coastal Australia, the arid interior was close to a wilderness. And yet here, where European men were close to starvation, the aboriginals lived in relative abundance. The aboriginals, moreover, probably obtained their food with less effort than was spent in 1861 by the average Londoner or Berliner.

III

Wanderers who owned no gardens, orchards, flocks, herds and agricultural machines could obviously produce only a fraction of the food which Australia produces today. Australia has perhaps fifty times as many people now as in the last phase of the nomadic era, and produces perhaps 100 times as much food as the aboriginals produced in a normal year. On the other hand the aboriginals' small output of food was probably sufficient. Most Australian regions several centuries ago were able to feed more aboriginals than actually lived there. That allowed a vital margin of safety. Drought could come without necessarily causing famine.

It is probable that on the eve of the European invasion, food was normally abundant in every Australian region except the central deserts. In Tasmania an enterprising explorer, who knew both the way of life of the brown Tasmanians and the food available to them, wrote that local fish, flesh and vegetables could have supported 70,000 or 80,000 aboriginals when in fact the peak population, in his estimation, had been only 7,000. One observer thought that the fertile Victorian riverflats near the junction of the Goulburn and Murray rivers could have fed twice as many aboriginals. Along the waterways of the Riverina the general impression in most years was that nature was lavish in providing food. In Arnhem Land, according to an outstanding observer of tribal life, the sources of food were so rich and varied that it was absurd to depict food-gathering as a lottery. Some plant foods could even be gathered by the ton, and they offered 'as regular a harvest of food as cultivated gardens'. Further north, on Melville and Bathurst Islands, the Tiwi people 'ate pretty well', especially those households with ten or twelve wives. Even the households consisting of only one or two wives—young women inexperienced in gathering plant foods—were not often hungry.

223

Conditions approaching famine were rarely observed by those Europeans who had the opportunity to see the aboriginals' tribal life before it disintegrated. Even when British explorers passed through countryside which was almost shaved bare by drought, they rarely noticed that aboriginals were on the brink of starvation. When they did report destitution their report was sometimes nullified by their own ignorance of what aboriginals ate. Thus the explorer Charles Sturt, seeing bark vessels full of the gum collected from the mimosa, concluded that 'these unfortunate creatures were reduced to the last extremity'. But the young explorer George Grey, who was inspired to explore partly by Sturt's exciting accounts, pointed out in 1841 that the gum of the mimosa was no more a sign of a bare cupboard than caviar or crayfish tails. The gum, wrote Grey, was so popular that in season it was the magnet for great gatherings in the southwest of Australia. He affirmed that the aboriginals generally 'lived well'. It was a popular mistake 'to imagine that they have small means of subsistence, or are at times greatly pressed for want of food'. When food became scarce they simply moved camp more frequently. That was the very advantage of the nomadic life: the ease with which scarcity in one area could be circumvented by moving to a new area.

Most aboriginals must have coped easily with brief interruptions to the normal sources of food. While a year of sparse rains imposed hardship it probably endangered few lives. Women and men could meet the scarcity by spending more hours in foraging and hunting; they could eat food which normally they shunned as unpalatable or inferior, kill the skinny dingoes that accompanied them, or accelerate the cycle of moving camp. But if the trying conditions persisted for several years, and the setback took on an intensity such as was experienced only once in every fourth or fifth lifetime, the population must have fallen in numbers.

IV

Aboriginals did not have a high standard of living by the present standards of Stockholm, Hamburg or Sydney. By the standards of the year 1800, however, the aboriginals' material life could be compared favourably with that of many parts of Europe. In essence much of the advance in the material comforts of western nations has come in the last two centuries. But for that recent advance Europeans could not have so readily dismissed the way of life of Australian aboriginals.

To attempt to compare the material well-being of two continents even today is hazardous. To compare them, as they were in the year 1800, is even more hazardous. Within each continent were wide variations in the abundance and variety of food and the adequacy of warmth and shelter in a normal year. In each continent, too, some regions had few lean years, and some had few fat years.

If we specify the main ingredients of a good standard of living as food, health, shelter and warmth, the average aboriginal was probably as well off as the average European in 1800. Aboriginals of course could not match the comfort and security of the upper classes of Europe, of the wealthiest one-tenth of the population, but they were probably much better off than the poorest one-tenth. In the eastern half of Europe the comparison favours the aboriginals, and they probably lived in more comfort than nine-tenths of the population of eastern Europe. Even in western Europe, with its strong patches of prosperity, the average person perhaps was no better off than the average aboriginal. If the average Scot in 1800 enjoyed as high a standard of living as aboriginals, the margin in favour of the Scots was entirely the result of economic advances in the eighteenth century. For as late as 1700 the Scots, according to G. M. Trevelyan's careful judgement, were 'always near the verge of famine'. And even in the following century when the welfare of many

225

Scottish people was dramatically improved, the improvement consisted mainly of augmenting the oatmeal porridge and milk with some potatoes, cheese, vegetables and sometimes a little meat. The aboriginals probably had the clearest advantage in food: almost everywhere in Australia they often ate foods which would have been rare luxuries to European peasants or town labourers, and at the same time they had plenty of the starchy foods which were the main or only course at most European tables. In winning that food the aboriginals must have spent fewer hours than the average Pole or Spaniard or Englishman of the year 1800; nor did the aboriginals rely so much on the child labour which was used throughout Europe in most rural and many town activities. Ample leisure was indeed one of the signs of the aboriginals' favourable standard of living.

Two of the advantages possessed by European workers or peasants several centuries ago were mainly illusory; but that illusion underlies the widespread idea that their living standards must have been far superior to those of aboriginals. Europeans, it is true, had shelter. Tiny cottages or hovels, they were larger and snugger than the shifting camps of aboriginals. And yet the cottages and shelters in most parts of Europe—and the tons of fuel burned annually in their fireplaces—merely attempted to repair the inadequacies of climate. Cottages, fuel and clothing represented the elimination of negatives more than the adding of positives. A fortunate peasant on the Prussian plain who, by work or inheritance, possessed a cosy cottage and a large stock of firewood and warm clothes did not necessarily have more comfort than a naked aboriginal whose normal shelter at night was a windbreak and whose fuel was scattered deadwood.

The other illusory advantage attributed to unmechanized farming societies—and the overwhelming majority of people in Europe in 1800 were farmers—is their reputed freedom from famine. Whereas nomads did not hoard foods, an agri-

226

cultural society had granaries, flocks and herds: a herd of course is a hoard. The evidence suggests that a nomadic society could perhaps cope more easily with famine. Even in Australia, where climates were erratic and poor seasons were more frequent than in Europe, aboriginals could meet those poor seasons by moving about more frequently or by eating many species of wild plants which normally they shunned. In contrast a poorer region of Europe, for all its silos and barns, could be desolated by one season of bad weather. As most of the food came from one plant, a disease or a wet summer or a dry spring could ruin the harvest and so lead to famines for which no relief was possible until the next harvest. In Finland in the 1690s famine killed perhaps one third of the people. In the 1840s the poor harvests of potatoes in Ireland caused catastrophe and death on a scale which might not have been equalled in the worst drought experienced in Australia in the previous thousand years. Even in Russia in 1891-2 a poor harvest and the accompanying cholera probably killed half a million people. Life was so precarious for Russian peasants that 'even a modest crop failure brought widespread starvation'.

In many other facets of daily life, the relative advantages of nomadic aboriginals and European peasants are not easily assessed. Aboriginals could not write and read but that was true of most European adults of the year 1800; furthermore the oral tradition in learning and in entertainment was compensatingly strong amongst illiterate peoples.* In the enjoyment of civil order perhaps the Europeans normally had an advantage: the likelihood that they would die violently was probably less. In longevity—a vital test of standards of living —it would be difficult to estimate what proportion of children in each society could expect to live to the age of forty: probably a new-born baby had a higher prospect of living to

* Thus in central Australia the possessor of aboriginal songs had great social prestige. According to T. G. H. Strehlow the traditional songs, handed on and on, 'took the place of private wealth'.

the age of forty in eastern Europe rather than in Australia, but after the child had reached the age of two the expectation of life probably favoured the Australian. In medical knowledge and skill the average village of eastern Europe in the year 1800 was perhaps slightly ahead of the traditional camps of aboriginals. Nor could aboriginal groups care adequately for the sick, for a proportion of their newborn, and for the very old: in contrast a settled society, because it did not have to move regularly to a new site, could care more easily for the helpless so long as it possessed sufficient food. But how often did the villages of Rumania or the Ukraine lack sufficient food? We have almost completed the circle of argument, for an insufficiency of food was perhaps more the mark of a primitive settled society than of a nomadic society.

The inability of most aboriginal groups to care for many of their helpless members was one of the flaws in their standard of living. A relatively high death rate was probably necessary in order to guarantee that their material comforts persisted. The fact that during vast stretches of time their population grew slowly, if at all, helps to explain why their food resources usually remained sufficient and why they lived abundantly.

While the unconscious solution of aboriginals to the pressures of population was to curb population, the solution of the advanced European nations, especially after 1800, was rather to increase the supply of food and raw materials. By applying science and an obsession with progress they could breed prolific plants and fatter animals, they could manufacture and construct and mine with less labour, they could carry commodities cheaply in trains and steamships over long distances, they could preserve meat and butter, they could exploit oil and gas and electricity, and they could make steel, rubber and other new materials. In the nineteenth century this strenuous harnessing of science was to lift the standards of living of the average person in many European nations and outposts high above the level achieved by Australians

or any other known nomads. The same harnessing of science
—the revolutions in industry and agriculture and transport
—was to pull stone-age Australia quickly into Europe's age
of steam and steel.

Ironically the innovations in western Europe in the period
1760-1860 not only made the aboriginals' material triumphs
and living standards seem unimpressive but they also set up
that demand for wool, minerals, and other raw materials
which led to the invasion of inland Australia and shattered
the aboriginals' way of life. For the original British occupation of Sydney and Hobart and a few points of coast had
small effect on the aboriginals. Only when those ports became depots for the industrial and financial cities of Britain
—for the woollen mills of Bradford and the copper smelters
of Swansea and the gold office of London's mint—did the
British migrants push deep into the interior and far along
the coast and so end the long reign of the nomads.

CHAPTER FOURTEEN

Sails of Doom

For more than thirty thousand years the aboriginals had been nomads. They maintained the tradition of wandering long after most people of the world had settled down to the sedentary life of garden, farm, village or town. Why they did not adopt the custom of cultivating plants and keeping herds is a puzzle. New Guinea had gardens and pigs, and several islands in Torres Strait grew vegetables in neat gardens, but the new way of life did not apparently penetrate Australia. The small groups of nomads were thus intensely vulnerable when, unscathed by the neolithic revolution, they were confronted less than two centuries ago by Europe's industrial revolution.

II

During the early phase of the rising of the sea, the nomads dominated the earth. In Australia and India, France and Mexico, there were no domesticated plants and animals. But in the last phase of the rising of the sea, gardens were tended and herds tamed in a few parts of the world. The long epoch of nomadic life was being challenged. For the domesticating of plants and animals was really the domesticating of men and women who now were chained, by the demands of crops and flocks, to one small district or pocket of ground for most of the year.

Perhaps the more settled mode of life was possibly spurred

partly by the rising of the seas and by the consequent scarcity of foods or the social dislocation near flooded areas. The full causes of the cultivation of plants, however, must remain speculative. Even the whereabouts of the first garden is not known though most of the likely sites are not far from the sea. According to the present precarious state of knowledge the first plants and trees were domesticated about ten or eleven thousand years ago. The first Garden of Eden was probably somewhere east of Suez or, less likely, somewhere north of Panama. In the next half century perhaps six or eight nations will, on the strength of archaeological research, lay claim to the site of that garden.

The old idea that this remarkable innovation was made entirely in the Middle East is no longer so convincing. Some disputed evidence suggests that a few plants and fruit trees were domesticated in north-west Thailand about 10,000 years ago. That a few Japanese were already making pottery seems to support the importance of East Asia in this neolithic revolution. At the same time the Middle East was probably taming plants and a few animals. It seems likely that sheep and goats were being domesticated in south-west Iran about 10,000 years ago. A little later cultivated patches of cereal grass were probably growing in the Indus Valley. About 10,000 years ago the town of Jericho covered about ten acres and those acres were perhaps the most crowded on earth, holding two or three thousand people who grew crops of emmer wheat and barley. The meat eaten at Jericho still came from hunted animals: the remains of the earliest domestic goats at Jericho have been dated as about 9,000 years old.

Agriculture appears not to have been a once-only invention which then spread to scattered places. It probably arose independently in the Middle East, East Asia and Central America at about the same time. About 9,000 years ago a few plants were perhaps cultivated by man in the highlands of Mexico. There the earliest garden plant—on present

231

knowledge—was the bottle gourd, grown for its qualities as a flask or receptacle. In the next two thousand years the Mexican highlands grew the domesticated pumpkin, squash, avocado, chili pepper and the maize. Far to the south, near the Andes Mountains, the common bean and the lima bean were already domesticated: an excavation in a cave there suggests that the beans were cultivated perhaps 8,000 years ago. The long list of cultivated plants from the Americas did not begin to reach Europe until about 1500 A.D., and in the following century a few reached the islands of the Indonesian archipelago and one even reached New Guinea but not the opposite Australian coast.

In that apron-shaped block of land between the Nile and the Persian Gulf were displayed—from 5,000 to 9,000 years ago—a series of innovations which were to reach Australia only in the last two centuries. To the herds and flocks of sheep and goats were added pigs and cattle. A wider variety of fruits, cereals, vegetables and herbs grew in gardens. In some of the more fertile regions the cultivated plants could now grow enough food to support a large village. The biggest villages attained a size which was as astonishing to a newcomer as Calcutta or Shanghai is to a peasant today. About 6,000 years ago, on the western fringe of the delta of the Nile, the town of Merimde was one of the most populous in the world. It held, according to estimates, about 16,000 people. That cramped town would have dumbfounded a nomadic hunter, for most nomads in Australia or Asia would not have set eyes on as many as perhaps 2,000 different people during their entire life. To defend such a town from outside attack, to police it or to organize its supply of water required a centralized government of a kind unknown, probably, to hunting societies. A town of such complexity required a system of recording transactions and obligations, and that record was greatly aided by an alphabet and the art of writing. The earliest evidence of the alphabet and of writing is in Mesopotamia more than 5,000 years ago. To feed a large town also called for efficient transport from the crop lands. That wonderful device, the wheel, was used in Mesopotamia about 5,600 years ago. The early wheels were solid; spokes were a later invention.

Today one of the best-preserved of the early cities is being excavated in eastern Iran, not far from the borders of Pakistan and Afghanistan. The scraping away of a sand-coloured crust of clay and salt is disclosing a city of rectangualr buildings separated by crooked alleyways in which worked new specialists in new crafts: the potters, weavers, dyers, masons, coppersmiths and cutters of precious stones. A microscopic inspection of some of the debris reveals that the inhabitants ate barley, millet, wheat, melons, cucumbers, grapes and the seeds of poppies. As a river had once flowed past the city the inhabitants caught fish, crabs, and such pond-birds as ducks, geese, and swans: the remains of food suggest that the river provided more flesh than did sheep, cattle, goats and gazelles of the pastures. The city appears to have been founded between 4,900 and 3,900 years ago, at a time when large towns were emerging in civilizations as far apart as China and Egypt. Known as Sharh-l-Sokhta this ancient city of Iran had traded with places as distant as the valley of Mesopotamia and the region now covered by Soviet Turkmenia. Indeed commerce must have been one of the ways by which the new form of economic and social life was advertised in remote nomadic regions.

While that city flourished in eastern Iran, the skills of the herdsmen and gardeners were approaching the outer islands of the Indonesian archipelago, thousands of miles to the south-east. The economic revolution reached the island of Timor about 5,000 years ago, perhaps earlier. Presumably the first pigs and cats arrived in the possession of migrants who sailed across the narrow sea. The keeping of pigs presupposed the growing of crops, for in most lands the pigs gained part of their food by foraging and part by eating the surplus food of the gardens. The skills of the potter appeared

233

in Timor about the same time as pigs. Whereas the possession of earthenware pots and bowls was a burden for nomadic people, gardeners often depended on pots for the storing of surplus grains and liquids gathered during the seasonal harvests.

III

In years to come archaeologists may be able to date more accurately the eastward movement of pigs from island to island. At present, however, we possess only scattered evidence: here a pig and there a pig, but few dates by which to indicate their antiquity. In the eastern highlands of Eastern New Guinea, pig bones were recently excavated in a rock shelter where generations of peoples had cooked and camped. The pig bones are perhaps 5,000 years old. In the same excavation at Kiowa, in a layer which is perhaps 10,000 years old, were found the bones of a thylacine 'the Tasmanian tiger'. Whether Tasmanian tiger and Asian pig ever met in the highlands of New Guinea is not known. But the spread of pigs, dogs and other domesticated animals from Asia to the island of New Guinea was possibly part of that slow ecological upheaval by which the Tasmanian tiger was ultimately extinguished, first in New Guinea, then in Australia and, in living memory, in Tasmania.

The razor-backed pigs had great prestige in many districts of New Guinea at the end of the nineteenth century, when Europeans began to govern much of the coast of the island. 'Pigs are our hearts', said the Enga men in the western highlands of Papua-New Guinea. In the Tor region of West Irian the households would not kill or eat the pigs which they themselves had petted and reared: 'Who would eat his own son or brother?' In trade the pigs were often the most valued of all items; and in social and ceremonial and festive life they were central. Pigs were a vital source of animal protein, and a valuable moving store for the surplus food of a good harvest, carrying that abundance into the following season. They had an additional merit: in the words of a New York anthropologist Andrew Vayda, they were 'effective garbage disposal units'.

Whether the venerated pigs and the tropical gardens quickly transformed life in New Guinea is open to doubt. Few excavations by archaeologists have been completed on the island, and it is not so easy to say whether pigs were widespread or whether pork contributed much to human diet. Even in recent years, in most parts of New Guinea, pork was reserved for feasts and ritual occasions; in a normal year it probably provided less than one or two hundredths of the people's food. The introduction of gardens was probably much more useful than the importing of the first pigs, but even the gardens probably augmented rather than replaced hunting and foraging. Though gardening probably came to New Guinea at least 5,000 years ago many tribes merely dabbled in or shunned cultivation even in living memory.

The early gardens in New Guinea were probably in tropical forest rather than grassland. The forest had fertile soil; furthermore the removal of big trees in order to plant a garden was not so forbidding to people for whom fire was sharper than any other of the tools which they owned. The large trees were probably ring-barked with a stone axe, the saplings were cut down, and the creepers cut at the base. A good fire cleaned the patch of forest and left a bed of ashes in which the cuttings of vegetables could be planted. A wooden fence had to be built around the garden if pigs or wild game were plentiful: the fence was the penalty for keeping pigs. While the taro or yams or other plant-foods were growing, the weeds had to be kept down with a hoe or digging stick.

Normally one crop lowered the fertility of the soil; furthermore the task of weeding, during the second year after the big burning, was demanding. Hence the gardeners were slightly nomadic and moved each year to a new edge of the forest, returning to their now-overgrown gardens perhaps a decade later. In poorer soil the ground might lie fallow for a quarter of a century. The adoption of gardening, however, enabled a region to support a larger population. Thus in the river valley near Madang in the early 1960s the density of the population was 64 to a square mile, or one thousand times the density of population in many hunting and gathering societies. The gardening economy, however, did not necessarily lead to a more diverse or abundant diet.

The invasion of domesticated plants and animals came close to Australia. From the coast of south-east New Guinea it began to cross the stepping stones in Torres Strait. When roots and plant-cuttings began to make the crossing is not known—some day excavations may throw up clues. J. R. Beckett, a Sydney anthropologist, concludes that pigs were also imported to a few islands, and in the nineteenth century the fences around some of the vegetable gardens certainly suggested either the presence or memory of pigs. On the islands in the strait the pigs were not considered essential. They do not appear in folk tales; they were not regularly exchanged in the complicated mesh of alliances and trading relationships. We cannot discard the possibility that pigs also reached northern Australia as gifts or as pets, but they did not multiply, and were presumably extinguished in one or two feasts. The wild pigs found in Cape York Peninsula in modern times, apparently, were the offspring of pigs released there by Captain Cook during his exploring voyage of 1770.

Gardening was not pursued in any part of aboriginal Australia but curiously it took root on islands in Torres Strait. The taro plant was cultivated on at least two islands which hugged the Papuan coast. Bananas and yams—some of the yams were longer than a forearm—were the main crops cultivated on other islands where the soil had sufficient moisture and fertility to support gardens. The islands at the eastern end of the strait had the prolific gardens. The Murray Islands, lying where the shallow waters of Torres Strait met the deep water of the Coral Sea, possessed volcanic soil, ample rains and dense vegetation. Much of the vegetation on the five square miles of the main island was periodically cleared for the gardens, and the island a century ago supported 800 to 1,000 people. Most of their meals came from the tiny gardens. The Murray Islanders also ate fish but they seemed less skilled in canoeing and fishing than islanders to the west, where fish and turtle were a larger part of the daily diet.

Gardens were also cultivated on islands which were so close to Australia that they could be clearly seen from high ground near Cape York. A few gardens were dug on Prince of Wales Island, which is divided from the mainland by a narrow strait that was often crossed by aboriginals. A Scottish woman named Barbara Thompson, saved from a shipwreck in 1844, lived with the aboriginals on Prince of Wales Island for nearly five years; and her evidence was indisputable that the islanders knew how to make gardens. She watched them burn the wood on the chosen ground, scoop holes in the rich ashes and soil, plant the cuttings or piece of yam, and place alongside a straight stick on which the plant could climb.

The gardens, she implied, were more an insurance, to be called upon if the yams on the higher rocky ground were not plentiful. Prince of Wales Island was certainly not an economic miracle, beckoning the 'under-developed' region on the mainland to sow and harvest.

There is a touch of drama about the way in which the world-wide advance of herds and gardens halted within sight of a strip of northern Australian coast. Two different ways of making a living stood side by side: economic systems which were as different as communism and capitalism. Moreover they co-existed in relative harmony for perhaps as long as several thousand years. Why the domestication of plants and animals did not affect Australia is one of the baffling questions in prehistory; and no sure answer may emerge.

The rising of the seas undoubtedly impeded the introduc-

237

tion of gardening to Australia. The gardeners and hunters faced one another on a very narrow front: Torres Strait was their only point of contact. Moreover gardens on the two islands nearest the Australian mainland were small and miserable, and so offered no inducement to the Cape York aboriginals to imitate the same hard work of clearing, burning, planting and weeding. In contrast the richer gardening societies lay at the eastern edge of Torres Strait, were ten times further from Australia than was Prince of Wales Island, and so were not a visible advertisement. Moreover the standard of living on Murray and Darnley islands might not have been higher than that of Cape York; and it is unlikely that those island fisherfolk and gardeners enjoyed the diversity of foods available to Australian aboriginals. Above all, the farming society of New Guinea and of the Torres Strait Islands was half-formed. The only edible domesticated animals were pigs, and they were not plentiful. Aboriginals in northern Australia had small incentive to adopt and keep pigs, because their grasslands provided them with much more meat than was available to the average Papuan.

We are also inclined to imagine that Cape York was probably too barren, too dry to support adequate gardens. It is tempting to conclude that even if aboriginals had wished to be gardeners, the harsh physical environment prevented them. This argument was dissected by Jack Golson. In the end he decided that the absence of gardens could not be explained by deficiencies in the environment, the absence of techniques or the scarcity of cultivable plants. Clearly the northern aboriginals must have preferred not to be gardeners. Perhaps more important, no outside conqueror arrived and forcibly imposed gardening and the new way of life upon them.

The cultural border between Australian aboriginals and the islanders of Torres Strait remained blurred. Torres Strait did not symbolize an iron curtain but rather a screen of pearl-shell: delicate and mottled. The curtain had often been penetrated. In the islands of Torres Strait most of the languages were related more to Australia than to Papua. Many aboriginals married islanders at the southern edge of the strait, and on Prince of Wales and Horn Islands the people were a cultural and racial mixture. In the large sail-powered canoes many commodities were exchanged between the tip of Cape York, the islands of Torres Strait and—two or three transactions later—the mainland of New Guinea. Southwards to the northern tip of Australia came special kinds of shells, plumes of the bird-of-paradise, stone clubs, bamboo pipes for smoking, a variety of trinkets and treasures; even outrigger canoes sometimes came south as part of the pattern of ceremonial exchange or simple exchange. From Cape York went many items including those pearl-shells so prized by Papuans for breast ornaments: for in the New Guinea Highlands pieces of pearl-shell were the traditional form of payment for pigs.* Australia also sent spears and spear-throwers to islanders who valued them highly, for in fishing and harpooning they were superior to the islanders' bows and arrows. The international trade in armaments is much older than is realized.

The Cape York Peninsula, extending south from New Guinea like a long causeway, led neither pigs nor cultivated crops into the continent, but its flanking waters and coastal plains were a passageway for new ideas, objects, and ceremonies. Thus in many parts of the peninsula the rituals of death were similar to those of Papua: the corpses were placed on platforms and allowed to putrefy and dry. The influence of Papua could be seen in the drums which were beaten at ceremonies, in the practice of the hero-cult and sometimes in the fuzzy hair and Papuan facial features of aboriginals. The

* Another export of Australian origin, a reluctant export, was human heads. The Scottish woman who was marooned on Prince of Wales Island once counted six severed Australian heads in a canoe of islanders. The heads were strung on cane loops: the head of a girl and of a woman were amongst them. They formed a valuable article of exchange in Torres Strait.

Northern Australia about 1780

PACIFIC

NEW
GUINEA

Madang

Kiowa

PAPUA

Gazelle
Peninsula

OCEAN

ADVANCE

TORRES STRAIT

ARAFURA
SEA

CORAL SEA

Gulf
of
Carpentaria

CAPE YORK PENINSULA

R S

L I A

PAPUA

Warrior Reefs

Darnley I

Murray Is

Banks I

TORRES STRAIT

Prince of
Wales I

Horn I

Cape York

GREAT BARRIER REEF

distinctive outrigger canoes were seen at the northern end of the peninsula, and sometimes the islanders themselves sailed south in order to exchange goods or see new faces and places. But the Papuan influences, resembling sea waves at the northern end of the Cape York Peninsula, were like ripples at the southern end.

IV

While Cape York Peninsula was the most obvious place of entry, it was not the only point at which the new way of economic life could enter. Long stretches of the northern and north-western coast of Australia were again within reach of the outside world; longer voyages were possible because seafaring skills were slowly improving. Three or four thousand years ago stronger craft and wiser navigators were partly bridging the gaps which had been widened by the rising seas. The long voyage from Timor or from western New Guinea to the north coast of Australia was hazardous but not impossible. Certainly in the last three thousand years in different parts of the Pacific Ocean, men from simple societies made sea voyages far more hazardous than the crossing of the Timor Sea and Arafura Sea. The Marquesas Islands, far to the north of Tahiti, had been settled by Pacific voyagers by the time of Christ. New Zealand also was reached in long sea voyages by the Maoris by about 1350 A.D. And somehow people from Borneo had sailed far around the Asian coast, finally settling in the island of Madagascar.

As we have long seen Australian history through a British telescope, we have been inclined to think that most of the continent was effectively cut off from the outside world until the coming of Captain Cook in 1770 or the making of the first British settlement near Sydney in 1788. The north coast of Australia, however, must often have felt tremors from the outside world; it was probably never cut off completely from human events in other lands. 'At every phase of its prehistory', wrote John Mulvaney, 'Australian isolation was more apparent than real.'

There is evidence that Chinese might have landed in northern Australia half a century or more before Christopher Columbus reached North America. The evidence is tantalising but slippery. Reports of a map of northern Australia, compiled by the captain of a Chinese trepang vessel in 1426 and last heard of in Peking five centuries later, will remain speculative until somebody succeeds in locating the map. Likewise the discovery in 1879 of a Chinese statuette near a north Australian harbour suggested the hypothesis that unknown Chinese navigators had visited the coast long ago. The statuette was found buried beside the thick roots of a large Banyan tree in Darwin. As the tree was near the sea, and as the statuette had been buried four feet below the surface, there seemed persuasive reasons for concluding that it had lain there for some centuries and had been deposited or lost by seafarers from China. The object, however, was of no great size—it can fit neatly into the pocket of a man's overcoat—and so alternatively it could have arrived in the possession of the Chinese coolies and gold seekers who settled in Darwin in the 1870s.

The statue was unmistakably Chinese. A bearded figure, the Taoist god of longevity, was mounted on a deer and his hand held a large peach. The god and deer and peach had been carved skilfully in a white stone which at first had been described as jade but is now confidently identified as soapstone. That stone is soft and easily damaged. Therefore the possibility that the statuette was left behind by a roaming Ming squadron of the 15th century, and was miraculously undamaged by four centuries of burial, is now considered untenable. Today the white carved stone stands in a crowded museum case in Sydney, without even an inscription outlining the glamorous theories which it had once nurtured. The label, sadly, dates it as a Chinese carving of the eighteenth century.

Chinese sailors could have reached Australia in the fifteenth century. Between 1405 and 1433 the Ming admiral, Cheng Ho, made a series of long voyages which were planned more elaborately and manned more massively than any European naval expeditions. The largest of the seven expeditions sailed from the 'Treasure-ship Yard' on the Yangtze River with about 300 ships and 28,000 officials, sailors, marines and gunners. Several of the Chinese vessels reached Malindi in east Africa; others visited Aden where a giraffe was taken aboard a junk and conveyed back to China for people to marvel at: and a few of the many-masted ships visited the coast of Timor.

The island of Timor was certainly known to the Chinese in the fifteenth century. It was the source of the white sandalwood which was widely used for incense or for wood-carving as far away as Calicut, Canton, and possibly south Arabia. Timor was shipping away the white sandalwood as early as the seventh century A.D., and perhaps the sandalwood trade was even older. In Chinese cities the scent of the sandalwood in the incense-burner was familiar in temples, and on hot days many Chinese women were cooled by the flutter of carved fans of sandalwood cut from slender trees on the ranges of Timor.

In the course of ten centuries of trading in sandalwood it is likely that several small ships were swept up by the north-west monsoon and driven towards the north-west coast of Australia about 350 miles away. There is evidence from Timor of sandalwood ships blown far off course. Moreover some traders or ship-masters might even have sailed to Australia in search of strands of sandalwood though the main Australian belts of that tree were too far from the coast to be accessible. Probably pieces of iron—a nail or needle or axe-head—reached northern Australia before the first European exploring vessels touched that coast in about 1600 A.D. Perhaps prized by some aboriginals, or passed on as gifts, the iron was a link with islands which themselves were on

244

the fringe of the trading network of south-east Asia; a network which, we easily forget, was vigorous long before Europeans themselves arrived to collect spices, silver, cloth, and kegs and sacks of tropical exotica.

Less than a century after the Chinese sent out their last armada of exploration, European ships began to appear in the waters of the Indonesian Archipelago. Portuguese, Dutch, and British ships came for spices and tried to exercise the kind of monopoly which the oil kingdoms of the Middle East seek today.

The islands closer to northern Australia grew no mace, nutmeg and cloves but Timor had the prized sandalwood tree and large supplies of beeswax. The Portuguese and Dutch fought for control of the sandalwood trade while Chinese and Indonesian smugglers quietly continued to help themselves to the wood. About the year 1566 a Portuguese fort was built on the island of Solor, seventy miles northwest of Timor, to protect the Dominican missionaries, the sandalwood traders and all their women. A century later the Portuguese also traded from a small fort on Timor—the modern Otussi—while the Dutch occupied the fort of Kupang which they had captured from the Portuguese in 1653. In the eighteenth century the Timor sandalwood was the commercial mainstay of the Portuguese colony of Macao which in turn sold the scented wood to the Chinese on their doorstep. In the alleyways of Macao lived scores of Timor women shipped there as slaves.

The capturing of slaves by black and white traders ultimately extended to aboriginal islands within sight of the northern coast of Australia. People on Melville and Bathurst Islands were taken as slaves to Timor where some might have been shipped to the slave markets at Djakarta and Macao. The slave trade in aboriginals is said to have ceased about the year 1800 and details of the trade are vague. Generally, slaves were not taken from hunting societies, partly because that way of living did not foster the physical stamina and the discipline imposed by gardens. As the aboriginals on Melville and Bathurst Islands were not gardeners the men were possibly exempted from slavery. No such exemption, apparently, applied to the women, for they were valued more as sexual property than as toilers.

In the two and a half centuries between 1519, when Portuguese captured the Malay spice emporium of Malacca, and the year 1769, when Captain Cook entered the Pacific Ocean on that voyage which led him to eastern Australia, many coastal aboriginals in northern Australia must have been affected occasionally by the activities of European or Indonesian traders. Aboriginals were taken as slaves. Europeans were marooned on the western Australian coast where Dutch ships ran aground while sailing between the Dutch-owned ports of Capetown and Djakarta. Indonesian vessels were possibly driven accidentally to the north coast by the summer monsoon. Ultimately more will be known about these contacts. Their main influence was possibly the introduction of a European virus or disease to which aboriginals had no immunity.

New Guinea, being less isolated than Australia, was more sensitive to the new influences in the Indonesian islands. Nevertheless it rejected Mohammedanism which had arrived not long before the European merchants and marines; perhaps New Guinea relied too much on pigs to be eager for a creed in which pork was taboo. New Guinea's gardens, however, accepted the sweet potato which the Portuguese had brought from America to the Indonesian islands. Sweet potatoes probably reached New Guinea in about 1600, and by 1900 they were probably the most prolific vegetable there, surpassing even the banana, taro and sago. As sweet potatoes could flourish in the mountain spine of the island they probably multiplied the island's food supply, allowing the population to increase. The sweet potato even invaded areas once dominated by hunters and gatherers, but certain areas remained unaffected. On the rugged foothills of the Central

246

Range, above the Sepik Plains, the sweet potato did not arrive until the coming of the first European explorers in about 1966. Nor did the gardening islands of Torres Strait apparently adopt the sweet potato; if by chance it did grow there is was no more than a minor supplement to their traditional root crops. Had another two centuries of isolation been allowed to New Guinea, the sweet potato might have spread further, reaching the islands of Torres Strait and perhaps even winning a few patches of ground on the northeast coast of Australia. But Europe's economic expansion, which had presented the sweet potato to New Guinea, was now too dynamic to allow this dead-end of the world to remain in isolation.

V

Cape York Peninsula had been the continent's causeway to the outside world for so many thousands of years that, in retrospect, it was surprizing that the invasion or infiltration should finally come from other points on the coast. And yet the first beachheads were made far from the outrigger canoes of Torres Strait. Far west, on the low-lying coast of Arnhem Land, Indonesian fishermen began to appear as regularly as the change of seasons. Near the exotic tamarind trees which mark their camping places the archaeologist Campbell Macknight has uncovered bronze coins, thousands of fragments of red Indonesian pottery, broken glass from green square-faced bottles and other pieces of now-prized litter left behind on Australian beaches. When these expeditions first visited the coast is still uncertain but was probably not earlier than 1700 A.D.

The Indonesian fishermen came mostly from the Dutch-governed port of Macassar at the southern end of the Celebes, and they made annual visits to northern Australia before the British made their first settlement in eastern Australia. The fisherman came in strange craft resembling low-roofed houses that had been swept out to sea. Driven by the moist winds of the north-west monsoon that blew from December to February, they could make swift passages to Australia or the near-shore islands. The 1,200 miles from Macassar were often covered in less than a fortnight by these vessels with squat sails of matting. As the south-east monsoon began to blow about March the vessels could also make a fast voyage home at the end of the summer fishing season.

Scattered along perhaps 700 miles of the Australian coast, from the Kimberleys to the Gulf of Carpentaria, the Indonesians fished in shallow waters for the sea-slug known as trepang or bêche-de-mer. They gathered the slug by wading in shallow water or by fishing from dug-out canoes which they brought across from Macassar. At favoured sites ashore —often marked today by groves of shady tamarind trees which had grown from the debris of Macassarmen's meals— they boiled the sea-slugs in cauldrons and cured them in smoke-houses made of bamboo rattan shipped from their home port. They were men of the iron age, these Macassarmen, for they chopped firewood amongst the shore mangroves with iron axes, shaped their dug-out canoes with iron adzes, and of course cooked their sea-slugs in iron cauldrons. They also belonged to an era of international trade, for their smoked trepang mostly reached the bazaars and merchant houses by the wide river at Canton where it commanded high prices as an ingredient of soup and as an aphrodisiac.

It is likely that the first decade of the trepang industry on the northern coast had greater influence on the aboriginals than did the first decade of British settlement (1788-98) on the Pacific coast. The Indonesian fishermen were scattered at many points and islands along some 700 miles of coast whereas British soldiers and convicts were confined to a small pocket of ground near Sydney. The Indonesian visitors numbered perhaps as many as 1,500 in busy summers, so in numbers they were comparable with the British who made the first settlement at Sydney. Although the Indonesians remained in Australia only during the summers they met aboriginals at many places from the Kimberleys to the Gulf of Carpentaria. One sign of the contact was the occasional presence of aboriginals in the crew of their ships.

The fleet from Macassar influenced aboriginals on the northern coast in many ways. Words from Macassar entered the aboriginal vocabularies; the visitors shaped aboriginal songs and rituals; bark-painters in eastern Arnhem Land borrowed motifs from the Macassarmen; and the 'Van Dyke beard' which became so popular on that coast is said to have been an imitation of the Macassarmen's beards. A few Indonesians fathered half-caste children but generally they did not interfere with the aboriginal women. The aboriginals and visitors had occasional fights near the beaches, but the fishermen had a strong incentive to foster cordial relations with aboriginals. They needed peace and security simply to be able to carry on their strenuous quest for sea-slugs and their curing activities on the shore. When ashore at their scattered smoking-sheds the Macassarmen, being outnumbered, must have been particularly vulnerable to surprise attack.

Those parts of northern Australia which were annually visited by the fleet from Macassar harvested useful items of equipment. Aboriginals accepted as gifts or stole or scavenged tobacco and pipes, beads, belts and pieces of cloth. They occasionally acquired a knife with an iron blade or an iron axe-head. They received scraps of iron which could be used to pierce or cut or scrape, fragments of bottle-glass which became as useful as machine-tools, and nails which could be twisted into fish hooks. Many of these articles temporarily increased the ability of the fortunate possessors to gather food: the axe could chop animals from hiding places in trees, the glass could tip a spear. Unfortunately the aboriginal bands on different points of the coast depended totally for their supply of iron and glass on the visiting fishermen. As the supply of these items was meagre and erratic, the iron and glass did not much alter the way of life. Nevertheless it is remarkable how avidly these new objects were accepted along the low-lying coast of Arnhem Land and the offshore islands. Our traditional picture is of an aboriginal lethargy, an undeviating resistance to change: the picture is obviously out of focus.

Dug-out canoes came with the Macassarmen. Each of their sailing vessels carried as many as eight or ten canoes. They were axe-made canoes, hacked from a long trunk of a tree. They were smooth underneath, possessing no keel, and were stable only if sailed skilfully by the men searching the shallow water for trepang. Some of these Indonesian canoes were more than twenty-four feet long and could carry six or eight men in the open sea. They were more advanced than any of the craft used by aboriginals in Arnhem Land where a canoe made in a few hours from a long oblong of stringy-bark was the most elaborate watercraft.

Some of the Macassarmen who sailed away at the end of the wet season gave a *lippa lippa* or dug-out canoe to aboriginals as payment for services rendered during the season: occasionally a canoe might have been seized in a sudden attack by aboriginals. More importantly, later visitors taught some aboriginals how to make a dug-out canoe and presented to them an iron axe with which to shape the log.* The dug-out canoes were to become the most complicated of all the manufactures of northern Australia and were usually the work of specialist craftsmen, but this activity belonged more to the first half of the twentieth century.

A few aboriginals sailed to Macassar with the departing fleets and lived in that strange city awaiting the change of monsoon which signalled the time for their return. Perhaps

* In Cape York Peninsula outrigger dug-out canoes were made but the people on that coast had a stronger cutting tool—a strong adze with a cutting edge consisting of tough shell. Even on the bays and beaches of that peninsula many of the canoes were imported from the Torres Strait Islands. Moreover a few unmanned canoes were blown south in storms, reaching Australia like gifts from heaven.

they had been taken to the homeport as a curiosity; perhaps they had been persuaded to man a vessel in which members of the crew had died or had been drowned in Australian waters. The first aboriginal to sail to and from Macassar is nameless but his visit across the seas was, in retrospect, momentous for a people who had lived for so many centuries in seclusion.

Even if no aboriginals were aboard, the departure of the Macassar fleet at the end of the wet season impressed itself on the spectators on the beaches; and some of the mystery of the embarkation was captured and woven into the ceremonies of groups in the north-east of Arnhem Land. The raising of the mast in the vessels about to sail, and the last farewells, were grafted on the burial ritual of aboriginals. Generations later a visitor to Arnhem Land was surprised to see several men, at a traditional funeral, lift up the dead body and move it up and down as if they were preparing to raise a mast. These movements were matched by a dance that imitated the hauling of those ropes with which a mast was raised. Later some of the mourners chanted an imitation of the prayer which the Macassarmen had sometimes recited; and the climax of the ceremony was the repeating of the cry which the Macassarmen had called out when the mast was at last erect and firmly placed on deck: a cry kept all those years in tribal memory and repeated even after the Macassarmen ceased coming with the wet monsoon. A day or two after the burial, the final symbol of the voyage was erected on the grave—a mast of Macassan design.

VI

Three thousand miles around the coast, in cooler seas, other masts were visible. In April 1770, off the hilly coast of New South Wales, an English ship was seen for the first time. The *Endeavour*, twenty months out from Plymouth, sailed slowly northwards, charting the coastline and searching for a suit-

251

able bay in which to anchor. Her master, James Cook, saw the smoke of aboriginal fires in the high hills, saw the lights of aboriginal fires near the beach at night, and through his telescope he scrutinized the faces of brown people whose future was to be powerfully shaped by the results of his voyage of exploration.

At Botany Bay two aboriginal men, seeing the English ship anchor in the harbour, were willing to defy the visitors. Watching thirty or forty men set out from the ship in rowing boats, they stood on the northern shore with their woomeras and long spears. For a quarter of an hour they stood on their ground, gesturing the boats to come no closer. The English officer wanted to go ashore to fetch fresh water but hesitated to land for fear that the resin which glued the sharp points to the spears was poisonous. In the end he ordered that a shot be fired over the heads of the warriors. At the loud sound of the musket the younger aboriginal dropped his bundle of spears in shock, then retrieved the spears and renewed his gestures and threats. The musket fired another two rounds, and the older aboriginal was wounded slightly by the small shot. Believing that he possessed the equipment to protect himself from any missile or spear, and undeterred by the numerical strength of the enemy, he ran to a nearby hut for reinforcements. He returned carrying a wooden shield. So the civilization of iron and gunpowder was confronted by the flimsy weapons of wood and bone.

Most of the contacts between British and aboriginals on the Pacific coast in 1770 were not so dramatic. On two occasions a few aboriginals threatened to fight, and several other groups fled at the sight of the British sailors. Other aboriginals neither fought nor ran. They treated the high sails of the great ship with an indifference that astonished those aboard. South of Sydney four fishermen with spears were riding their tiny canoes in a small inlet when the largest man-made object in all Australia sailed into sight. The

Endeavour even sailed within a quarter of a mile of their bark vessels; but to the astonishment of the botanist Banks and all who were lining the side of the ship the fishermen 'scarce lifted their eyes from their employment'. Further to the north the high drama of indifference was replayed. The officers in the *Endeavour* could see through their spy-glasses a line of aboriginals carrying bundles of palm-leaves along a beach, up a path, and over a gentle hill. For nearly an hour the aboriginals ashore were within clear view, and even a turn of their heads could be observed through these field glasses of no great power. But none of the score of aboriginals seemed to be in the least impressed or frightened by the sight of a white-eared monster such as they could not previously have seen. 'Not one', wrote Banks, 'was once observed to stop and look towards the ship'. In many of the later journals and diaries of explorers one can see, in addition to fear or fearlessness, the same calm apathy of aboriginals who had lived so long in isolation that intruders were inconceivable.

Influenced by the reports written by James Cook and the botanist Joseph Banks, the British government made a permanent settlement at Sydney in 1788. More and more white sails were seen along that coast, bringing the people, plants, flocks and herds, skills and weapons, cures and diseases, and the wide-armed organization of a different world. Whereas for thousands of years there had been some prospect that the economic and social life of the aboriginals would be reshaped by the entry of gardening and pig-raising from New Guinea, the real reshaping was to be drastic. Whereas gardening could be grafted onto a semi-nomadic life, the economic activities and energies of England of 1800 would shatter the social and economic customs of the aboriginals. Tragically, the largest region of nomads in the world was now face to face with the island which had carried to new heights that settled, specialized existence that had arisen from the domesticating of plants and animals. People who could not boil

253

water were confronted by the nation which had recently contrived the steam engine.

On the hot coast of northern Australia many aboriginals had celebrated the approach of the matting sails of the Macassarmen, for they were merely summer birds of passage. But on the east coast the white sails of the English ships were a symbol of a gale which in the following hundred years would slowly cross the continent, blowing out the flames of countless camp-fires, covering with drift-sand the grinding stones and fishing nets, silencing the sounds of hundreds of languages, and stripping the ancient aboriginal names from nearly every valley and headland.

Notes and Sources

In setting out sources of information used in the book, the following abbreviations are used:

A.A.A.S.   Official report of the Australasian Association for the Advancement of Science—the present ANZAAS.

A.D.B.   *Australian Dictionary of Biography* (Melbourne, 1966-).

A. & P.A.   *Archaeology and Physical Anthropology in Oceania.*

Arnhem Land   C. P. Mountford ed., *Records of the American-Australian Scientific Expedition to Arnhem Land*, vol. 2, 'Anthropology and Nutrition' (Melbourne, 1960).

Bass Strait   *Bass Strait: Australia's Last Frontier* (A.B.C. talks, Sydney, 1969) by S. Murray-Smith et al.

Beveridge   Peter Beveridge, 'Of the Aborigines Inhabiting the Great Lacustrine and Riverine Depression of the Lower Murray, Lower Murrumbidgee', etc., in *R.S.N.S.W.*, 1883, vol. 17, pp. 19-74.

Buckley   John Morgan, *The Life and Adventures of William Buckley* (Melbourne, 1967, ed. C. E. Sayers).

Cotton   B. C. Cotton ed., *Aboriginal Man in South and Central Australia* (Adelaide, 1966) Part 1.

Curr   E. M. Curr, *The Australian Race* (Melbourne, 1886) 4 vols.
            E. M. Curr, *Recollections of Squatting in Victoria* (Melbourne, 1965, H. Foster ed.).

E.B. Encyclopaedia Britannica, editions of 1910-11 or 1962.

Grey George Grey, *Journals of Two Expeditions of Discovery in North-West and Western Australia* (London, 1841) 2 vols.

Jones Rhys Jones, 'The Geographical Background to the Arrival of Man in Australia and Tasmania', *A. & P.A.*, 1968, vol. 3, pp. 186-215.

MacGillivray J. MacGillivray, *Narrative of the Voyage of H.M.S. Rattlesnake* (London, 1852) 2 vols.

Mitchell T. L. Mitchell, *Three Expeditions into the Interior of Eastern Australia* (London, 1839) 2 vols.

Mulvaney D. J. Mulvaney, *The Prehistory of Australia* (London, 1969): a revised edition is to appear in 1975.

Mulvaney and Golson D. J. Mulvaney and J. Golson, ed., *Aboriginal Man and Environment in Australia* (Canberra, 1971). A series of papers at seminars which brought together recent research from a variety of disciplines.

N.Mus.Vic *Memoirs of the National Museum of Victoria.*

Plomley N. J. B. Plomley, *Friendly Mission: the Tasmanian Journals and Papers of George Augustus Robinson 1829-1834* (Hobart, 1966).
Friendly Mission: a Supplement (Tas.Hist.Res. Assocn., Hobart, 1971).

Q.Vic.Mus. *Records of the Queen Victoria Museum*, Launceston.

R.S.N.S.W. *Proceedings of Royal Society of New South Wales.*

R.S.V. *Proceedings of Royal Society of Victoria.*

R.S.W.A. *Journal of the Royal Society of Western Australia.*

Smyth R. Brough Smyth, *The Aborigines of Victoria,* with notes on other parts of Australia (Melbourne, 1878) 2 vols.

Thomson D. F. Thomson, *Economic Structure and the Ceremonial Exchange Cycle in Arnhem Land* (Melbourne, 1949).

256

Notes and Sources

Torres Strait   D. Walker ed., *Bridge and Barrier: the Natural and Cultural History of Torres Strait* (Canberra, 1972)—containing 16 papers given at a Canberra symposium in Dec. 1971.

In the following notes the verbose titles of articles are sometimes shortened, and details of publications are not always given in full when they appear in the notes for a second or third time.

Page   Chapter 1—FIRE ON THE LAKE

4   Lake Mungo: J. M. Bowler, 'Pleistocene Salinities and Climatic Change', Mulvaney and Golson, p. 59.

4   Aboriginals at Lake Mungo: J. M. Bowler, Rhys Jones, Harry Allen and A. G. Thorne, 'Pleistocene Human Remains from Australia', *World Archaeology*, 1970, vol. 2, pp. 39-60.

6   Thorne on crushed bones: ibid., p. 57.

7   Ice ages affected animal evolution: D. B. Ericson and G. Wollin, *The Ever-Changing Sea* (London, 1971), p. 199.

7   Europe in last ice age: ibid., pp. 138-9.

7   Australian climate 30,000 years ago: A. B. Costin, 'Vegetation, Soils and Climate', in Mulvaney and Golson, pp. 35-7.

8   Low sea level during last cold epoch: R. W. Galloway and E. Löffler, 'Aspects of Geomorphology and Soils in the Torres Strait Region', in *Torres Strait*, p. 25. They suggest that, about 20,000 years ago, the sea level was perhaps 600 feet lower than now. In contrast 400 feet is closer to the figure sometimes preferred; see J. N. Jennings in Mulvaney and Golson, p. 4.

10   Australia's continental shelf: J. N. Jennings, 'Sea Level Change and Land Links', in Mulvaney and Golson, pp. 3-6.

10   Dating of recent volcanoes in south-east Australia: information from Bernard Joyce, Geology Dept., Melbourne University.

11   Mexican volcano: C. Ollier, *Volcanoes* (Canberra, 1969), p. 18.

13   Grooved axe at Tower Hill: D. J. Mulvaney, 'Prehistory of the Basalt Plains', in *R.S.V.* vol. 77, pp. 427-32.

Chapter 2—THE DISCOVERERS

17   D. J. Mulvaney, *The Prehistory of Australia*, p. 58.

17   J. N. Jennings, 'Sea Level Changes and Land Links', in Mulvaney and Golson, pp. 6-7.

19   W. E. Harney, *Taboo* (Sydney, 1943), pp. 200-2.

19   Tasmanian raft-canoes: exhibit in Tasmanian Museum, Hobart. See also D. F. Thomson, 'Notes on Some Primitive Watercraft in Northern Australia', *Man*, 1952, vol. 52, pp. 1-5.

19   Ocean voyages of Tasmanians: Plomley, *Friendly Mission*, pp. 379, 465. For a drawing of a Tasmanian raft-canoe see Plomley, *Friendly Mission: a Supplement*, p. 16 and plate 2.

21   Polynesian voyages: G. M. Dening, 'The Geographical Knowledge of the Polynesians', *Journal of the Polynesian Society*, vol. 71, 1962, Supplement on 'Polynesian Navigation', esp. p. 131.

21   Analogy between discovering islands and mining fields: G. Blainey, 'A Theory of Mineral Discovery: Australia in the Nineteenth Century', *Economic History Review*, 1970, vol. 23, pp. 304 ff.

22   G. A. Robinson in Plomley, p. 300.

23   Indonesia's frequent volcanoes: G. A. Macdonald, 'Volcano', in *E.B.*, 1962, vol. 23, p. 243.

24   Rhys Jones, editorial in *Mankind*, 1969, vol. 7, no. 2.

24   Oenpelli camp site: Carmel White, 'Man and Environment in North-west Arnhem Land', Mulveney and Golson, p. 147 ff.

25   Tropical axes: ibid., p. 153.

25   J. Golson, 'Australian Aboriginal Food Plants', in Mulvaney and Golson, pp. 196-209.

27   Seeds eaten on plains: R. Jones, 'Emerging Picture of Pleistocene Australians', *Nature*, 30 Nov. 1973, p. 281.

29   M. J. Meggitt, *Desert People: a Study of the Walbiri Aborigines of Central Australia* (Sydney, 1962), pp. 50-1.

29   Fluid tribal boundaries: E. C. Black, 'Population and Tribal Distribution', in B. C. Cotton ed., *Aboriginal Man in South and Central Australia* (Adelaide, 1966), p. 105.

31   Fragmentation by languages: D. T. Tryon, 'Linguistic Evidence and Aboriginal Origins', in Mulvaney and Golson, esp. pp. 350-2.

31   Sydney languages: A Capell, 'Aboriginal Languages in the South Central Coast, New South Wales: Fresh Discoveries.' *Oceania*, 1971, vol. 41, pp. 22-4.

Chapter 3—THE TASMANIANS: OUTLINE OF A PUZZLE

32   French visit: L. A. Triebel, 'Marion du Fresne: Pioneer Explorer', *Papers of Tasmanian Historical Research Association*, 1972, vol. 19, pp. 126-8.

33   Hair of Tasmanians and mainlanders: Plomley, pp. 15, 19-20; R. M. and Catherine H. Berndt, *The First Australians*, (Sydney, 1967 edn.), p. 31.

33   Fair hair: A. A. Abbie, 'Physical Characteristics' in B. C. Cotton, pp. 19-20.

33   Shaler's ice sheets: P. K. Weyl, *Oceanography: an Introduction to the Marine Environment* (New York, 1970), p. 453.

34   Date of the Deluge: *Beeton's Dictionary of Universal Information* (London, c. 1859) vol. 1, p. 1. According to Archbishop Usher the world had been created on 23 Oct. 4004 B.C.: Noah entered his Ark in 2349 B.C.

34   'Longest . . . isolation': Rhys Jones, 'Bass Straight in Prehistory', in *Bass Straight*, p. 27.

34   Belief that primitive peoples were static: D. J. Mulvaney, 'Discovering Man's Place in Nature', in *The Australian Academy of Humanities, Proceedings 1971* (Sydney, 1971), pp. 50-1.

36   'One of the Makolo': Curr, *Australian Race*, vol. 1, p. 167.

36   Negro ancestry of Australians: Curr, vol. 1, pp. 152, 158, 183-4 and vol. 3, p. 604.

37   Quaint notes on Andaman Islanders: *E.B.* 1910-11, vol. 1, p. 956.

37   Cook's theory of common origin of Pacific languages: J. C. Beaglehole ed., *The Journals of Captain James Cook*, vol. 3, part 2, pp. 784, 789.

38   William Bligh, *A Voyage to the South Sea* (London, 1792), p. 51.

38   Tasmanian languages: Rhys Jones, 'The Demography of Hunters and Farmers in Tasmania', Mulvaney and Golson, pp. 279.

39   Dravidian theory: A. W. Howitt, 'On the Origins of the Aborigines of Tasmania and Australia', in *A.A.A.S.* (Sydney, 1898), pp. 747-9.

40   C. Arnold, in *E.B.*, 1910-11, vol. 2, p. 756.

40   J. B. Birdsell, 'Preliminary Data on the Trihybrid Origin of the Australian Aborigines', *A. & P.A.*, vol. 2, 1967, pp. 100-55.

45   Air raids: A. G. Thorne, in Mulvaney and Golson, p. 317.

46   Tasmanians possibly modified by isolation: S. L. Larnach and

N. W. G. Macintosh, 'The Keppel Islanders: A Supplement to the Craniology of the Aborigines of Queensland', in *A. & P.A.*, 1972, vol. 7, p. 12.

46   Keppel Islands; ibid., pp. 8-14.

46   African pygmies: R. Oliver and J. D. Fage, *A Short History of Africa* (London, 1966), p. 19.

47   A. G. Thorne, 'Mungo and Kow Swamp: Morphological Variation in Pleistocene Australians', *Mankind*, 1971, vol. 8, pp. 86-9.

Chapter 4—THE DEATH OF THE GIANTS

51   Clarke and the diprotodon: Clarke's correspondence in *Further Papers Relative to the Discovery of Gold in Australia* (Brit. Parlt. Papers, London, Dec. 1854), pp. 33, 38-42.

51   Leichhardt and giant fauna: M. Aurousseau ed. and translator, *The Letters of F. W. Ludwig Leichhardt* (Cambridge, 1968), vol. 3, pp. 745, 756, 770-3.

52   Leichhardt to Owen, ibid., p. 773.

53   J. H. Calaby, 'Man, Climate and Fauna', in Mulvaney and Golson, p. 82.

54   Finds by Gallus and Gill: cited in Rhys Jones, *A. & P.A.*, vol. 3, pp. 202-3. Jones's article includes a fascinating survey of man's possible effects on the environment.

54   China-clay quarry: information from palaeontologists, National Museum of Victoria, Sept. 1974.

54   Larry G. Marshall, 'Fossil Vertebrate Faunas from the Lake Victoria Region', *N.Mus.Vic.*, 1973, vol. 34, pp. 163, 169.

55   D. Merrilees, 'Man the Destroyer: Late Quaternary Changes in the Australian Marsupial Fauna', *R.S.W.A.*, 1968, vol. 51, pp. 1-24.

56   Rhys Jones, 'The Arrival of Man', p. 204.

58   Thylacines in museums: my description of the skin is based on the stuffed specimens in the W.A., Hobart and Launceston museums.

59   Thylacine in New Guinea: R. Schodde and J. H. Calaby, 'Australo-Papuan Birds and Mammals' in *Torres Strait*, p. 299.

59   Thylacine depicted in Pilbara: B. J. Wright, 'Rock Engravings of Striped Mammals: the Pilbara Region', in *A. & P.A.*, 1972, vol. 7, pp. 15-23.

60   E. J. Brandl, 'Thylacine Designs in Arnhem Land Rock Paintings', in *A. & P.A.*, 1972, vol. 7, p. 30.

60   Thylacine, Arthur River: M. Sharland, *Tasmanian Wild Life* (Melbourne, 1962), pp. 8-9.

61   Arrival of dingoes: Mulvaney in *Prehistory*, p. 179.

62   Habits of dingoes: J. H. Calaby, 'Man, Climate and Fauna' in Mulvaney and Golson, p. 90; E. C. Rolls, *They All Ran Wild: the Story of the Pests on the Land in Australia* (Sydney, 1969), ch. 16.

63   F. Wood Jones, *The Mammals of South Australia* (Adelaide, 1923-5), p. 355.

63   P. J. Trezise, 'A Preliminary Analysis of Aboriginal Rock Art Styles of the Deighton River', roneod, ANZAAS Conference, Brisbane, 1971, p. 7.

64   Lake Nitchie necklace, research by N. W. G. Macintosh, cited by Rhys Jones in *Nature*, vol. 246, p. 281.

65   Bush flies: information from Dr. D. F. Waterhouse, Divn. of Entomology, C.S.I.R.O.

Chapter 5—A BURNING CONTINENT

67   Tasman on burnings: A. Sharp ed., *The Voyages of Abel Janszoon Tasman* (Oxford, 1968), pp. 41 n., 111.

68   W. Bligh, *A Voyage to the South Sea*, p. 49.

68   Smoke seen from Cook's ship: *The Endeavour Journal of Joseph Banks*, vol. 2, pp. 50-2.

68   Aboriginal fires ashore: Banks, ibid., vol. 2, p. 56; J. J. Auchmuty ed., *The Voyage of Governor Phillip to Botany Bay*, (Sydney, 1970), p. 25; S. Parkinson, *A Journal of a Voyage to the South Seas* (London, 1773), pp. 133, 136, 138; J. Bach ed., *An Historical Journal of Events at Sydney and at Sea . . . by Captain John Hunter*, (Sydney, 1968), p. 55.

69   G. A. Robinson: Plomley, p. 567.

69   Water on camp-fires: Plomley, p. 765.

70   Fire-making in desert: R. A. Gould, *Yiwara: Foragers of the Australian Desert*, (London, 1969), pp. 122-3.

70   Fire drill: W. L. Warner, *A Black Civilization: a Social Study of an Australian Tribe* (New York, 1937), p. 495; Smyth, vol. 1, p. lvii.

70 Fire by percussion: G. Völger, 'Making Fire by Percussion in Tasmania', *Oceania*, 1973, vol. 44, p. 61.

71 'Tobacco, iron tomahawks . . .': Curr, *Recollections*, p. 132.

71 The many uses of fire: see Curr, p. 133; Warner, pp. 473, 496; Plomley, passim; and R. A. Gould, 'Uses and Effects of Fire among the Western Desert Aborigines of Australia', in *Mankind*, 1971, vol. 8, pp. 14-24.

72 C. P. Mountford, *Brown Men and Red Sand: Journeyings in Wild Australia* (Melbourne, 1967), pp. 87, 122.

73 Anthropologist on smoke signals: R. A. Gould, 'Uses and Effects of Fire', pp. 19-21.

73 Steamship and signals: Smyth, vol. 1, p. 153; T. A. Parkhouse, 'Native Tribes of Port Darwin and its Neighbourhood', *A.A.A.S.*, (Brisbane, 1895), pp. 646-7.

74 J. McLaren, *My Crowded Solitude* (Melbourne, 1966), p. 103.

76 R. A. Gould, 'Uses and Effects of Fire', pp. 19-21.

77 R. L. Jack, *Report on Explorations in Cape York Peninsula, 1879-80* (Queensland Parlt. Paper, 1881), p. 3.

78 Curr on the firestick: Curr, *Recollections*, p. 88.

79 Effects of absence of fire: Curr, ibid., pp. 86-88; T. F. Bride ed., *Letters from Victorian Pioneers* (Melbourne, 1898), p. 150.

79 Changes in Tasmanian landscape: J. B. Walker, *Early Tasmania: Papers Read before the Royal Society of Tasmania* (Hobart, 1950 impression), p. 268; Rhys Jones, 'The Arrival of Man', pp. 207-10; Plomley, p. 54.

80 Darling Downs in 1844: *The Letters of F. W. Ludwig Leichhardt*, vol. 2, p. 719.

80 Reversion of mainland's savannah grasslands to scrubby forest: M. R. Jacobs, cited by R. Jones, op. cit., p. 207.

80 Firesticks on American grasslands: R. F. Spencer, J. D. Jennings et. al., *The Native Americans: Prehistory and Ethnology of the North American Indians* (New York, 1965), p. 55.

80 Spinifex and mulga: J. S. Beard, 'Drought Effects in the Gibson Desert', *R.S.W.A.*, 1968, vol. 51, p. 44; J. B. Cleland, 'Ecology and Diseases', in B. C. Cotton, pp. 123-5.

81 Fire and eucalyptus seeds: S. G. M. Carr, 'Geography of Tropical Eucalypts', in *Torres Strait*, p. 171.

Chapter 6—THE RISING OF THE SEAS

84　The relative antiquity of Austn. cremation and art: D. J. Mulvaney, 'Discovering Man's Place in Nature', *Aust. Acad. Humanities*, 1971, p. 55.

84　Koonalda Cave: R. V. S. Wright ed., *Archaeology of the Gallus Site, Koonalda Cave*, (Canberra, 1971).

86　Sequence of inundation in Bass Strait: J. N. Jennings, in Mulvaney and Golson, pp. 7-9.

87　Prehistoric course of Yarra and Tamar rivers: J. N. Jennings, 'The Geological History of Bass Strait', in *Bass Strait*, pp. 20, 22.

87　Hunter Island: Sandra Bowdler, 'An Account of a Geological Reconnaissance of Hunter's Isles', *Q.Vic.Mus.*, 1974, No. 54, pp. 1-22.

87　Frenchman's Cap deglaciation: Rhys Jones, 'The Arrival of Man', p. 192.

88　Extreme pace of advancing shoreline: the suggestion that the shoreline in northern Australia could have advanced at a maximum of about three nautical miles a year is based on low gradients of coastal land and the idea that the total rise of the sea in 10,000 or 15,000 years was not 400 feet (as sometimes suggested) but 600 feet. See R. W. Galloway and E. Löffler, *Torres Strait*, pp. 25-28.

89　The dating of Torres Strait: J. N. Jennings, *Torres Strait*, p. 29. He assigned a date range of 11,000-5,000 years ago with a preference for 8,000-6,500 years ago.

Chapter 7—BIRTH AND DEATH

92　Regions of closer settlement: Mulvaney, *Prehistory*, p. 40.

92　A. R. Radcliffe-Brown, 'Former Numbers and Distribution of the Australian Aborigines', Commonwealth *Official Year Book*, 1930, no. 23, pp. 687-96. According to his estimate Vic, Tas, and S.A. together held less than 10 per cent of the total.

93　T. R. Malthus, *An Essay on the Principle of Population* (London, 1890) pp. 15-20.

94　D. Collins, *An Account of the English Colony in New South Wales* (London, 1798). An example of Malthus's copying is his third paragraph on p. 16, taken almost verbatim from Collins, p. 557.

94   'Lowest stage of human society': Malthus, caption to ch. 3.
95   Oenpelli: B. P. Billington, 'Health and Nutritional Status' in *Arnhem Land*, vol. 2, p. 50.
95   Herbal medicine: J. McLaren, *My Crowded Solitude*, pp. 48, 100.
96   Paroo River abortions: Curr, *Australian Race*, vol. 2, p. 183. The efficacy of aiding abortion by putting pressure on the stomach was doubted by a physician during discussion at a meeting of the Royal Society of Tasmania, 1 October, 1974.
96   Abortion in 350 societies: G. Devereux, cited by S. Polgar, 'Population History and Population Policies from an Anthropological Perspective', *Current Anthropology*, 1972, vol. 13, p. 206.
97   Bangerang infanticide: Curr, *Recollections*, p. 116.
97   More old people near river: Curr, p. 111.
98   Infanticide in Geelong district: Buckley, pp. 40, 51.
98   Deformed children: Buckley, p. 51; M. J. Meggitt, *Desert People*, p. 272.
98   Ways of killing babies: M. J. Meggitt, *Desert People*, p. 272; Buckley, p. 51; Curr, *Australian Race*, vol. 1, p. 76 and vol. 2, p. 182.
98   When human milk ceased: Curr, *Australian Race*, vol. 1, p. 352; D. Collins, *An Account of the English Colony*, vol. 1, p. 607; T. R. Malthus, *Essay*, p. 19.
99   Graeme Pretty, 'The Cultural Chronology of the Roonka Flat: a Preliminary Consideration', ronoed, Conference of Austn. Inst. of Aboriginal Studies, May 1974.
100   Mother carrying urchin: Curr, *Recollections*, p. 116.
101   Ground-down teeth were common amongst aboriginals, being largely the result of the sand and grit mixed with foods cooked over the open fire or in hot ashes.
101   A gift of gruel: *W. C. Gosse's Explorations, 1873,* (Libraries Board of S.A., 1973), p. 22.
101   Old woman burned: Curr, *Recollections*, pp. 124-5.
102   James Woodburn, in R. B. Lee and I. De Vore, ed., *Man the Hunter* (Chicago, 1968), p. 91.
102   Anthropologists argue that epidemics were infrequent: S. Polgar, *Current Anthropology*, vol. 13, p. 205; Moni Nag, 'Anthro-

pology and Population', *Population Studies*, 1973, vol. 27, p. 61 ff; C. O. Sauer, *Land and Life* (Berkeley, 1965), p. 175.

103   Spread of epidemics amongst isolated aboriginals: Buckley, p. 68; E. C. Black in B. C. Cotton, pp. 102-3; J. Hawdon, *Journal of a Journey in 1838* (Melbourne, 1952), p. 27.

103   Pioneer sheep-owner hears of epidemic: Peter Beveridge, *R.S.N.S.W.*, vol. 17, p. 35. Beveridge's observations covered the years 1845-68.

104   Fatal European diseases were spread from a few points on the seaboard to a vast part of the remote interior several decades ahead of the first explorers and shepherds and drovers. If those diseases were deadly, the population in many parts of the interior might have been resultantly low at the very time when it was first observed by Europeans. If that is so, then it is risky to estimate the maximum population of aboriginal Australians on the basis of observations and hand-counts made by the inland explorers.

105   Plague seen as a work of sorcery: P. Beveridge, p. 35.

105   Power of sorcery: D. F. Thomson, 'The Native People', in C. Pearl ed., *Australia*, (Sydney, 1965), pp. 36-8.

106   Buckley's early life: M. J. Tipping, 'Buckley', in *A.D.B.*, vol. 1, p. 174; C. M. Tudehope, 'William Buckley', *Victorian Historical Magazine*, 1962, vol. 32, pp. 216 ff.

108   Buckley's report of war deaths: my computations come from the evidence in Buckley, esp. pp. 26-61.

108   Estimate of population of Buckley's roaming area: based partly on population density in Mulvaney, *Prehistory*, p. 40.

109   Arnhem Land deaths: W. L. Warner, *A Black Civilization*, pp. 158-63. Warner did not convert his estimates of war deaths into an annual war-death-rate based on total population of the area, nor compare Arnhem Land's rate with that of other parts of the world. As no prehistorian, to my knowledge, tried to convert the fighting deaths of hunter-gatherers into percentages, the illusion easily arose that in such societies fighting deaths, being numerically few, were not of great significance.

110   European war casualties are based on my computations. For deaths in World War Two, see *E.B.* (1962), vol. 23, p. 793 Q.

111   New York professor: Moni Nag, in *Population Studies*, 1973, vol. 27, p. 61.

112   Evidence of heavy fighting in other parts of Australia is easily
       found. For instance see D. Thomson, in C. Pearl ed., *Australia*,
       pp. 37-8; M. J. Meggitt in *Desert People*, p. 42; A. W. Howitt,
       The Native Tribes of South-East Australia (London, 1904),
       p. 348; and W. E. Roth, *Ethnological Studies Among the
       North-West-Central Queensland Aborigines* (Brisbane, 1897),
       p. 139 ff.

112   Cannibalism: index to Curr, *Australian Race*, vol. 3, p. 702;
       Buckley, p. 50; R. M. and C. H. Berndt, *The First Australians*
       (Sydney, 1967 edn.), p. 134; T. G. H. Strehlow, *Songs of
       Central Australia* (Sydney, 1971), pp. xlii n., 611 n; Baldwin
       Spencer and F. J. Gillen, *The Arunta: a Study of a Stone Age
       People* (London, 1927), vol. 2, p. 495; W. E. Roth, *Ethno-
       logical Studies*, p. 166.

112   Carl Lumholtz, *Among Cannibals: an Account of Four Years'
       Travels and of Camp Life with the Aborigines of Queensland*
       (London, 1889), pp. 271-4.

115   Population pressure as alleged causes of war: G. Blainey, *The
       Causes of War*, (London, 1973), pp. 10-11.

116   Discussions of Birdsell's views: Mulvaney, *Prehistory*, p. 50; A. P.
       Elkin, 'Man and his Past in Aboriginal Australia', *A. & P.A.*,
       1967, vol. 2, p. 42.

119   Iron age reaches Cape York: R. L. Jack, *Report on Explorations
       in Cape York Peninsula, 1879-80* (Brisbane, 1881), p. 41.

Chapter 8—THE HUNTERS

125   *Sydney Gazette*: Sunday, 23 December 1804.

126   George Grey, *Journals*, vol. 2, p. 282.

126   Regions where boomerangs not used for hunting: D. Thomson,
       Economic Structure, p. 64; Curr, *Australian Race*, vol. 1, pp.
       395-6; Mulvaney, *Prehistory*, p. 132; R. A. Gould, *Yiwara*, p.
       76.

128   Regions where woomera not used: Curr, *Australian Race*, vol. 2,
       pp. 143-4, 182 and vol. 3, p. 90; information from Dr. I.
       McBryde of A.N.U.

128   Spearsmen in Gibson Desert: Gould, *Yiwara*, p. 78.

129   Aboriginal cricketers: D. J. Mulvaney, *Cricket Walkabout: The
       Australian Aboriginal Cricketers on Tour 1867-8* (Melbourne,
       1967) pp. 31, 64-5.

129   Alice M. Brues, in Y. A. Cohen, *Man in Adaptation: the Bisocial Background* (Chicago, 1968), pp. 186-94.
130   Tasmanian mimicry: Plomley, p. 197.
130   T. L. Mitchell, *Three Expeditions*, vol. 2, p. 277.
131   Uses of mimicry in hunting: W. E. Harney, *North of 23°: Ramblings in Northern Australia* (Sydney, n.d.) pp. 155-6; W. E. Harney, *Brimming Billabongs: The Life Story of an Australian Aboriginal* (Sydney, 1947), pp. 52-3, 56-7; R. H. Mathews, 'Aboriginal Tribes of New South Wales and Victoria', *R.S.N.S.W.*, 1904, pp. 255-6.
132   Sign language: W. E. Roth, in *Records of the Australian Museum* (Sydney, 1908-10), vol. 7, p. 82 ff, W. E. Roth. *Ethnological Studies*, preface.
132   Platypus egg: F. Wood Jones, *The Mammals of South Australia* (Adelaide, 1923-5), p. 29. For a contrasting example of aboriginals' ignorance—about the nesting habits of lyrebirds—see A. H. Chisholm, in *A.D.B.* vol. 1, p. 86.
132   Ida Mann, cited by A. A. Abbie in B. C. Cotton, p. 41.
134   Increasing use of bone-tips: Mulvaney, *Prehistory*, pp. 84-91.
134   J. MacGillivray, *Narrative*, vol. 1, pp. 167-8.
135   Turtle-hunting, W. E. Harney, *Taboo*, p. 197.
135   Stranded seal: P. P. King, *Narrative of a Survey of the Intertropical and Western Coasts of Australia* (London, 1827), vol. 2, pp. 126-7.
136   Tasmanian shell fish: Plomley, p. 79; A. J. Dartnell, 'Marine Molluscs of Tasmania', in *Tasmanian Year Book*, 1973, pp. 55-6.
137   South Australian shellfish: J. B. Cleland, in B. C. Cotton, pp. 129-30.
137   Wilson's Promontory: G. S. Hope and P. J. F. Coutts, 'Past and Present Aboriginal Food Resources at Wilsons Promontory, Victoria', *Mankind*, 1971, vol. 8, pp. 104-14.
138   Shellfish mounds: P. P. King, *Narrative of a Survey*, vol. 1, p. 87; R. B. Smyth, vol. 1, p. 241; R. V. S. Wright, 'Prehistory in the Cape York Peninsula', in Mulvaney and Golson, pp. 133-6.
139   Toe-fishing in Darling River: Mitchell, *Three Expeditions*, vol. 1, pp. 305-6.
140   Fish traps and weirs: P. Beveridge, p. 48; T. F. Bride ed., *Letters from Victorian Pioneers* (Melbourne, 1969 edn), p. 271.

141   Glyde River fish trap: D. F. Thomson, 'A New Type of Fish Trap from Arnhem Land . . .' *Man*, 1938, vol. 38, pp. 193-8.

142   The simplest vessels: P. P. King, *Narrative of a Survey*, vol. 2, p. 69; J. L. Stokes, *Discoveries in Australia* (London, 1846), vol. 1, p. 112; D. F. Thomson, 'Notes on Some Primitive Watercraft', *Man*, 1952, vol. 52, p. 1 ff.

143   Robert Edwards, *Aboriginal Bark Canoes of the Murray Valley* (Adelaide, 1972), pp. 29-30.

144   Lake Boga fleet: Mitchell, *Three Expeditions*, vol. 2, p. 142.

144   Dug-out canoes: W. E. Roth, 'North Queensland Ethnography', in *Records of the Australian Museum* (Sydney, 1910-13), vol. 8, pp. 11-16; D. F. Thomson, *Economic Structure*, pp. 52, 57-60.

145   Goose hunters in Arafura Swamp: unpublished notes by Donald Thomson on magpie geese in N.T., 1935-7, kindly supplied by Miss Judith Wiseman of Melbourne University: D. F. Thomson, 'The Tree Dwellers of the Arafura Swamps: A New Type of Bark Canoe from Central Arnhem Land', *Man*, 1939, reprint article; D. F. Thomson, 'Arnhem Land: Explorations among an Unknown People', *Geographical Journal*, 1949, vol. 114, pp. 31-34; H. J. Frith and S. J. J. F. Davies, 'Ecology of the Magpie Goose', *C.S.I.R.O. Wildlife Research*, 1961, vol. 6, pp. 91-141.

148   'It was an unforgettable experience': D. F. Thomson, 'Arnhem Land . . .' p. 33.

149   G. Orwell, *The Road to Wigan Pier*, esp. part 6.

151   'Eggs innumerable': P. Beveridge, p. 36.

151   Mitchell, *Three Expeditions*, vol. 2, p. 153.

152   Duck netting: P. Beveridge, p. 46.

153   Bogong moth: W. K. Hancock, *Discovering Monaro: a Study of Man's Impact on his Environment*, (Cambridge, 1972), pp. 21-2; R. B. Smyth, vol. 1, p. 207 n.

154   Laarp: P. Beveridge, pp. 63-5.

Chapter 9—HARVEST OF THE UNPLOUGHED PLAINS

155   The woman's hand bag: Mitchell, *Three Expeditions*, vol. 2, p. 270.

155   Possum meat: Ibid, pp. 344-350.

155   1860 expedition: A Moorehead, *Cooper's Creek* (London, 1963), pp. 39, 165, 189.

156   E. Palmer, 'On Plants Used by the Natives of North Queens-
        land'; *R.S.N.S.W.*, 1883, vol. 17, p. 93 ff.

156   Varying importance of plant foods: a valuable study is R.
        Lawrence, 'Habitat and Economy: a Historical Perspective', in
        Mulvaney and Golson, pp. 254-7.

156   The Bangerang: Curr, *Recollections*, p. 116.

156   Beyond Geelong: Buckley, pp. 27, 51; T. F. Bride, ed., *Letters
        from Victorian Pioneers*, p. 395.

157   Western Australian coast: Sara J. Meagher, 'The Food Resources
        of the Aborigines of the South-West of Western Australia',
        Records of the W.A. Museum, 1974, vol. 3, pp. 14, 24-27.

157   Hutt River: G. Grey, *Journals*, vol. 2, pp. 12-13.

157   Variety of plant foods: J. Golson, 'Australian Aboriginal Plant
        Foods', in Mulvaney and Golson, p. 204.

157   Wilson's Promontory: G. S. Hope and P. J. F. Coutts, in
        Mankind, 1971, vol. 8, pp. 105-109.

158   Victorian plant foods: Smyth, vol. 1, pp. 209-14.

158   Adelaide oxalis: John Stephens, *The Land of Promise* (London,
        1839), p. 77.

160   Central Australia: *Gosse's Explorations, 1873*, pp. 11, 13; J. Gol-
        son, in Mulvaney and Golson, p. 204.

160   Bunya pine: *The Letters of F. W. Ludwig Leichhardt*, vol. 2,
        pp. 666 ff, 704, 707-9; R. B. Smyth, vol. 1, pp. 218-19.

161   Desert greens and seeds: Golson, p. 204.

162   Nardoo: Smyth, vol. 1, p. 216; exhibit in the S.A. Museum.

163   Food gathering in Arnhem Land: F. McCarthy and Margaret
        McArthur, 'The Food Quest and the Time Factor in Abo-
        riginal Economic Life', *Arnhem Land*, vol. 2, p. 145 ff (Fish
        Creek). John Calaby rightly calls this chapter a unique study
        of food-gathering.

165   Toxic yams at East Alligator: J. Lewis, *Fought and Won*
        (Adelaide, 1922), p. 131.

166   Hemple Bay: F. McCarthy and M. McArthur, pp. 180-8, See
        also p. 127.

167   'The quantity of food': M. McArthur, *Arnhem Land*, p. 92.

168   Betty Hiatt, 'The Food Quest and the Economy of the Tas-
        manian Aborigines', *Oceania*, 1967-8, vol. 38, pp. 99-133, 190-
        219, esp. p. 216; Betty Hiatt, in Fay Gale ed., *Woman's Role in
        Aboriginal Society* (Canberra, 1970), pp. 7-12.

169   Carl O. Sauer, *Land and Life* (Berkeley, 1965), p. 161. Of the
       seven reasons I offer for the inadequacies of surviving evidence,
       the first two come from Sauer.

170   Rhys Jones, 'Tasmanian Aborigines and Dogs', *Mankind*, 1970,
       vol. 7, p. 267.

Chapter 10—MEDICINES, DRUGS, LIQUIDS AND
COSMETICS

171   L. J. Webb, 'The Use of Plant Medicines and Poisons by Aus-
       tralian Aborigines', *Mankind*, 1969, vol. 7, pp. 137-46.

172   Knowledge of boiling: on the eve of the European coming,
       Macassarmen possibly introduced the boiling of liquids to
       part of Arnhem Land. See *Arnhem Land*, vol. 2, pp. 182 n.,
       293.

172   T. T. Webb, 'Aboriginal Medical Practice in East Arnhem
       Land', *Oceania*, 1933, vol. 4, p. 95.

173   Cider gum: Plomley, pp. 534, 536, 542, 556-7, 580.

174   Victorian alcohol: Smyth, vol. 1, pp. 210-11.

174   J. B. Cleland, in B. C. Cotton, p. 120.

175   Pituri: T. H. Johnston and J. B. Cleland, 'The History of the
       Aboriginal Narcotic, Pituri', *Oceania*, 1933-4, vol. 4, pp. 201-23,
       269-89; exhibit in S.A. Museum, Adelaide.

176   Narcotics in fishing: J. B. Cleland in B. C. Cotton, p. 120; E.
       Palmer, 'On Plants Used by the Natives of North Queensland',
       R.S.N.S.W., 1883, vol. 17, pp. 106-8; W. H. Hovell and H.
       Hume, *Journey of Discovery to Port Phillip* (Adelaide, 1965),
       p. 39 n.

177   C. O. Sauer, *Land and Life*, p. 263.

178   Quest for water: A. T. Magarey, 'Aborigines' Water Quest in
       Arid Australia', *A.A.A.S.*, 1895, vol. 6, pp. 647-58; J. B.
       Cleland, in B. C. Cotton, pp. 114, 142; L. C. E. Gee, *Bush
       Track and Gold Fields* (Adelaide, 1926), esp. 61-3.

180   Water from a frog: Magarey, p. 655; Cleland, p. 142.

181   T. G. H. Strehlow, *Songs of Central Australia*, p. 461.

182   Wilgie Mia ochre: K. R. Miles in A. B. Edwards ed., *Geology of
       Australian Ore Deposits* (Melbourne, 1953), pp. 242-4.

182   Tasmanian minerals: Plomley, pp. 600-1, 688, 903-5; Plomley,
       Supplement, p. 17.

183   Kangaroo dung as paint: R. A. Gould, *Yiwara*, p. 147.

183   B. Spencer and F. J. Gillen, *The Arunta*, vol. 2, pp. 552-3.

183   Gold nugget: E. J. Dunn, *List of Nuggets Found in Victoria*, Memoirs of Geological Survey of Victoria, No. 12, 1912, pp. 4, 45. In a long search of mining literature this is probably the only unassailable reference I've found to aboriginal respect for gold.

184   Australites: C. P. Mountford, *Brown Men and Red Sand*, pp. 35-6; E. J. Dunn, *Australites*, Bulletin 27 of Geological Survey of Victoria (Melbourne, 1912), p. 14.

Chapter 11—THE LOGIC OF UNENDING TRAVEL

185   D. F. Thomson: 'The Seasonal Factor in Human Culture: Illustrated from the Life of a Contemporary Nomadic Group', *Proceedings of the Prehistoric Society*, 1939, pp. 209-221.

187   Vegetables in dry season: D. F. Thomson, ibid, pp. 215-6; D. F. Thomson, *Economic Structure*, pp. 21-2.

189   Seasons in Arnhem Land: D. F. Thomson, 'Arnhem Land: Explorations Among an Unknown People', *Geographical Journal*, 1948, vol. 112, pp. 26-8 and folding table.

191   Darge's testimony: M. Alexander, *Mrs Fraser on the Fatal Shore* (London, 1971), pp. 134-40.

192   J. B. Cleland, 'Some Aspects of the Aboriginal Inhabitants of Tasmania and Southern Australia', *Procs. Royal Society of Tasmania*, 1939, p. 9.

192   Aboriginals in cold weather: Buckley, p. 68; C. Lumholtz, *Among Cannibals*, p. 140; George Grey, *Expeditions*, vol. 2, p. 262; A. A. Abbie, in B. C. Cotton, p. 38; P. Beveridge, pp. 27-8.

193   Shoulder capes: Christine Cornell tr., *The Journal of Post Captain Nicolas Baudin* (Adelaide, 1974), pp. 303, 339.

193   Rug of 81 skins: Mulvaney, *Prehistory*, p. 80.

193   Fire in frost: Mitchell, *Three Expeditions*, vol. 2, p. 145.

194   Wik Monkan hoard: D. F. Thomson, 'The Seasonal Factor', p. 216.

194   East Alligator yams: J. Lewis, *Fought and Won*, p. 131.

195   Preserving plums: D. F. Thomson, *Economic Structure*, pp. 23-4.

195   Western desert: R. A. Gould, *Yiwara*, p. 20.

195   Cycad palm: F. R. Irvine, 'Evidence of Change in the Vegetable Diet of Australian Aborigines', in A. R. Pilling and R. A.

Waterman, *Diprotodon to Detribalization* (East Lansing, 1970), p. 280.

195   Portulac: A. W. Howitt, cited in Smyth, vol. 2, p. 302.

196   Jerked meat: J. MacGillivray, *Narrative*, vol. 2, p. 23.

196   Lake Victoria mussels: K. N. G. Simpson and Sir Robert Blackwood, 'An Aboriginal Cache of Freshwater Mussels at Lake Victoria, N.S.W.', *N.Mus.Vic.* 1973, no. 34, pp. 217-8.

196   Aboriginal dams: A. T. Magarey, *A.A.A.S.*, 1895, p. 656; R. J. and J. M. Rowlands, 'An Aboriginal Dam in Northwestern New South Wales', *Mankind*, 1969, vol. 7, pp. 132-6.

198   Hunting rights among Wik Monkan: D. F. Thomson, 'The Seasonal Factor', pp. 211, 216.

199   Foods as sex symbols: D. McKnight, 'Sexual Symbolism of Food among the Wik-Mungkan', *Man*, 1973, vol. 8, p. 197.

199   Taboo on W.A. *unio*: Smyth, vol. 1, p. 237.

199   Marine biologist: Dr Frank Talbot of The Australian Museum.

200   Doubts about extent of Tasmanian fish taboo: see Plomley, *Supplement*, p. 8; E. D. Gill and M. R. Banks, 'Cainozoic History of Mowbray Swamp', *Q.Vic.Mus.*, 1956, no. 6, p. 38.

201   Grey, cited in Smyth, vol. 1, p. 237.

201   Groote Eylandt; M. McArthur, *Arhem Land*, vol. 2, pp. 124-5.

Chapter 12—TRADE ROUTES AND RITUALS

203   Shell trade: F. D. McCarthy, '*Trade* in Aboriginal Australia and *Trade* Relationships with Torres Strait, New Guinea and Malaya', *Oceania*, 1938-9, vol. 9, pp. 434-5; Mulvaney, *Prehistory*, p. 96 (map).

204   Mt William axes: G. Clark, 'Traffic in Stone Axes', *Economic History Review*, 1965, vol. 18, pp. 14-15.

204   Melton Mowbray: J. B. Walker, *Early Tasmania* (Hobart, 1950), p. 285.

205   New England axe traffic: R. A. Binns and Isabel McBryde, *A Petrological Analysis of Ground Edge Artifacts from Northern New South Wales* (Canberra, 1972), esp. pp. 16-19, 92, 97.

206   Blue Mud Bay: Thomson, *Economic Structure*, p. 65.

206   14-pound stones: Buckley, p. 57.

206   The physician: W. E. Roth, *Ethnological Studies*, (Brisbane, 1897), pp. 104, 134.

207   Cape Leveque trade: F. D. McCarthy, 'Trade', p. 435.

207   Central Australian trade: B. Spencer and F. J. Gillen, *The Arunta*, vol. 2, pp. 518, 521, 528.

208   Trade in food: F. Micha, in *Diprotodon to Detribalization*, p. 286, argued that there was no trade in food in Australia, and his seems to be the common view. The evidence in Buckley, pp. 38-9, contradicts this view.

209   Parade of daughters: Buckley, p. 41.

209   Thomson, *Economic Structure*, esp. ch. 5.

210   'Each individual': Thomson, ibid., p. 67.

210   W. E. H. Stanner, 'Ceremonial Economics of the Mulluk Mulluk and Madngella Tribes of the Daly River', *Oceania*, 1933-4, vol. 4, esp. pp. 156-75, but also 19-21 and 458-71.

212   'Defections': Stanner, p. 161.

214   Defined tribal boundaries in Tasmania: Plomley, p. 969; J. B. Walker, *Early Tasmania*, p. 278.

Chapter 13—THE PROSPEROUS NOMADS

218   Native nut and spinach: F. R. Irvine, in *Diprotodon to Detribilization*, p. 279.

220   Wills' journal, in *The Argus*, ed., *The Burke and Wills Exploring Expedition* (Adelaide, 1963 reprint), pp. 14-32.

220   Effects of nardoo: Wills, pp. 31, 32.

221   Padlu: Wills, p. 28.

221   Portulac plant: Wills, p. 30; Burke and Wills Commission, Vic. Parlt., 1861, no. 97, evidence of John King, Q. 900-2, 921; A. Moorehead, *Cooper's Creek* (London, 1963), pp. 72, 99.

221   Mussels: Wills, p. 29.

221   Fishing equipment: Kathleen Fitzpatrick, 'The Burke and Wills Expedition and the Royal Society of Victoria', *Historical Studies*, 1963, vol. 40, p. 471; A. Moorehead, *Cooper's Creek*, p. 36.

222   Fish caught: Wills, pp. 28-30. The S.A. Museum displays a fishing net of remarkable quality made by aboriginals at Cooper's Creek.

223   Tasmanian food: J. E. Calder, *Some Account of the . . . Native Tribes of Tasmania* (Hobart, 1875), pp. 25, 31. Whereas Calder thought Tas had 7,000 people, it probably had closer to 4,000.

223   Victorian river flats: Curr, *Recollections*, p. 120; P. Beveridge, p. 74.

223 Arnhem Land plenty: D. F. Thomson, *Economic Structure*, p. 22.
223 Tiwi: C. W. M. Hart and A. R. Pilling, *The Tiwi of North Australia* (New York, 1966), pp. 34-5.
224 George Grey, *Journals*, vol. 2, pp. 259-61.
225 G. M. Trevelyan, *English Social History* (London, 1944), pp. 432, 450, 452.
227 Finland's famine: F. Braudel, *Capitalism and Material Life 1400-1800* (New York, 1974), p. 42. Even France in the 18th century (p. 39) reputedly suffered 16 'general famines'.
227 Russian 'Starvation': J. L. H. Keep, 'Russia', in *New Cambridge Modern History*, vol. 11, p. 367.
227 T. G. H. Strehlow, *Songs of Central Australia*, p. 677.

Chapter 14—THE SAILS OF DOOM

231 Thailand plants: B. A. V. Peacock, 'Early Cultural Development in South-East Asia', *A. & P.A.*, 1971, vol. 6, p. 115; P. I. Boriskovsky, 'New Problems of the Palaeolithic and Mesolithic of the Indochinese Peninsula', *A. & P.A.*, 1971, vol. 6, p. 105.
231 Jericho: *Report on the British Museum (Natural History), 1969-1971*, pp. 40-2.
232 Mexico and Andes: Betty J. Meggers, *Prehistoric America* (Chicago, 1973 edn.), pp. 29-33.
233 River City of Iran: *The Times*, London, 11 Dec. 1972, pp. 1, 4.
233 Timor pigs: I. C. Glover, 'Prehistoric Research in Timor', in Mulvaney and Golson, p. 177.
234 New Guinea pigs and gardens: A. P. Vayda, 'Pigs', in *Encyclopaedia of Papua and New Guinea* (Melbourne, 1972), vol. 2, p. 907; S. Hatanaka and L. W. Bragge, 'Habit, Isolation and Subsistence Economy in the Central Range of New Guinea', *Oceania*, 1973, vol. 44, pp. 38-57; M. J. Meggitt, 'The Sun and the Shakers', *Oceania*, 1973, vol. 44, pp. 2-19; Ester Boserup, *The Conditions of Agricultural Growth* (London, 1965), p. 33.
236 J. R. Beckett: 'The Torres Strait Islanders', in *Torres Strait*, p. 316.
237 Prince of Wales Island; D. R. Moore, 'Cape York Aborigines and Islanders of Western Torres Strait', *Torres Strait*, pp. 339-43; J. MacGillivray, *Narrative*, vol. 2, pp. 25-6.
238 Why North Australians did not become gardeners: the question is too complex to discuss adequately in this short space, and

moreover it is linked to explanations of why other lands did or did not adopt gardens and herds. My aim is eventually to publish a separate article on this issue.

238   J. Golson, 'The Relationship of Australian and New Guinea Prehistory' in *Torres Strait*, pp. 387-91. See also J. P. White, in Mulvaney and Golson, pp. 182-4.

239   Six severed heads: D. R. Moore, in *Torres Strait*, p. 339.

243   D. J. Mulvaney, *Prehistory*, p. 20.

243   Chinese map of 1426: J. V. G. Mills ed., *The Overall Survey of the Ocean's Shores* (Cambridge, 1970), p. 21.

243   Darwin statuette: Mulvaney, *Prehistory*, pp. 31-2. The statuette can be seen in the Museum of Applied Arts and Sciences, Sydney.

244   Chinese voyages: J. V. G. Mills, *The Overall Survey*, pp. 9-22; C. G. F. Simkin, *The Traditional Trade of Asia* (London, 1968), pp. 142-3.

245   Timor sandalwood trade: I. C. Glover, in Mulvaney and Golson, p. 178; J. R. McCulloch, *Dictionary of Commerce* (London, 1854 edn.), p. 1134; Mills, p. 22.

245   Coming of Portuguese: C. R. Boxer, *Fidalgos in the Far East 1550-1770* (Hong Kong, 1968), pp. 180 ff; C. M. W. Hart and A. R. Pilling, *The Tiwi of North Australia*, pp. 97-8; C. R. Boxer, *Portuguese Society in the Tropics* (Madison, Wisconsin, 1965), esp. pp. 56-9.

247   Trepang trade: G. Blainey, *The Tyranny of Distance* (Melbourne, 1966), pp. 82-88; J. D. Mulvaney, 'Bêche-de-mer, Aborigines and Australian History', *R.S.V.*, 1966, vol. 79, pp. 449-57.

249   Macassarmen's influence: W. L. Warner, *A Black Civilization*, pp. 157-8, 166-7, 468; M. McArthur, in *Arnhem Land*, vol. 2, pp. 2-3; D. F. Thomson, *Economic Structure*, pp. 52, 56-60.

251   Burial ceremony: W. L. Warner, pp. 430-4, 466.

252   Conflict at Botany Bay: J. C. Beaglehole ed., *The Endeavour Journal of Joseph Banks 1768-1771*, vol. 2, pp. 54-5, 134.

253   Aboriginals ignore *Endeavour*: ibid., pp. 54, 62-3.

Index

abalone, 136-7
Abbie, A. A., 33n
abortion, 95-6, 114, 115
acacia, 27, 172, 194
Adelaide, 10, 31, 53, 203
Adelaide River, 146
adhesives, 129, 177-8
Africa, as homeland of Tasmanians, 35-6
Alberga River, 101
alcohol, 173-4
Alexandra Headland, 160
Alice Springs, 101, 203, 207
Andaman Islands, 36-7
Arafura Sea, 52, 91, 104, 209
Arafura Swamp, 145-51
archaeological discoveries, at Lake Mungo, 3-6; Tower Hill, 13; Oenpelli, 24-5; Niah Cave, 25; Keppel Islands, 45-6; Kow Swamp, 47; Wellington, 51; Condamine River, 51; Lake Callabonna, 53, 57; Keilor, 54; Bacchus Marsh, 54; Balladonia, 55; Koonalda Cave, 84; Hunter Island, 87; Roonka flat, 99-100; Bateman's Bay, 134; Glen Aire, 134; Wilson's Promontory, 137; Hanover Bay, 138; Port Essington, 138; Weipa, 138-9; Milingimbi, 138; Lake Victoria, 196; Great Victoria Desert, 196; Melton Mowbray, 204; Moore Creek, 204-5

Archer River, 185
Arnhem Land, 18, 24, 26, 41, 60, 64, 70, 71, 72, 95, 109, 110, 111, 126, 134, 141, 144, 145, 146, 156, 157, 158, 165n, 189, 206, 207, 209, 210, 223, 247, 249, 250, 251
Arnold, Channing, 40
arrows, 129
art, 59, 60, 84-5
Arthur River, 60
Aru Island, 17
Australia, discovery of, 15-24; exploration of, 26-8, 30-1
Australia Felix, 13
axes, stone, 13, 19, 129, 143, 177, 204, 205, 206; edge-ground, 25, 205; iron, 209, 212, 248, 249, 250
Ayers Rock, 160

Bacchus Marsh, 54
Bali, 15, 16, 23
Balladonia, 55
Banda Sea, 23
Bandicoots, 24, 129, 131, 164, 165
Banks, Joseph, 253
bark, as building material, 82, 186; canoes, 18, 19, 40, 82, 139, 142-4, 145-6, 151, 186; paintings, 249; parcels, 206
barter, see trade
Barwon River, 208
Bass Strait, 33, 34, 86, 87, 88, 89, 98
Bateman's Bay, 134

277

Index

Bathurst Island, 223, 245, 246
bats, 75
Beckett, J. R., 236
beetles, green, 153-4
bettong, 5
Binns, R. A., 205
birds, hunting of, 125, 126, 131, 144-53
Birdsell, Joseph, 40-1, 44, 116
birth rate, 111
Blanche Town, 99
Bligh, William, 38, 67-8
Blue Mountains, 51
Blue Mud Bay, 206, 210
Bogong Moth, 153, 194
bone, 130, 134
boomerangs, 35-6, 39-40, 125-7, 207
Borneo, 8, 16, 17, 25
botanical   knowledge,   171-81
    passim
Botany Bay, 68, 252
Boulia region, 140
Bourke, 205
Bowler, Jim, 6n
bows and arrows, 129
Brandl, E. J., 60
Brues, Alice M., 129
Bruny Island, 37, 174
Buckley, William, 103, 106-8, 192-3, 208
Bulloo River, 197
Bunbury, 98
Bungary, 126
Bunya Bunya pine, 30, 160-1, 194, 195
burial customs, 3, 6, 64, 99-100, 251
Burke and Wills expedition, 162, 218-222
bush flies, 65
bushfires, 66, 67-8, 75-82

Cairns, 41, 144
Calaby, J. H., 53
Caldwell, Robert, 39
camp-sites, discoveries at, *see under*
    archaeological discoveries

cannibalism, 112-13
canoes, bark; 18, 19, 39-40, 82, 139, 142-4, 145-6, 151, 186; dug-out, 18-19, 144, 248, 250; raft, 19, 21; outrigger, 144, 250n
Cape Grafton, 144
Cape Grim, 182
Cape Leeuwin, 115
Cape Leveque, 207
Cape Otway, 86, 134
Cape York Peninsula, 63, 71, 74, 77, 95, 104, 119, 138, 156, 157, 185, 194, 203, 236, 237, 238, 239, 242, 247
Carpentarians, 41
casuarinas, 179
catamarans, 142
cats, native, 5; wild, 75
Celebes, the, 16, 17
ceremonial dress, 217
'Ceremonial Exchange Cycle', 209-14, 239
childbirth, 96
child-rearing, 97-8, 115
children, treatment of, 100
Chinese voyages, 243-5
cider eucalypt, 173-4
clans, 28, 29. *See also* nomadic groups
Clarence Valley, 128
Clarke, W. B., 51
Cleland, J. B., 174, 176, 192
climatic changes, effects of, 7-8, 22-3, 56-7, 85, 117
Cloncurry, 159
Cloncurry River, 159, 176
clothing, 72, 193, 217
clubs, 129
Clutterbuck Hills, 73
coastline, changes in, *see* sea levels
Cobar, 205
cockatoos, 126, 153
cockles, 137
Colac, 208
Cole-be, 99
Collins, David, 94
commerce, *see* trade

278

Index

279

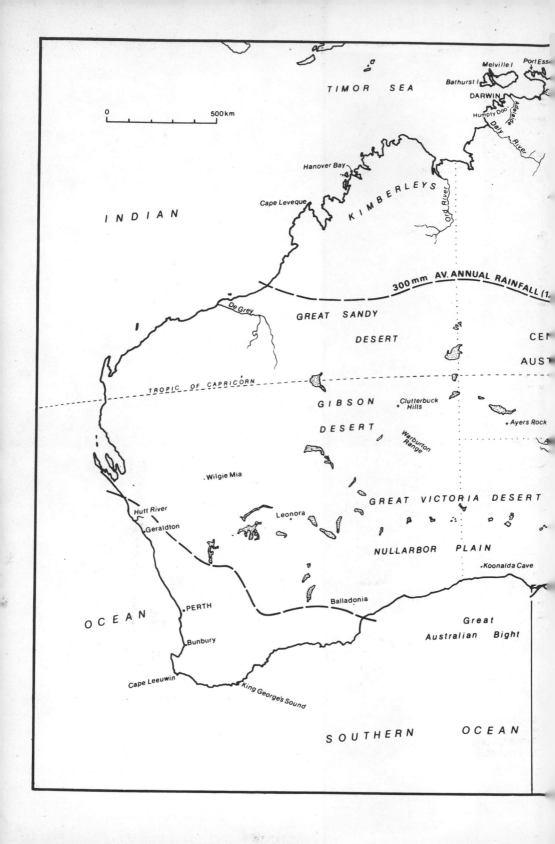